Voices of
Foreign Brides

Voices of Foreign Brides

The Roots and Development of Multiculturalism in Korea

Choong Soon Kim

ALTAMIRA
PRESS

A division of
ROWMAN & LITTLEFIELD PUBLISHERS, INC.
Lanham • Boulder • New York • Toronto • Plymouth, UK

Published by AltaMira Press
A division of Rowman & Littlefield Publishers, Inc.
A wholly owned subsidiary of The Rowman & Littlefield Publishing Group, Inc.
4501 Forbes Boulevard, Suite 200, Lanham, Maryland 20706
http://www.altamirapress.com

Estover Road, Plymouth PL6 7PY, United Kingdom

British Library Cataloguing in Publication Information Available

Library of Congress Cataloging-in-Publication Data

Kim, Choong Soon, 1938–
  Voices of foreign brides : the roots and development of multiculturalism in Korea /
Choong Soon Kim.
    p. cm.
  Includes bibliographical references and index.
  ISBN 978-0-7591-2035-8 (cloth : alk. paper)—ISBN 978-0-7591-2037-2 (electronic)
  1. Multiculturalism—Korea (South) 2. Foreign spouses—Korea (South) I. Title.
HM1271.K55 2011
306.84'5095195—dc23   2011015233

∞™ The paper used in this publication meets the minimum requirements of American
National Standard for Information Sciences—Permanence of Paper for Printed Library
Materials, ANSI/NISO Z39.48-1992.

Printed in the United States of America

For Chŏng-a, with love and gratitude

Contents

Acknowledgments

As I worked on this book, I incurred debts to many people and organizations. Without their understanding, support, and permission, I would have been unable to complete it. Hence, I came to the conclusion that a book should have many authors.

As this book is an unexpected outcome of the Cyber University of Korea's (CUK) e-Learning Campaign for Multicultural Families, supported by financial aid from the P'ohang Iron and Steel Company (POSCO) and Goldman Sachs, I am indebted to these two organizations. Without their financial support, I would have been unable to initiate the Campaign. I owe many thanks to Yun Sŏkman, the former president of POSCO, and John J. Kim and Christopher Jun, managing director and executive director, respectively, at Goldman Sachs, for their generous arrangement for the grants.

When I began the Campaign, permission and assistance from various provincial, regional, and local governments was instrumental. I am grateful for the enthusiastic support and administrative assistance from two governors, Kim Kwan-yong of north Kyŏngsang province and Park Chun-yŏng of south Chŏlla province. Also, many officials in provincial and municipal government helped to advance the Campaign. Chŏn Man-gil, who represents a support group for foreign brides, helped me meet many foreign brides. I am indebted to her assistance. Since so many people and organizations assisted me directly and indirectly during the course of the Campaign, I cannot list them all. Even so, I extend my gratitude to them.

When the idea to initiate the Campaign first occurred to me, my colleague at the CUK and a fellow anthropologist, Cho Kyung-jin (Kyŏng-jin Cho), encouraged me to go ahead with the Campaign and did preliminary work for it in two rural towns: Kumi in north Kyŏngsang province and Tamyang in south Chŏlla province. She and I drafted a preliminary Campaign proposal and approached several funding agencies seeking financial support. Yi Hyŏn-rak, who was chairman of our board of trustees then, was effective in persuading POSCO to understand the significance of the project. POSCO made a commitment to support our Campaign for three years from 2007 to 2010. As POSCO's funding phased out, Goldman Sachs began to back the Campaign financially.

During the Campaign, four of our deans, Cho Kyŏng-jin, Lee Jae-yŏl, Na Hong-sŏk, and Kim Sang-ki, were involved. Yŏm Ch'ŏl-hyŏn took on the position of director of the project until March 2010. Other supporting members of the Campaign team gathered much information that appears in this book. The team captain in the general affairs' section, Ryu Si-hyŏk, traveled with me on my frequent trips, including trips to Japan and Vietnam. I thank him for his work and for tolerating my nagging demands. For strong support for my research and writing, I owe a great deal to the CUK. I am thankful to many colleagues and friends at the CUK for encouraging me to engage in research and publication activities. My principal secretary, Ŏm Hae-sŏn, was instrumental in gathering a lot of basic data and arranging and analyzing it. For this, I am grateful.

AltaMira Press was essential in its enthusiastic support and expeditious evaluation. I am indebted to Jack Meinhardt, acquisition editor, and Marissa M. Parks, assistant editor, for pressing me to submit my project to AltaMira Press. Wendi Schnaufer has been a wonderful executive editor, shepherding this book through the final development stages. I am thankful to Desiree Reid for meticulous copyediting. My appreciation also extends to the anonymous readers for their constructive criticism that has improved this book.

Whatever the weakness of this book, rest assured they would have been far greater without the assistance and suggestions made by Roy Richard Grinker at George Washington University, Kendall Blanchard and Connie Blanchard at Georgia Southwestern State University, Nancy Abelmann at the University of Illinois, and Kyŏng-jin Cho at the CUK, who read the prospectus of the book and the draft version of the manuscript. They made valuable comments and suggestions about how I might further develop my raw ideas. Robert Brown read the roughest version of the manuscript and assisted me in polishing my rough writing into readable form.

My deepest debt of gratitude is to the many unnamed foreign brides whose accounts are included in this book. For their hospitality and cooperation, without which this book could not have been written, I will be forever grateful. Nevertheless, for the purpose of concealing their identities, I will not name them. Still, I deeply regret not being able to credit them by name.

I owe special gratitude to my wife, who had to carry a heavy burden when I was away from home doing fieldwork and then again while I was writing this book. My two sons, John and Drew; two daughters-in-law, Karen and Nancy; and five grandchildren, Matthew, Ryan, Jack, Luke, and Caroline, have been inspirational. Chŏng-a has been my energizer. I am forever grateful.

Introduction

The developed nations of the twenty-first century are predominantly multicultural: nations within nations, kaleidoscopes of ethnicities, complex collections of religious and political ideologies, and innumerable combinations of family values and traditions. Modern transportation, increased human mobility, and the shifting economic and political fortunes of many countries have contributed to this phenomenon of demographic heterogeneity. More than fifteen years ago, Will Kymlicka, a political philosopher and one of the utmost authorities on "multiculturalism," observed that "most countries today are culturally diverse. According to recent estimates, the world's 184 independent states contain over 600 living language groups, and 5,000 ethnic groups. In very few countries can the citizens be said to share the same language, or belong to the same ethnonational group."[1]

At the same time, however, Kymlicka noted that "Iceland and the Koreans [both North and South Korea] are commonly cited as two examples of countries which are more or less culturally homogeneous."[2] Later, in a book on multiculturalism that he published in 2007, he reiterated this claim, indicating that Korea, as are Iceland and Portugal, is mononational.[3] However, recent research and a closer look at the demographics of modern-day Korea give one reason to question Kymlicka's conclusion. Despite the popular view that Koreans are culturally and biologically homogenous, there is now evidence that would challenge this view and that is the principal subject of this book.

The view that Korea is a single ethnocultural nation is popular among native Koreans, especially so-called ethnic nationalists who argue for a type of "ethnic nationalism," the notion of Koreans as a single ethnic group of "pureblood" (*sunhyŏl*) that is descended from a common ancestor. Koreans of my generation and older have been deeply indoctrinated by a school of thought of national historiography (*minjok sahak*) that stresses the origins of Korean national identity as rooted in a single race (*tan'il minjok*).[4] Terms such as *mixed-blood* (*honhyŏl*) and *pure-blood* (*sunhyŏl*) have long been used to identify the ethnic origin of people who live in Korea. This tradition has raised concerns among human rights activists who argue that such terms lend themselves to social and economic discrimination. For this reason, in 2007, the UN Committee on the Elimination of Racial Discrimination (CERD) asked Korea to avoid the use of such expressions as "mixed-blood" and "pure-blood."

Despite the prevailing view among the traditionalists in Korea, the evidence from Korean prehistory, history, and contemporary demographics suggests that the conventional view of Korea as a racially and culturally homogeneous society may have no foundation in fact. According to newly revealed archaeological evidence, during the prehistoric Paleolithic period through the Neolithic era and into Bronze Age, the Korean peninsula was inhabited by two major racial groups, Caucasoid and Mongoloid, who appear to have lived side by side. Also, during the historical periods, various groups of foreigners—the Han Chinese, Mongolians, Manchurians, Vietnamese, Jurchens, Khitans, Yen, Japanese, Arabs, and various groups from the south and southeast—immigrated to the Korean peninsula and were naturalized. The descendants of those foreign immigrants have been identified and represent almost twelve million of South Korea's total forty-six million residents who were counted in the 2000 census. In other words, the descendents of those individuals who immigrated to Korea during the last several hundred years make up 26 percent of the country's total population. This figure alone should give one reason to question the accuracy of South Korea's description as monoethnic.

International marriages have a long history in Korea and have contributed to the diversification of the Korean gene pool. According to the *Samguk yusa* (*Memorabilia of the Three Kingdoms*), a Korean history written by Ilyon (Iryŏn), a thirteenth-century monk, the first-century Korean Kim Suro, the king of Kaya, married a princess of Ayodhya, India, in AD 48.[5] Later, during the period of the Koryŏ dynasty (918–1392), a succession of four kings married Yüan princesses. These foreign immigrants introduced their native cultural traditions to Korea, thus enriching and enlarging the inventory of Korean culture.

It is estimated that Korea's current population includes approximately 1.4 million immigrants or foreigners who have come from 180 different countries around the world. Of this number almost 182,000 are foreigners whose moves to Korea were occasioned by marriage. Some 162,000, or 89.2 percent of that total, are foreign brides who have come from a total of sixty-seven countries throughout the world.[6] The total number of foreigners makes up 2.5 percent of the current South Korean population. Obviously, these numbers pale in comparison to the number of foreigners who have immigrated to countries such as the United States, Australia, or Canada, both in absolute terms and percentages. However, this number is significant, especially in comparison to Korea's history. The country's foreign population has doubled twice within the last five years[7] and continues to grow steadfastly.

In response to such shifting demographics, multiculturalism has become one of the most talked-about issues in Korea. Increasingly, the public, government, and many civic organizations are demanding that the country recognize and affirm its ethnic diversity.[8] The notion of single ethnic nationalism in contemporary Korea is being replaced by an emergent multiculturalism. Because the topic has become so popular among the public, a growing number of scholars and intellectuals have begun to pursue studies of Korea's multiethnic and multicultural roots. Many historians, prehistorians, and archaeologists whose orientations are not grounded in the nationalistic historiography are pointing out that even traditionally Korea was not a monoethnic society. Also, they are raising questions about the roots of Korea's self-identification as ethnically pure and its xenophobic attitudes toward foreigners. Recently published writings reveal that before the later nineteenth and early twentieth centuries, Koreans did not have such a disparaging view of foreigners, nor did they discriminate against foreigners on the basis of ethnic origin.

ABOUT THE BOOK

In many ways, this book is a response to the growing interest in Korea's multiculturalism and helps to fill the void of scholarship relative to the topic. In its exploration of ethnic diversity in Korea, the work focuses on 161,999 foreign brides from sixty-seven countries who married Korean men and the 121,935 children born to these international marriages. The analysis does not include those marriages that involved foreign men marrying Korean women. It is not that these are considered insignificant. Indeed, they are. However, the focus of my fieldwork and analysis has been on the foreign brides, their experiences in Korea, and their impact on the increasing diversity of Korean society and culture. The principal aim of this book is to examine and attempt to understand Korean attitudes toward foreigners and the changing nature of Korean culture. An equally important objective is to analyze the way in which multiculturalism is being implemented in South Korea and to identify the difficult challenges the country is facing and the equally difficult decisions it is making.

Although this book is a typical descriptive, ethnographic work, I have made an effort to characterize and analyze a Korean version of multicultural-ism as it compares with the prevailing liberal democratic model of Western multiculturalism. The questions I address include the following: First, how do the Korean advocates of multiculturalism understand the meaning of the term? It appears that Koreans use the term *multiculturalism* to describe an increasingly diverse Korea as the antithesis or counterconcept of a single ethnic nationalism.[9] This book will attempt to isolate and describe Koreans' epistemological understanding or *emic* perception[10] of multiculturalism.

The second major question addressed in the book is simply why the term *multiculturalism* is one of the most talked-about issues in contemporary Korea and why Koreans are increasingly embracing and affirming multicul-turalism while several European countries such as Britain, Germany, and the Netherlands seem to be retreating from multiculturalism, especially "immi-grant multiculturalism," as Kymlicka has noted.[11] Korea's public discourse and rhetoric on its growing multiculturalism are centered on the country's demographic trends: its low birthrate (the lowest in the world at 1.15);[12] its increasing life expectancy (79.6),[13] which is creating an "aging society";[14] and its critical shortage of marriageable women in farming and fishing villages that has resulted largely from the massive exodus of rural peoples to the cities and industrial zones.[15]

The third question the book addresses is how the concept of multiculturalism that is being implemented in Korea reflects the needs, wishes, and expectations of those who are the subjects of that policy, particularly the foreign brides. Scholars characterize the process as the development of multiculturalism policies that are government-led[16] and that are largely political rhetoric and slogan,[17] are paternalistic, and as one that overlooks or undermines the views of immigrants even as it adopts policies that will have direct effects on their lives.[18] Even the nongovernmental organization (NGO) groups who advocate multiculturalism compete with each other, and often their programs overlap with one another. Also, most of their projects are supported by government funds—usually one-time or temporary. The projects themselves are mostly cultural events, including cooking and tea ceremonies at local fairs, and they offer little to the foreign brides except for an opportunity to dress up and parade around in their native costumes, an exercise these women sometimes resent.

The fourth question raised in this book is: What do the Koreans mean by multiculturalism? Is there a distinctively Korean concept or model, and if so, how does it reflect Korean culture, and how is it unique among the many other models that exist? As Will Kymlicka has indicated, the "various senses of culture are reflected in the different meanings attached to the term 'multiculturalism' in different countries. In Canada, it typically refers to the right of immigrants to express their ethnic identity without fear of prejudice and discrimination: in Europe, it often refers to sharing of powers between national communities; in the USA, it is often used to include the demands of marginalized social groups."[19] One major goal of this work is to describe what multiculturalism means in today's Korea.

The fifth question posed in this book is: "What is the future of multiculturalism in Korea?" Can a Western-like, liberal model of multiculturalism be successfully implemented in Korea? This issue is the main topic of the final summary chapter and conclusion.

UNDERSTANDING OR MISUNDERSTANDING MULTICULTURALISM

Definition of Multiculturalism

The term *multiculturalism* is becoming a household word in contemporary Korea. However, I must confess that even though I am a cultural anthropologist, I myself was not certain what the term meant when I first undertook this project. Those scholars who were the first to write about multiculturalism, such as Charles Taylor, Will Kymlicka, and others, were predominantly philosophers or political scientists. Their academic orientations are different than mine, and as one would expect, so, too, are their academic jargons. To most cultural anthropologists, the concept of cultural relativism is central to their worldview. This tenet is based on the assumption that all patterns of culture are equally valid and therefore should be viewed objectively and without ethnocentric bias. In some ways I was of the opinion that this tenet in itself is sufficient for dealing with cultural diversity. I had never considered the need for an additional concept like multiculturalism.

Some intellectuals are openly critical of the term *multiculturalism*. For one, Alain Finkielkraut, a French essayist and one of France's prominent public intellectuals, has written: "Multiculturalism! This is the key word used in the struggle against those who strive for national purity. Multi-culturalists exalt the spice and variety of plurality of cultures over the dull monopoly of cultural sameness. Do not be deceived, however. However different the two sides may seem, and however strained their relationship, they both adhere to the same relativism. Their credos are opposed, but their versions of the world are similar. Both see cultures as all-embracing totalities, whose virtue lies in their multiplicity."[20]

Kymlicka dismisses Finkielkraut's criticism by arguing that "the emerging international discourses and norms are fundamentally liberal in character. As such, they are broadly consistent with theories that have been developed by recent Western political theories in which multiculturalism is understood as a concept that is both guided and constrained by a foundational commitment to principles of individual freedom and equality."[21]

Even though the term *multiculturalism* has become fashionable today, some organizations intentionally avoid using the term. For instance, according to Kymlicka, "One reason why IQs (international intergovernmental organizations) do not use the term 'multiculturalism' is that in many countries it has more limited connotations. In Europe, for example, 'multiculturalism' is often seen as a distinctly New World term that does not cover older European ideas of 'minority protection.' Even within the New World, 'multiculturalism' is sometimes used only in the context of immigrant groups, and does not cover policies towards indigenous peoples."[22] Others who dislike the term *multiculturalism* prefer to use terms such as *minority rights, diversity politics, interculturalism, cultural rights,* or *differentiated citizenship.*[23]

I do not have any particular predisposition to like or dislike the term. Nor am I inclined to insist on using the concept of cultural relativism simply because it has been the underlying metaphor guiding the fieldwork I have done as an anthropologist. Instead, I would admit to the weakness of the concept. Cultural relativism is not tied to any normative standards that allow for the objective ethical evaluation of cultural patterns and behaviors, since in its classic version, cultural relativism assumes there are no universal principles of morality and instead insists on tolerance for all cultures. The problem is that while cultural relativism seems to be a universally fair and just ethical principle, the fact is there have been some universally "wrong" cultural traits. Consider such practices as human slavery, anti-Semitism, torture, and genocide. In other words, it may in some circumstances be necessary to reconcile the concept of cultural relativism with an international code of human rights. The concept of multiculturalism is not constrained by the assumption that all cultural patterns are equally valid and thus perhaps better suited to understanding and developing policy for ethnically diverse societies.

Charles Taylor, one of the early proponents of multiculturalism, assumes that multiculturalism policy can be built "on the already established principles of the politics of equal respect"[24] and thus include implicitly the perspective of cultural relativism. Finkielkraut is more explicit in his argument that cultural relativism has actually been included in multiculturalism theory. He notes that "all cultures had to be declared equivalent. . . . The modern philosophy of decolonization, by denouncing the deep-seated inhumanity of humanism, and by seeking out the particular, the historical and regional differences behind everything which suggests universality, thus links up again with Herder."[25]

Even though the term *multiculturalism* is so often and widely used, as political theorist David Miller points out, it remains vague, with no clear or fixed meaning that is easy to define in a single sentence.[26] Charles Taylor has defined multiculturalism as "the politics of recognition" and equal respect.[27] In a book by that title that Taylor published in 1993, he considers initially whether the institutions of liberal democratic government make room—or should make room—for recognizing the worth of distinctive cultural traditions, which was the centerpiece of his concept of multiculturalism. Later, in the 1994 edition of his essay, Taylor adds: "A number of strands in contemporary politics turn on the need, sometimes the demand, for recognition. The need, it can be argued, is one of the driving forces behind nationalist movements in politics. And the demand comes to the fore in a number of ways in today's politics, on behalf of minority or 'subaltern' groups, in some forms of feminism and in what is today called the politics of 'multiculturalism.'"[28] Susan Wolf is a scholar who has dealt extensively with the issue of feminism and multicultural education.[29]

Kymlicka uses Taylor's descriptor, "the politics of recognition," when he defines the concept of multiculturalism, noting that "in some contexts, the term multiculturalism is used to cover a broader range of forms of diversity, including gender/sexual orientation/disability and so on. On this broader view, 'multiculturalism' is virtually coextensive with 'the politics of recognition.'"[30] Kymlicka views the adjective *multicultural* as applicable not only to ethnic cultures but also to nonethnic groups, such as "disabled, gays and lesbians, women, the working class, atheists, and Communists."[31] Summing up the definition of *liberal multiculturalism*, Kymlicka avers[32]: "Liberal multiculturalism rests on the assumption that politics of recognizing and accommodating ethnic diversity can expand human freedom, strengthen human rights, diminish ethnic and racial hierarchies, and deepen democracy."[33]

However we might define multiculturalism, if there were no multicultural policies—for example, Taylor's "political recognition,"—multiculturalism would remain only an ideology, orientation, or morality in much the same way as anthropology's "cultural relativism." As Kymlicka and his associates have addressed the challenges of defining what is meant by multicultural policies,[34] they have conducted an insightful empirical study. Using eight different criteria as a way of categorizing multicultural policies, they rated twenty-one countries. The results were interesting. The outcomes of the study indicate that the countries with the strongest and most comprehensive policies include Australia and Canada. Countries with moderately strong policies include Belgium, the Netherlands, New Zealand, Sweden, the United Kingdom, and the United States. Austria, Denmark, Finland, France, Germany, Greece, Ireland, Italy, Japan, Norway, Portugal, Spain, and Switzerland are characterized as having the weakest multicultural policies. South Korea was not included in the study, but its ranking will be analyzed and categorized in a later chapter.[35]

Rhetoric on Multiculturalism in Korea

One question that must be raised is whether the notion of multiculturalism in Korea is a diffused version of Western liberal multiculturalism either in word or deed or both. Is the Korean version of multiculturalism different in meaning than the way it is used in the West in a descriptive, normative, and/or ideological sense? Some native Korean scholars, notably cultural anthropologists, suggest that Koreans use the term *multiculturalism* in their own way (i.e., an *emic* category of perception) to describe an increasingly ethnically and racially diverse Korea. Multiculturalism in this sense is being used in Korea as a counterconcept or in contrast to the idea of a single ethnic nationalism that seems to have originated in response to Japanese domination and to have persisted from the beginning of the nineteenth century until the early 2000s.

Kim Hyun Mee writes that "the term 'multiculturalism' was coined in Korea after the racial, sexual, and class violence stemming from ethnic nationalism based on pure-blood ideology was thought to seriously encroach on the rights of migrant workers, biracial people, and migrant women. Multiculturalism in Korea is thus used as a counter concept to Korea's violent mono-ethnicity, rather than its general meaning of recognizing or having a mutual understanding of cultural difference."[36] Han Geon-Soo is critical of the way Koreans use multiculturalism: "[In Korea] multicultural society and multiculturalism are not used as analytical concepts reflecting the reality of Korean society, but merely as rhetoric concepts or political slogans for future visions of Korea."[37] Han Kyung-Koo, on the other hand, characterizes Korean multiculturalism as a weak form of "state sponsored multiculturalism" or "government-led multiculturalism."[38]

Koreans until recently have not been keenly aware of the complexities that are involved in the concept of multiculturalism. The prefix *multi* was introduced at first to refer to the growing number of international marriages involving unions between Koreans and persons of various non-Korean ethnic and racial groups. The phrase *multicultural family* was adopted before the term *multiculturalism*. Kim Hyun Mee reports:

> The word "multicultural family" first appeared in government documents at the suggestion of an NGO. In 2003, "Hifamily," an activist organization focused on families, submitted a petition to the National Human Rights Commission saying that the use of the word "mixed blood" (*honhyeol* or *honhyŏl*) was a human rights violation, and sought to replace the term with "the second generation of a

multicultural family." Since 2005, migrant women have been at the center of the Korean government's attention, and hence started using the word "multicultural family." . . . [Beginning in January 2006], "multicultural family" became the official term used by the government and NGOs, a consensus was reached that systematic support for multicultural families should be provided.[39]

Since then, "The official discourse has taken a positive turn and advocated for multiculturalism, which is a far cry from the official affirmation of a single nation-state."[40]

Because the term *multiculturalism* originated in and evolved from the concept of the multicultural family, most of Koreans tend to think that multiculturalism is applicable only to foreigners who married Koreans and their children. The only legal foundation that regulates multiculturalists is the Multicultural Families Support Act (*Tamunhwagajok chiwŏnbŏp*), which provides services exclusively for multicultural families. Except for some activists in various NGOs, few members of the Korean public or officials in the Korean government recognize some 557,000 foreign workers, both legal and illegal, as multicultural or as issues for multiculturalism policy. Little effort has been made to protect their human rights while they are in Korea. They are governed by the Act on the Employment of Foreign Workers (*Woegukinkŭlojaŭi koyongdŭngae kwanhan pŏplyul*) and are not allowed to stay any longer than five consecutive years. Otherwise, they would be eligible for naturalization. Obviously this suggests that Korea's commitment to multiculturalism has its limitations and that the country's rhetoric on the subject does not reflect the reality of its policies.

Regarding the introduction of Western multiculturalism in Korea beginning in the early 2000s, a few words are in order about Korea's history of adopting foreign ideas. Throughout its history, Korea has not been a good teacher of its own culture to others—except to the Japanese during the Three Kingdoms—but Koreans have been good students of foreign ideas: ideologies, religions, and philosophies such Confucianism, Taoism, Christianity, Buddhism, democracy, communism, capitalism, and now multiculturalism.

Multiculturalism, as it is understood in this study, was the invention of Western political philosophers in the twentieth century. Multiculturalism was a political and social response to accommodating ethnically and culturally diverse immigrants, and in some countries, indigenous minority groups. Because Koreans have been indoctrinated since the early twentieth century to believe that Korea is a homogeneous, monoethnic society, there has previously been no word in the Korean language equivalent to "multiculturalism" as it is used in liberal Western democratic societies. Recently Koreans have come up with the term *tamunhwa*, which is more or less a literal translation of *multiculturalism* in English. However, the Korean word cannot carry the same meaning as the English word because Koreans encountered the term without first understanding all the implications and ramifications of it.

Multiculturalism is not the only Western concept that Koreans have adopted before fully understanding its full meaning. The term *democracy* is a classic example of an idea that Koreans encountered before grasping its full meaning. This is evident in Korea's republican governance. Korea instituted its first republican government after World War II: the Constitution of 1948 was based on the principle of democracy. Nonetheless, Korea experienced the strong authoritarian rule of Syngman Rhee, the first president of the republic, for twelve years and then military rule for thirty-two years thereafter. Finally, as of 1993, Koreans have enjoyed a genuinely democratic society. After encountering the idea of democracy, it took some sixty years for Koreans to adapt to the democratic principle in both word and deed. Perhaps it will also take some time for Koreans to implement a genuine multiculturalism equivalent to that practiced in liberal democratic societies of the West. I hope that the readers do not believe there is no chance of implementing multiculturalism in Korea, given that Korea did eventually implement fully democratic governance. I only hope that it does not take as much time for multiculturalism to become a reality in Korea as it took for democracy to firmly take root.

WHY FOREIGN BRIDES?

This study focuses on 161,999 foreign brides (about 89.2 percent of the total international marriages in Korea) from sixty-seven countries who married Korean men and 121,935 children who were born into international marriages. Why study foreign brides and their children? First, the phenomenon is a major challenge to Korea that is part of its effort to give its "rural bachelors a chance to marry,"[41] as the government slogan has it. Providing brides for Korean men, especially those in remote farming and fishing villages, has become a national agenda and priority of the Korean government at all levels.

Korea has for some time been experiencing a critical shortage of marriageable women in its farming and fishing villages due largely to the massive exodus of rural peasant farmers from the countryside to the cities and industrial zones during the nation's recent economic development. Despite the desperate effort of the Korean government to revitalize rural villages through its New Village Movement (*Samaŭl undong*),[42] beginning in 1970, unprecedented economic growth and industrialization brought about devastating consequences for rural villages. The lower income and poor living conditions in rural areas motivated peasant farmers to leave their homes for urban areas and industrial zones, as these locales promised higher wages and modern living conditions along with the prospect of a better education for their children. As a result, urban and industrial zones became "black holes" into which massive numbers of rural migrants, especially young people (and young women in particular), were drawn.

Consequently, the number of farm households decreased from 2,483,000 in 1970 to 1,194,000 in 2009—a reduction of 1,289,000 (a 51.9 percent decrease). Also, the overall farming population decreased from 14,422,000 in 1970 to 3,118,000 in 2009—a decrease of 11,304,000 (a total of 78.4 percent reduction). In the early 1990s, the exodus of younger Koreans out of rural farming villages became severe: the population of younger people whose ages range from fifteen to fifty in rural farming villages was 5,291,000 in 1990, but it has since decreased by 2,439,000 to 2,852,000 (a 46 percent reduction). The exodus has led to an imbalance of the sexes in the farming population. Men outnumber women, especially among those of marriageable age, twenty-five to thirty-nine.[43] Today, most farmers who remain in rural villages tend to be older, as the younger ones have left. There are fewer women of childbearing age in rural areas (16.6 percent of the total rural female population). This situation has created a critical shortage of farm labor and a paucity of female partners for marriage. This paucity is, of course, a concern central to this study.[44]

To compensate for the shortage and to attempt to keep men on the farm, the Korean government, especially local government, has spearheaded a campaign to recruit foreign brides, relying heavily on international marriage brokers. The success of this effort has ensured that Korea would become a multicultural society. While the program itself has been a success, the Korean government has not responded effectively to the needs and expectations of the foreign brides themselves. Until recently, the government did not have a formal mechanism for addressing and coordinating the affairs of foreign brides. Now this responsibility belongs to the Ministry of Gender Equality and Family (*Yosŏng kajokpu*). However, there is still some confusion since several branches of government that often compete with one another monitor the affairs of the international brides. What is more, scholars have not yet developed an adequate strategy for transforming Korea from a society that once believed itself to consist of a single ethnicity into one that is truly multicultural. Analyzing and understanding the challenges and conditions of foreign brides in Korea can provide valuable insight into the dynamics of Korea's growing multiculturalism.

A second justification for the ethnographic study of foreign brides in Korea is the fact that, as noted earlier, that the term *multiculturalism* in Korea has evolved from the concept of multicultural families. Most Koreans still tend to understand the concept of multiculturalism as something pertaining almost exclusively to foreign brides. For that reason, the various programs, aids, and campaigns related to multiculturalism are still built largely around the foreign brides and their circumstances. Other immigrants, such as migrant workers, foreign students, or even North Korean escapees are not considered critical to the development and implementation of multiculturalism. Therefore, understanding the meaning of multiculturalism and the development of related operational policies is most effectively achieved by a focus on foreign brides.

The third reason for my focus is the fact that foreign brides in Korea face a "double jeopardy" situation, in that they are women on the one hand and members of ethnic and racial minority groups on the other. The conventional multiculturalism theory and practice of the past thirty years within the academic community has dealt largely with issues of ethnocultural diversity, to include immigrants, national minorities, and indigenous peoples. Until recently the plight of women as minorities has not been central to this discussion. However, the latest scholarship on multiculturalism addresses nonethnic groups such as "disabled, gays and lesbians, *women* (emphasis mine), the working class, atheists, and Communists."[45] Susan Wolf expresses a fundamental feminist concern that the early proponents of multiculturalism failed to recognize females as minorities and thus understated their plight.[46] Such an oversight in Korea is especially unfortunate in that foreign brides are playing positive roles in a rapidly evolving society. Not only are they filling a void created by a critical shortage of Korean women, but they are also playing important traditional roles as filial daughters-in-law and submissive wives in a culture still rooted in a gender-biased Confucian paternalism. The voices of these foreign brides thus provide valuable data and an insightful perspective on the evolving role of women as part of the multicultural movement in Korea.

A fourth and practical reason for the focus of my study is the fact that I had an opportunity to conduct fieldwork on foreign brides as an unexpected outcome of a public service campaign I recently conducted (e-Learning Campaign for Multicultural Families). This campaign was designed to help foreign brides improve their Korean language skills and develop a better understanding of Korean culture. While I was working to provide these services I had the opportunity to observe the efforts made by local governments, NGO activists, and volunteers to teach the Korean language to foreign brides. As a result, I came to understand the difficulties encountered in these efforts. Because foreign brides are so widely dispersed throughout the country, often in remote villages or on small islands, it is difficult, if not impossible, to assemble them at a specific time and place. The rural residents simply do not have the means of transportation that allow them to drive to and from classes. Also, since most of them are working full time and raising young children, they cannot allocate the time to study. This is especially a problem during the farming season.

These handicaps are exacerbated by the reluctance of families who host foreign brides to allow them to attend classes. They worry that such public outings would give the brides an opportunity to meet other countrywomen and gossip disparagingly about their in-laws. Also, some Korean husbands worry that if their foreign brides are given the freedom to associate with outsiders, they may be tempted to leave them, searching for more lucrative jobs in the cities or industrial zones.

As a result of these challenges, I decided to shift the educational paradigm from traditional "off-line" education to "on-line" education via the Internet. Such online or distance learning is convenient, inexpensive, and continuous, without any time or term limitations as long as immigrants can access computers and connect to the Internet. They can also choose the curriculum that best fits their level of competency in the Korean language, and they can repeat the lessons as needed. On-line education in Korea is especially appropriate because Korea has a robust infrastructure for supporting Internet communication.[47]

Having come to this conclusion, I decided to use my authority and resources as president of the Cyber University of Korea (CUK) to implement an online education program for assisting foreign brides in their adaptation to Korean society. This program, entitled e-Learning Campaign for Multicultural Families (hereafter the CUK's Campaign or Campaign) was designed to teach the Korean language and culture to foreign brides via the Internet. Financial support for the Campaign came from P'ohang Iron and Steel Company (POSCO), the largest steel company in Korea, and Goldman Sachs, the world's well-known investment banking company. Administrative assistance for the project came from central, provincial, municipal, and local governments.

During this process, I observed and interviewed numerous foreign brides, their husbands, and other family members. During the Campaign, I also acquired an unusual empathy for and understanding of the lives of married immigrants in Korea. At the same time, the Campaign led me to gather the information necessary to write this book. In fact, the life stories of foreign brides told in this book are based on those of the "students" who have been and are enrolled in the Campaign. I was able to interact with them frequently, conduct in-depth interviews, and observe them in both formal and informal settings. Thus, in many ways, this book is the unexpected outcome of the Campaign.

The Campaign, besides becoming a serendipitous fieldwork setting, has proven to be a programmatic success. As of the end of November 2010, some

71,175 foreign brides from fifty-five countries are taking Korean lessons offered by the CUK free of charge. The total number of enrollees is increasing by about one hundred a day. With additional funding from Goldman Sachs, the Campaign is developing an advanced Korean language course. This curriculum is advanced enough to help foreign wives prepare for the language exam required for Korean citizenship and other Korean language proficiency tests. Also, the Campaign has begun to develop courses on foreign brides' native languages and cultures, beginning with the Vietnamese language and culture. This part of the Campaign is meant to promote cross-cultural understanding. In addition, since the Korean language package is on the Internet, some 4,813 people from fifty-two countries, including 359 cities throughout the world, are taking the Korean language courses.

INFLOW OF FOREIGN BRIDES

As noted earlier, Korea's effort to recruit foreign brides was prompted largely by the shortage of marriageable women in Korea, especially in rural farming and fishing villages, a circumstance resulting from the promise of economic opportunity in the cities. What further compounds the problem is that in rural regions many women are either postponing their marriages or choosing to remain single for life.[48] A drastic decrease in the traditional custom of arranged marriage—wherein marriage decisions were made by parents, other relatives, and acquaintances—has become a hindrance for rural men seeking mates. As Korea transforms itself from a premodern to a modern society, younger generations of Koreans are opting out of arranged marriages and choosing mates independently. This makes the situation that much more difficult for rural men who are looking to marry since now they must depend on their ability to convince someone to marry them rather than have a match made for them. A variety of demographic changes have complicated rural men's efforts to find Korean mates. Many of those seekers have turned to foreign brides and often have looked to local government agencies for help. These government agencies have a vested interest in such marriages since they ultimately serve to keep local young people from immigrating to the city. They also intervene to raise fertility rates and stabilize declining populations.

Between 2004 and 2008, the number of foreign spouses married to Koreans increased nearly forty-four times over and continues to rise rapidly.[49] Currently, approximately 40 percent of Korean men who work in agriculture, forestry, or in the fishing industry are married to foreign women. The number of children born into these families is increasing at a rapid pace. By 2010, the total had reached 121,935.[50]

Since the fall of the former Union of Soviet Socialist Republics (USSR) in 1990 and the establishment of independent satellite states beginning in 1991, out-immigration policies in these states have been lax. As a result, several former satellite states, including Uzbekistan, Russia, Kyrgyzstan, Kazakhstan, Ukraine, and Tajikistan have allowed their women to emigrate and marry Korean men. The largest number of foreign brides came from China, the vast majority of these since the country normalized its relations with China in 1992. Of these, 59,346, or 32.7 percent of the total foreign brides, are *Chosŏnjok* (Korean Chinese).[51] They are followed closely by the Han Chinese foreign brides (51,348 or 28.3 percent). So, without normalized relations between the two countries, over 110,000 foreign brides (over 61 percent of all the foreign brides in Korea) would most likely not have been able to marry Korean men and enter Korea.[52] Even though the normalization between China and Korea took place in 1992, most *Chosŏnjok* and Chinese have entered Korea since the year 2000. Without question, the policy of détente helped to promote cross-racial and cross-ethnic marriage.

Seeking foreign women as mates is a logical, practical choice for many single Korean men in rural villages. At the same time, there are factors that make the option of marrying a Korean man attractive to a non-Korean woman. According to a study conducted by the Korean Ministry for Health, Welfare and Family Affairs in July 2005, 41 percent of all the foreign women who have married Korean men are searching for economic betterment, hoping eventually to send money to their natal families back home. Over 73 percent of those who married via international marriage brokers were seeking to improve their economic status.[53] In some areas of Southeast Asia, finding foreign husbands for young brides is believed to be the best route out of poverty. By marrying foreigners from richer countries, brides believe they can save their parents back home.[54]

The Korean economy is doing better than that of most countries from whence the immigrants hail, with the exception of Japan. But, many of the married immigrants come to realize that the financial situation of their Korean families is worse than they had expected during courtship and before coming to Korea. The rosy picture of the Korean economy and its living standards publicized via a Korean pop culture phenomenon called *Hallyu* may give some of the immigrants a distorted impression of life in Korea.[55] People from East and Southeast Asian countries in particular have been exposed to Korean television, mainly soap opera series, music, and dance. This exposure to the *Hallyu* wave has helped to create an image of Korea as a land of wealth, prosperity, and lavish spending, an image that resonates well with economically deprived women who are desperate to find a way out of poverty.

ORGANIZATION AND PRESENTATION OF THE BOOK

The expansion and acceptance of multiculturalism in Korea has faced little systematic or organized resentment. Many Koreans tend to believe that this apparent tolerance is accidental and attributable largely to the changing demographics themselves. However, to accept this simple explanation is to overlook the Korean historical tradition that tolerates foreign immigrants. It also fails to take into account the deliberate effort to actively recruit foreign human resources. These are important factors in understanding the current Korean multicultural movement and the affirmation that is sustaining it.

Even though there are over a million foreigners in Korea today, there are over six times that many Korean immigrants in other countries around the world.[56] So, the experience of immigration is not difficult for Koreans to understand. Since some 6.8 million Koreans and their descendants live outside Korea as a result of the so-called Korean diaspora—mostly in China (about 2.3 million), the United States (2.1 million), Japan (0.9 million), Canada (22,300), and Russia (22,000)—most Koreans are predictably empathetic toward immigrants, travelers, and ethnic minorities.

In the years between 1963 and 1977, some 8,600 poverty-stricken South Korean men went to West Germany as coal miners and 10,400 women went as nurses. Many of these Korean immigrants married each other, while some of nurses found German husbands. During the 1980s, some seventeen thousand Korean brides, mostly economically underprivileged divorcees or women who had missed the opportunity to marry in early age, went to Japan under many of the same circumstances facing the foreign brides who married Korean men and came to Korea in the early years of the current century.[57]

Understanding traditional Korean history and culture as it relates to immigrants is essential to the effort to understand why Koreans have been so receptive to the country's growing multiculturalism and why there has been so little resentment and so few protests. Analyzing the current demographics of Korean society outside the context of the country's culture and history is an example of what anthropologist Francis L. K. Hsu describes as "pebble analogy": "Some of our scientific investigations are not unlike counting, classifying and 'computerizing' pebbles on the beach to determine the causes of rising and ebbing of tides."[58] However, counting, classifying, and computerizing pebbles on the beach will never lend itself to explaining the invisible forces of the moon's gravity that cause tides to rise and fall.

Certainly, the formation of Korea's traditional view on multiculturalism did not occur in a historical vacuum. An ethnohistorical analysis is critical to understanding Korean immigration and naturalization. As Søren Kierkegaard has observed with reference to the value of history, "Life is lived forward but it is understood backward."[59]

For this reason, the first part of this book, including chapters 1 and 2, is devoted to describing the historical roots of Korea's ethnic and racial diversity. The second part, chapters 3, 4, 5, and 6, relates in case-study format the life histories of selected foreign brides. The concluding chapter, chapter 7, characterizes the current state of Korean multiculturalism and makes some remarks on the future of Korean multiculturalism.

ORIENTATION AND METHODOLOGY OF THE BOOK

This book may be unique in that it is written by a self-reflexive anthropologist who has a dual identity as both an insider and an outsider. I am, in a sense, an insider who was born, raised, and partly educated in Korea for twenty-seven years. However, I am also an outsider who lived for thirty-six years in the United States until my return to Korea in 2001, although during the years I resided in the United States I spent two years in Korea as a senior Fulbright Scholar (1988 to 1989 and 1993 to 1994), and several months doing anthropological fieldwork. During my prolonged years of living in the United States studying, teaching, and doing research, I acquired self-reflexivity—a sense of critical distance from myself that minimizes subjectivity and maximizes my ability to see through the eyes of the people I am studying. In describing the life histories of foreign brides I have made an effort to present a balanced view of their lives and those of their Korean in-laws. Since I lived so long in the United States as an ethnic minority, I have the ability to empathize with the foreign brides. Moreover, my family is a multicultural family. I have a Caucasian daughter-in-law and two grandsons from a cross-racial marriage. Thus, both my objectivity and sensitivity in writing this book arise from my own personal experience.

While this is an ethnographic work, generalizations are not its principal focus. Inevitably, though, the use of some historical comparisons has led to some generalizations. Some seasoned anthropologists have admitted, "Ethnography is always more than description. . . . [It is] also a way of generalizing."[60] According to James W. Fernandez, the works of anthropologists like Bronislaw Malinowski, Ruth Benedict, E. E. Evans-Pritchard, Marcel Griaule, and Clyde Kluckhohn are considered "major *'points de repère'* in anthropology," not because of their theoretical contributions but because of their "skillful presentation of local points of view."[61] Fernandez notes that "they did not allow that essential academic interest to override local realities."

I want to relate local realities as much as I can instead of using a specific theory or model. I think I have been successful in doing so in my previous work when telling poignant stories of dispersed Korean families before, during, and after the Korean War (1950–1953).[62]

In this study, various information-gathering techniques have been used:

(1) A collection of ethnohistorical methods for reconstructing the ethnic origins of Koreans.

In order to reconstruct an ethnohistory of Korea, genealogies of various Korean surname groups (*sŏng-ssi*) were gathered and analyzed. In addition, many volumes of archaeological, prehistoric, and historical research were consulted. Although some historians and other social scientists have used genealogy (*chokpo*) in their studies as a valuable source of information, it has seldom been used in anthropological research because anthropologists traditionally have studied mostly preliterate and simple societies where there are no written genealogies. However, some historians, sociologists, and legal scholars have recognized that genealogies are a useful source of information for their studies.[63] Still, issues concerning validity and reliability sometimes arise. This was the case with some genealogies compiled, published, and updated during the Japanese domination of Korea and after its liberation from Japan in 1945. This case will be revisited in the following chapter. Nevertheless, since they are written records, genealogies were indispensable in my efforts to trace the origins of immigrants to Korea, to describe the process of their naturalization, and to identify their status and occupation after they settled on the Korean peninsula.

(2) The ethnographic method.

As the basis for my ethnographic description, I have employed various data-gathering techniques such as participant-observation and in-depth interviews with the people being studied or informants who are knowledgeable about them. I have also used various available written documents, ranging from sensational newspaper stories to thoughtful scholarly writings.

(3) Participant-observation as a part of the CUK's campaign.

In order for participants to take part in the CUK's Campaign, they must have at least minimal computer skills and the ability to connect to and navigate the Internet. The Campaign team and I visited individual homes, village halls, and municipal, county, and provincial offices to make sure that the appropriate equipment and skills were in place. This gave us ready access to the world of our subjects. In addition, the training teams and I brought in assistants who were natives of the immigrants' culture of origin and could serve as interpreters and "cultural brokers." In the process, I observed and interviewed numerous foreign brides, their spouses, and other family members. I also had the opportunity to get to know many officials of local, municipal, and central government who are responsible for dealing with the affairs of foreign brides.

In addition, I talked to and worked with many civic group volunteers who are involved in the implementation of multicultural programs. These experiences allowed me to collect important information and valuable data and thus better understand the problems of foreign brides and the challenges faced by Korea as it adjusts to and accommodates its new residents.

(4) The collection of life histories.

In addition to collecting information through participant-observation and interviews, I have used a method of collecting individual life histories as a valuable technique for delineating the life patterns of several specially selected foreign brides. The method of life history as a major research tool in anthropological field research is legitimate and well established in anthropological studies.[64] Anthropologists have often found life histories to be "useful for examining the patterning of general values, foci of cultural interests, and perceptions of social and natural relationships."[65] Some nonanthropologists may be skeptical about the validity and reliability of life history materials. Nonetheless, "to the objection that life-history data frequently cannot be checked against objective observations of real behavior," Pertti Pelto contends that "very frequently a chief anthropological concern is the patterning of peoples' beliefs and conceptualizations of past events, rather than the truth or falseness of these accounts."[66]

In the ethnography section of the book, I narrate the life histories of foreign brides, focusing on four categories or types of such histories: First, an epic journey of an archaeologist in search of his ancestress "believed to be from India"; second, the tales of foreign brides who married via international marriage brokers; third, stories of foreign brides who married as a result of arrangements made by religious organizations; and fourth, stories of foreign brides who married Korean men because they fell in love with them.

In narrating these tales I cannot claim that these selected foreign brides are representative of all 161,999 who have immigrated to Korea. Nor am I representing this as a statistical analysis that relies on the randomness of data selection and collection. My primary interest is in telling the rich and personalized life histories of these individuals in a way that sheds light on their circumstances and those of the larger Korean society to which they are adapting. Some might question the value of an approach that focuses on the experience of a relatively small group of informants. However, some important sociological and anthropological theoretical insights have resulted from this approach. Anthropologist Oscar Lewis, for instance, was successful in theorizing about and providing a valuable window on "the culture of poverty" by studying only five families.[67] In a similar fashion I have, in an earlier book, successfully described the lives of ten million dispersed Korean families through the life histories of five individuals.[68]

At the same time, I would remind the reader that my descriptions in this book are not limited to the life histories of people in the four categories listed above. I have incorporated stories of many additional people: workers in various civic organizations, reporters, intellectuals and scholars, laypersons, and officials who are involved in assisting foreign brides. I have studied vast quantities of prehistoric, historic, and contemporary documents, including articles in the daily press and in weekly and monthly journals, stylistically ranging from crass sensationalism to thoughtful discussion. Books and essays that narrate stories of foreign brides are uncommon, especially in English. However, Korean newspapers have provided an invaluable source of information, and I have quoted from them extensively.

Parenthetically, some readers may wonder why multiculturalism in Korea is a subject suited to publication in English. In truth, the content of this book is not limited to Korea and the Korean people. Rather, it includes stories of brides from sixty-seven countries and their children. Were this book not written in English, people from those countries would not have access to realistic accounts about their daughters, sisters, and friends who are living in Korea. Also, they would miss the lessons to be learned about the preparation for and movement to Korea for those women contemplating marriage to a Korean man.

In addition, issues raised in this book are global issues and English has become the dominant global language. As more and more of the world's people cross national boundaries, a detailed description of Korean multiculturalism will become an increasingly valuable case study.

In order to give the book a universal appeal, I have made every effort to tell, with compassion, compelling tales of foreign brides in an alien land. They are stories that deserve to be told, and who better to tell them than an anthropologist who has lived and studied in different worlds. As my good friend Miles Richardson, a humanistic anthropologist, once said, "If the anthropologist does not tell the human myth, then who will?"[69]

ETHICS, USAGE, AND READERSHIP

Throughout this book, for person's names and places, even though there is a new Korean romanization system developed by the National Institute of the Korean Language in July 2000, I have romanized in accordance with the more traditional McCune-Reischauer system. This will ensure that this book is consistent with most Western works about Korea. The exceptions are the names of a few Koreans, including myself, who have established different romanizations for themselves (e.g., Syngman Rhee) as personal names or particular places (e.g., Seoul, the capital city of South Korea). When I have quoted directly from original sources with the new romanization, I have not altered the originals. However, in such cases I have indicated the use of the McCune-Reischauer system in parentheses.

Also, following Korean and Japanese usage, when I refer to Koreans and Japanese, I give their surnames (family names or *sŏngssi*) first, before their personal names. However, when the publications of Korean and Japanese authors are in English, I follow the Western practice of personal names before family names. Consequently, in some cases a person's name may appear in two different ways in the book. Readers can assume that if any Korean author's surname appears first his publication is in the Korean language. The same principle has also been applied in the bibliography: Korean and Japanese authors whose works were written in their native languages are listed by their surnames without placing a comma before their personal names. Otherwise, I follow the Western practice.

In referring to the names of individuals included in this book, in accord with the ethic of my discipline, I have tried to protect their privacy and defend the dignity of the individuals, their cultural values, and their geographical locations. For this reason, I have used pseudonyms for individuals, clans, lineages, and locations, even though Korean custom considers using a fictitious name an intolerable insult. At the same time, in many cases I have used accrual names for certain individuals (e.g., colleagues, assistants, and supporters of this work), organizations, and locations that would be difficult to conceal. Because of the contextual information provided such a disguise would be futile.

Although this book is written by an anthropologist and academician, I want it to be accessible to a diverse audience, especially readers from those countries from whence the many women who come to Korea to marry Korean men hail. Accordingly, I have tried to minimize disciplinary terminology and maximize the usage of footnotes. The detailed footnotes enable interested readers to pursue the subject in greater depth. The target audience for this book includes three groups: 1) scholars and students in anthropology, sociology, history, ethnic and racial studies, East Asian studies, and Korean studies in particular; 2) professionals in immigration and naturalization, social workers, policy makers, human rights advocates, and civil service workers; and 3) general readers who are interested in globalization, international migration, multiculturalism, and international marriage.

1

The Multicultural Roots of Koreans

In February 2007, while I was attending an Internet training session for foreign brides and conducting preliminary fieldwork in Kumi, north Kyŏngsang province, a twenty-three-year-old bride from Mongolia commented that she might be one of the first Mongolian women to marry a Korean man and move to Korea. Apparently, the Mongolian bride was unaware of the fact that in 1274 a Yüan princess named Holdrogerni-misil, the daughter of the Yüan emperor Kublai Khan, married the Koryŏ prince who eventually became the twenty-fifth king, Ch'ungyŏl (1274–1308). Holdrogerni-misil became his queen. The Mongolian bride I was speaking to came to Korea some 733 years later than Holdrogerni-misil.

It is possible that this bride could be one of the remote descendants of the 206,000 Koryŏ people who were captured by the Mongolian army and taken to Mongolia in 1254. Since over two hundred thousand is a large number, particularly during these days of low population density and considering that many of the foreigners married Mongolians, it is likely that Korean blood flows in the classic bloodlines of Mongolia. Considering such a possibility, I have made an effort to locate Mongolian brides who bear Korean surnames such as "Kim," "Lee [Yi]," "Pak [Park]," and others. However, I have been unable to find one out of the total 2,806 brides from Mongolia who are entered the CUK's e-Learning Campaign. Whenever I met a Mongolian bride, I asked her to tell me if she knew of any Mongolian bride who claims to be a descendant of a remote Korean ancestor. So far, none of these women has reported knowing such a person.

Nevertheless, as I have observed the many Mongolians I have met during the course of my research I have been impressed by the fact that they seem to have many physical features similar to those of Koreans. They seem to share more of these features with Koreans than do the Chinese, Japanese, or other East Asians. Also, I have been impressed that Mongolians who speak Korean do so with a less-pronounced accent than do other East Asian speakers of Korean. I have been particularly impressed by one of the Mongolian assistants who worked with us in the CUK's Campaign. Her fluency I would rate as remarkable, and as a result I found myself feeling a kinshiplike bond with this young woman. The situation reminded me of conversation I once had with Francis L. K. Hsu, a prominent Manchurian-born anthropologist and former mentor of mine. Hsu told me, "You and I look more alike than any other fellow Chinese and I. Your ancestors and my ancestors might have belonged to the same tribe."[1] It was a casual comment, yet as I thought back to Hsu's remark, I realized that I could make the same comment about the possible connection between the Mongolian assistant and me. Indeed, because of her physical features and her comfort with the Korean language, I could not help but speculate that she and I might have a common ancestral connection. This response, be it somewhat accidental and emotional, reinforced my suspicions regarding the possibility of strong prehistoric and historic ties between the Mongolians and the Koreans.

On another occasion, a Vietnamese bride told me that she was one of the first Vietnamese to move to Korea, having immigrated to the country in the early 2000s. Not unlike the Mongolian bride, she was unaware of an interesting bit of history. Some centuries ago, a Vietnamese nobleman, Yi Yong-sang, a prince of the Lý kingdom (1009–1226) of Vietnam, had come to Korea, naturalized, and became the progenitor of the Hwasan Yi clan, whose membership today numbers over five thousand.

During two field trips to Vietnam, one in November 2009 and another in November 2010, I met many faculty members and students at the National Hanoi University. During this time I made a deliberate effort to find anyone with the surname "Lý," but I was never successful. Later, I learned that when the Lý dynasty fell and was replaced by the Chin dynasty there was a massive political purge to eliminate the remnants of the Lý families. Some of Lý families were executed indiscriminately. In order to survive, some members of Lý dynasty, such as Yi Yong-sang, went to other countries as political exiles, some changed their surnames from Lý, and some fled for refuge into the deep mountains and fishing villages located along the upper tributaries of the Mekong River.[2] That being the case, it is not surprising that it is so difficult to find many contemporary Vietnamese whose surnames are Lý.

In general, not many foreign brides are aware of the fact that Korea has a rather long history of immigration and international marriage. In fact, most Koreans themselves are unaware of the fact that not long ago a good many Korean brides married foreign men for exactly the same reasons that most foreign brides marry Korean men. They wanted to improve their economic conditions. They felt they were too old to be attractive to Korean men. Or they were divorced and convinced that the stigma attached to that status would prohibit their finding another Korean husband. These reasons are not new.

At the same time, neither the Korean government nor its agencies has encouraged Korean women to emigrate for the purpose of marrying to improve their economic conditions. An agency worker at aid organizations in a city in north Kyŏngsang province that assists foreign brides told me, "Even in the 1960s, when our per capita income was around $100 a year, which is about one-tenth of the current per capita income in Vietnam ($1,052 in 2009), we did not encourage Korean women to go overseas for work or to marry foreign men in order to improve their economic conditions."

Nevertheless, Koreans have a history of immigrating to other countries to find work or other means of improving their economic situations. For example, from the mid 1960s through much of the 1970s over ten thousand Korean nurses went to West Germany to earn foreign currency, which was desperately needed in Korea. Not long ago, in 1980, some seventeen thousand Korean women, most of whom were relatively well educated but economically deprived, relatively older than what was considered the ideal marriageable age, or divorced, married Japanese men using the services of Japanese marriage brokers.[3] The characteristics of the Japanese men they married were almost identical to those of the Korean men who marry foreign women today. They were relatively older, economically deprived, and living in remote prefectures such as Yamagata.[4] In 1997, an additional three hundred Korean women went to Japan to marry Japanese men for the same reasons and under the same conditions. At that time, Korea's economy was struggling with the challenges of the foreign currency crisis that swept across Asia that year. The outflow of brides to Japan was stemmed when the International Monetary Fund (IMF) stepped in and bailed out the Korean government.

Those Korean women who married Japanese men during the last two decades of the twentieth century have since relocated to cities such as Tokyo and Osaka. However, some two thousand still live in Yamagata prefecture and have had their share of problems. They suffered from an initial cultural shock due to the cultural differences. They struggled with the limitations of their limited fluency in the Japanese language. They were isolated and estranged from their Japanese mothers-in-law in a strongly paternalistic and male-centered Japanese family system. They also were the subjects of prejudice and discrimination because they were "ethnic Koreans," *zainichi kankokujin.* "Although many younger ethnic Koreans were born and grew up in Japan, and became assimilated into Japanese society, they remain noncitizens."[5] The tendency for the Japanese to look down on and discriminate against ethnic Koreans in Japan is well documented.[6] These Koran brides were also subjected to prejudice not only from the Japanese but also from other ethnic Koreans in Japan. The Korean brides were viewed by their fellow Koreans in Japan as opportunists who had come to Japan for the sole purpose of marrying and escaping the miserable conditions of their lives in Korea.

In an effort to overcome the adversities they have faced in Japan, the Korean brides in Yamagata have brought many Korean innovations to their new communities. For example, they introduced Korean ethnic food such as *kimch'i* (the Japanese pronounce it as *kimuchi*), a very popular Korean dish of pickled Chinese cabbage and radish seasoned with spices and condiments, especially hot pepper. Several scholars surmise that even in the Early Village period (6000–2000 BC) of Korean prehistory inhabitants in the peninsula made large storage vessels that were used primarily as *kimch'i* pots (*onggi*).[7] Some suggest that *kimch'i* can be used in tracing Korean ethnic identity.[8] Now, thanks to the women who have immigrated to Japan it has become very popular in Yamagata, especially among tourists. In the course of its growing popularity, the *kimuchi* made by Korean brides has had an impact on the Japanese economy. Its popularity has prompted the cultivation of its essential ingredients, including Chinese cabbage, red pepper, and radish. It has also become an important commercially produced commodity.

In 1996, a group of twenty-five Korean brides introduced a special *kimch'i* under the brand name Umaech'an kimuchi. The brand is now distributed to seventy-eight large supermarket chains in Japan and brings in revenues of over $1 million annually. *Kimuchi matsuri* (*kimch'i fair*) has become an integrated part of the annual fall fair in Yamagata. It features an online home page that promotes both the fair and the purchase and consumption of *kimuchi*.[9] At least one of the Korean brides has been conducting cooking classes for the last ten years in the prefecture, teaching Japanese cooks how to prepare Korean food. In this regard, the Korean women who have immigrated to Japan in recent decades have become culture brokers and emissaries for South Korea in Japan. Now in Korea, some Japanese who married Korean men are playing a similar role as Korean brides played such roles in the Yamagata prefecture in Japan. The experience of the Korean brides in Japan is something with which Koreans, like the lady who works in an agency in north Kyŏngsang province, should be familiar. If nothing else it should make them more empathetic to foreign brides in Korea.

In addition, Korea's long history of such marriages and its multiethnic and multicultural roots should also lend themselves to a greater understanding and appreciation for those persons who have chosen, for whatever reason, to immigrate to Korea. For that reason, I review in this chapter Korea's racial and ethnic history and present evidence that challenges the conventional view that the Korean people belong to a single ethnic group or that Koreans are a "pure race" (*tan'il minjok*).[10]

THE MULTICULTURAL ROOTS OF TRADITIONAL KOREA

For over a century now, the nationalistic school of thought has dominated the discourse about Korean history. As a result, until the beginning of this millennium, not many scholars disputed the prevailing viewpoint that Koreans were a singular ethnic group or pure race. No one wanted to be accused of being antinationalistic or sympathetic to Japanese imperial history. Because of these constraints, scholars were reluctant to attempt any objective analysis of Korea's multicultural history and be forced to admit to that history's complex ethnic and racial intermixing. But recently, thanks in part to the popular rhetoric on multiculturalism, a growing number of historians, prehistorians, and archaeologists whose orientation is not embedded in the nationalistic historiography have begun to address the diversity of Korea's social history and to publish the results of their researches. Kim Byung-mo (Pyŏg-mo Kim), a prominent Korean anthropologist, is one of those scholars. However, in his case, he had begun addressing the myth of Korea's racial and cultural purity even before the term *multiculturalism* had become fashionable and popular in Korea.

According to Kim Byung-mo, in 1965 archaeologists excavated skeletal remains found under the dolmen at Hwangsŏk-ri, Chech'ŏn-gun, in north Ch'ungch'ŏng province. Their first conclusion was that the remains were those of a forty-year-old male with a "long skull (Cephalic index of 66.3 while average Korean's is 81.5)." It was speculated that the person lived around 410 BC. Characteristics of the skull actually suggested a Caucasoid identification, not a Mongoloid. Yet, because of the prevailing mood in the academy, the excavation team was reluctant to contradict the conventional view that the Korean peninsula was never home to Caucasians. So, researchers simply labeled the remains Hwangsŏk-ri Man (*Hwangsŏk-ri-in*), naming it after the site where it was found. Recently, however, an anatomist named Cho Yong-jin, a professor at Seoul National University, reconstructed the skull using digital technology. He concluded that Hwangsŏk-ri Man was Caucasian. Also, according to Cho Yong-jin's investigation, contemporary inhabitants living in the same area were found to have skulls similar to Hwangsŏk-ri Man.[11]

Other scholars have looked beyond the popular paradigm of nationalistic history and courageously pursued the reality of Korea's multicultural roots.[12] Among them, Kim Byung-mo has done the most notable work. Conducting his research in the early 1960s, Kim ardently pursued his research to prove that his remote ancestress, Queen Hŏ Hwang-ok, wife of King Kim Suro of the Kaya kingdom, had come from Ayodhya, India. Kim's work has generated great interest among many other Koreans who want to trace their genealogy and are not intimidated by the possibility that their roots may be interwoven with persons of other cultures and nationalities. This new interest among Koreans is not unlike that among African Americans who were inspired by Alex Haley's 1976 book *Roots* and the 1977 TV miniseries based on the book.[13]

Before multiculturalism became a popular topic in Korea at the beginning of the current century, Lee Hee Soo (Hŭi-su Yi), a Korean anthropologist, traced Korea's contact with Muslims to the latter part of the United Silla period (AD 661 to 935).[14] Ch'oe Sang-Su, a Korean folklorist, has traced the life history of a Muslim named Chang Sun-ryong, who came to Korea from Mongolia in 1274 and later became the progenitor of the Tŏksu Chang lineage.[15] Park Ok-kol (Ok-kŏl Pak), a Korean historian, has published work on Koryŏ's policies on immigration and naturalization.[16] Because of Koryŏ's openness to the outside world, foreigners adopted the name *Korea* because of the phonetic similarity between "Koryŏ" and "Korea."[17]

Several foreign scholars such as Bruce Cumings,[18] John M. Frankl,[19] and Andre Schmid[20] have researched Korean history as well as played a significant role in tracing Korea's multiethnic past. Gi-Wook Shin's *Ethnic Nationalism in Korea* is also an important contribution to this scholarship, as it rethinks and reevaluates the consequences of ethnic nationalism in contemporary Korea.[21] According to this work, Korea was open and indeed welcoming to foreigners, at least prior to the late nineteenth or early twentieth century. Apparently, there was not a strong nationalistic sensibility in traditional Korean society. Until the late nineteenth century, when William Elliot Griffis introduced the epithet "hermit nation,"[22] Korea's international interaction was not limited to its geographical neighbors.[23] Frankl states that even Hŭngsŏn Taewŏngun, known to be the chief architect of the hermit nation, was tolerant enough to allow his wife to convert to Catholicism and hire a Catholic nurse for his son.[24]

Korean isolationism or exclusionism[25] in many ways was a by-product of the early Mongol invasion of the thirteenth century and the later Hideyoshi invasion of Japan in the sixteenth century. An increasing Western pressure in the nineteenth century was another contributing factor. Bruce Cumings has observed, "In earlier periods Korea was thought very *worldly* (emphasis mine) and very wealthy, as we learned from the Arabic travelers who fell in love with Silla."[26] Cumings has found evidence of possible hybrid bloodlines between Arabs and Koreans: "Arab travelers also discovered and wrote about the wonders of Silla, coming to Korea overland from China and by ship (*dhow*). . . . Presumably these Arab sojourners also married, putting a bit of Semitic seed into the hallowed Korean bloodlines."[27] Yi Hŭi-kŭn substantiates Cumings's view that the morphology of a statue erected in Kyŏngju appears to be Arab and infers from it that some Arabic people lived in the Silla domain.[28]

John M. Frankl, as a result of examining traditional Korean literature, reports that traditionally Koreans did not make any effort to distinguish between foreigners and Koreans on the basis of national boundaries.[29] They did not consider themselves to be ethnically unified as a homogeneous group of people and did not discriminate against foreigners simply on the basis of their ethnic origins. Instead, Koreans were tolerant, open, and even hospitable to foreigners.[30] Because there was a large number of naturalized Koreans who came from elsewhere, Frankl legitimately refers to Korea as a society of "cultural hybridity," not a society of ethnic homogeneity. The only concern and criteria for traditional Koreans were whether the immigrants or potential immigrants were *orangk'ae* (barbarians).[31] The criterion for being an *orangk'ae* was, in accordance with Han Kyung-Koo, "theoretically based on one's intention to assimilate, not on place of birth or ethnic origin."[32]

According to Andre Schmid, a North American historian who specializes in Korean history, the term *minjok*, meaning "ethnic nation," rarely appears in the canonical texts of Korean nationalists in the ten years before the Protectorate Treaty of 1905 with Japan.[33] Recently, with a trend toward multicultural studies, anthropologists, archaeologists, and historians have begun to scrutinize nationalistic historiographies. Yi Hŭi-kŭn challenges the myth of a homogenous people, claiming it is "made," if not outright "fabricated."[34] Yi has documented and provided ample historical evidence of foreign immigrants in Korea.[35]

THE PREHISTORIC ROOTS OF KOREANS AND KOREAN CULTURE

The search for the ethnic and cultural origins of Koreans on the Korean peninsula—who were they, when did they arrive—is not an easy task when one is constrained by the concept of the modern nation-state. Lothar von Falkenhausen has asked, when we speak of Korea, "What territory do we mean?"[36] The prehistoric inhabitants of East Asia, including Koreans, did not have the same territorial boundaries that exist today. Their sphere of occupancy stretched from the eastern border of Mongolia via Manchuria, a northern part of China proper, into central Japan. Even the word *Asia* may be irrelevant, for people were in the region long before the designation was introduced.[37]

There are more questions about the earliest inhabitants of the Korean peninsula than there are definitive answers. Sarah M. Nelson, an American archaeologist who specializes in Korean civilization, surmises that the Korean peninsula was perhaps inhabited by its earliest settlers half a million years ago.[38] Human remains from a Paleolithic (the Old Stone Age) site in North Korea have been dated to about 200,000 years BP and appear to be Mongoloid. However, a skull that was uncovered at a Paleolithic site in Mandal-ri near P'yŏngyang in North Korea was determined to be a "long skull" characteristic of a Caucasoid. Thus the evidence suggests that during the Paleolithic period the Korean peninsula was inhabited by both Caucasoid and Mongoloid, who lived side by side.[39] Nonetheless, "It is not known . . . whether the Korean people today are the ethnic descendants of these Paleolithic inhabitants of the land."[40]

The inhabitants of the Korean peninsula during the Neolithic period (the New Stone Age, 6000 to 2000 BC) might be possible ancestors of modern Koreans.[41] According to Kim Byung-mo, the Neolithic inhabitants were categorized as Paleoasians, with the characteristics of both Mongoloid and Caucasoid.[42]

The Bronze Age (the dawn of civilization)[43] may have begun on the Korean peninsula around the fifteenth century BC.[44] The era was marked by the presence of intensive agriculture, possibly rice cultivation.[45] While some archaeologists believe that rice was probably brought from south China across the Yellow Sea to southern Korea,[46] others such as Kim Byung-mo assume that it had been introduced from the South, most likely from Southeast Asia. Kim surmises that in introducing rice, people from South and/or Southeast Asia came to Korea and introduced the necessary techniques of cultivating rice and fashioning dolmens.[47] Although there is no conclusive archaeological evidence that Southeast Asian migrants brought rice cultivation to Korea, there is reason to believe that Southeastern ethnic groups mixed with a resident, ethnic gene pool of Koreans. Kim has identified linguistic evidence of a possible South Asian connection: identical phonemes in certain words related to rice cultivation in the Korean language and India's Dravidian language. For example, *pyŏ,* raw rice still bearing husks, and *ssal,* rice without husks, have parallels in the words *ssi,* which means "seed," and *kare,* a word that refers to a farming tool for tilling soil. Kim has listed about four hundred likely cognates between the two languages.[48]

Another possible sign of an influx of Southeast Asians can be seen in the distribution of dolmens.[49] Since dolmens are found in Taiwan, Southeast Asian countries, and India, they appear to be cultural characteristics of Southern, not Northern peoples, as similar dolmens are not found in inland China, Mongolia, and Siberia.[50] It appears that the know-how to fashion dolmens came to the Korean peninsula and southern Manchuria during the later period of the Neolithic age brought by people from South and Southeastern settlements.[51] Even if there is no definite archaeological evidence to prove or disprove the hypothesis of a migration from the south, it seems certain that some Southern people came as a large group to the Korean peninsula and established contact with Korean and Southern and Southeastern peoples of Asia. However, according to Kim Byung-mo, traditionally Koreans have believed that the major migration came from the north rather than the south.[52]

Interestingly, there has been a mitochondrial DNA (mtDNA) study using forty-five individuals from seven ethnic groups in East Asia in isolate female lineages in Korea and the ancient state of Koguryŏ. Based on the distribution pattern of mtDNA haplogroups, Koreans show both a high proportion of northern haplogroups and southern haplogroups of East Asia. Koreans appear to be more closely related overall to Korean-Chinese and Manchurians than to Han Chinese. The results of the study also indicated a strong genetic affinity between the modern Korean population and the ancient population of Koguryŏ.[53]

Recently, some ninety scientists from ten countries, including Mahmood Ameen Abdulla at the Singapore-based Human Genome Organization (HUGO) Pan Asian SNP Consortium, published the results of their studies on human genetic diversity, focusing on Southeast Asian (SEA) and East Asian (EA) populations. The results of the study show that genetic ancestry is strongly correlated with linguistic affiliations as well as geography. More than 90 percent of EA haplotypes could be found in either SEA or Central Asia (CA) populations and show a clinical structure with haplotype diversity decreasing from south to north. Furthermore, 50 percent of EA haplotypes were found in SEA only, and 5 percent were found in CSA only, indicating that SEA was a major geographic source of EA populations. This study also indicates that Koreans resembled Japanese people more than Chinese.[54] This is another piece of scientific evidence that supports the idea that some Korean ancestral lines might have originated in the south. The evidence supports the Kim Byung-mo hypothesis.

Information regarding the ethnic origins of Paleolithic foragers in the Korean peninsula is scanty,[55] but it seems that a major population influx may have occurred during the Neolithic period when people from the Lake Baikal region of the north moved into the peninsula. However, there is no direct evidence supporting this theory of migration.[56] Some archaeologists such as Se-jin Na have tried to study physical traits of present-day Koreans,[57] but others such as Chong Pil Choe [Chŏng-p'il Ch'oe] argue that physical traits cannot delineate boundaries between ethnic groups.[58]

From a physical and archaeological standpoint, there is not enough evidence to reach solid conclusions about the origins of Koreans in the peninsula. However, it is certain that no shred of evidence indicates that prehistoric inhabitants in the Korean peninsula belonged to a single ethnic group with "pure blood." Sarah M. Nelson sums it up well: "There is no evidence that a single ethnic group swept into Korea. . . . It seems much more consonant with the evidence at hand to postulate that over the course of 2,000 years various groups entered the peninsula and found a niche in the mosaic of a developing complex society."[59]

THE HISTORIC ROOTS OF KOREANS AND KOREAN CULTURE

Unlike scholars of the prehistoric period, scholars of the historical era can make use of various written documents, including genealogies. In addition to various articles,[60] several books on the subject of multicultural origins have been published since multiculturalism became a hot topic in early 2000.[61] Almost all Korean daily newspapers have published serial feature stories on the subject. A synthesis of these publications indicates that a significant number of contemporary Korean surname groups (*sŏngssi* or *sŏng* in abbreviation) and clan-seats (*pon'gwan* or *pon* in shortened form) are the descendants of naturalized foreigners.

Kim Chŏng-ho has calculated that, on the basis of the latest Korean census of 2000, 140 of 286 *sŏng* (surname groups) are naturalized, not native, and 516 of 4,190 *pon* (clan-seats) are naturalized. As of November 2000, over twelve million contemporary Koreans have ancestors who were naturalized foreigners. This amounts to over 26 percent of the total Korean population.[62]

THE ORIGINS OF KOREAN SURNAMES (*SŎNGSSI* OR *SŎNG*) AND CLAN-SEATS (*PON'GWAN* OR *PON*)

Sŏng is equivalent to "surname" in a Western sense and is also the word for *clan*,[63] denoting a consanguineous tie (blood relations), while *pon* (clan-seat) indicates a place from whence one's ancestors came.[64] In Korean society *sŏng* has to be addressed or written while *pon* can go unidentified or unacknowledged. Before Koreans adopted the surname system of the Chinese, they used only the name of one's geographical origin; this served as a surname of sorts. Since *pon* indicates a place, *pon* helps Koreans trace their genealogies. Since *pon* predates *sŏng*, *pon* was (and still is to a certain extent) an important indicator of a person's heritage.[65]

The Origins of Korean Surnames and Personal Names (*sŏng-myŏng*)

Until Korea adopted the Chinese system of surnames in the seventh century, Korea had neither a written language nor surnames for its people.[66] In the seventh century, Silla borrowed common *sŏng* from T'ang China (618–906).[67] Even after surnames were introduced in Korea, not every Korean had one. The royal family took one first, followed by *yangban* (the nobility) and other elite groups.[68] In the Chosŏn dynasty (1392–1910), *yangban* oversaw the government, the economy, and the culture at large.[69] In all aspects of social life, *yangban* members were a privileged class.[70]

Up until the fifteenth and sixteenth centuries, during the Chosŏn dynasty, only 10 percent of Koreans were *yangban* while over 40 percent of Koreans were *sangmin* (the class of commoners).[71] The remaining half of the population belonged to *ch'ŏnmin* (the lowest class).[72] During this period, large numbers of Koreans still lacked surnames. In the late nineteenth century, the reform of *Kabo* (*Kabo kyŏngjang,* 1894) abolished social classes.[73] In 1909, the last year before the Chosŏn dynasty fell to Japan, the civil registration law (*minjŏkpŏp*) mandated that every Korean had to take a surname as well as a personal name.[74] Thenceforth, farmhands and slaves who did not have *sŏng* either adopted the surnames of their masters or simply made up their own in reference to the most common surnames around them.

Consequently, some well-recognized surnames were widely adopted.[75] Many individuals who belonged to a particular *sŏng* had no blood kinship with others sharing the same surname. Although surnames were introduced to Korea relatively recently, Koreans consider them somewhat sacred. However, during Japanese occupation (1910–1945), Japan instituted policies of deliberate Korean cultural genocide under the slogan of *naesŏn ilch'e,* meaning "Japan and Korea are one entity." These policies were aimed at completely eradicating Korean national identity, which included forcing Koreans to adopt the Japanese style of naming, called *ch'angssi,* or identity creation, beginning in 1940.[76]

Following the passage of the Civil Registration Law (*Minjŏkpŏp*) in 1909, Korea adopted the *hojŏk* system, a male-oriented family registry. Under this system only male members could be the family head (*hoju*), and children had to take their father's *sŏng*. However, on February 3, 2005, the Constitutional Court ruled that the *hojŏk* system was unconstitutional and violated the spirit of gender equality in the Korean Constitution. In keeping with this court decision, on March 2, 2005, the Korean National Assembly passed a statute abolishing the *hojŏk* system, effective on January 1, 2008. Now, children are able to choose their mother's *sŏng* if they wish or combine their father's and mother's *sŏng*. This will inevitably increase the number of Korean *sŏng*.

Today among the *sŏng* and *pon* of naturalized Koreans, if one already has a Chinese-styled *sŏng,* that person can retain the name and only *pon* will be given, mostly named after the place where the person settled. For those who do not have a Chinese-styled *sŏng*, they can follow the process that Korea's *sangmin* (commoners) and *ch'ŏnmin* (lowest class) went through.[77] Most *sŏng* of naturalized Koreans are common names in Korea. In the past, over 90 percent of naturalized Koreans had a Chinese-styled *sŏng*, but now Japanese, Filipino, and Vietnamese names have begun to appear.[78] In 2009 alone, 25,044 foreigners from 49 nations were naturalized.

Of 25,044, some 4,884 naturalized new Koreans created their own *sŏng* and *pon*. Most took on common Korean surnames like Kim, Lee, and Park, but others used the names of their native countries, such as Mongol Kim, meaning Kim from Mongolia, or T'aeguk T'ae, referring to T'ae from Thailand. In creating a new *sŏng* and *pon,* some used their current place of residence, such as Kuri Sin, meaning Sin who lives in Kuri, a place in the vicinity of Seoul. This trend indicates that, even if naturalized, immigrants like to carry the names of their homeland, which would be helpful in identifying their origin in the future.[79]

Although genealogies have some limitations,[80] some of them have valuable information for tracing the origins of Koreans.[81] Hwang Un-ryong, for instance, used his genealogy to trace his own roots. He discovered that his ancestors came from Han China around AD 28 after his ancestors shipwrecked on the Korean seashore during a diplomatic trip to Vietnam.[82]

Naturalized *Sŏng* in Korean History

According to Kim Chŏng-ho, from the ancient period of Samhan (Three Han)[83] to the beginning of the Koryŏ dynasty, 46 *sŏng* and 119 *pon* were naturalized, almost all of them coming from China. Most of the immigrants were political refugees who left China to avoid political strife amid the rise and fall of successive dynasties or to avoid conscripted labor in the construction of the Great Wall. Arthur Cotterell describes the misery of building the Great Wall and "the sufferings of the conscripted laborers who toiled and died in the thousands building the Great Wall."[84] It is no wonder that the workers would go to any odds to escape and that so many of them ended up in Korea. According to one source some 5,079,708 contemporary Koreans would belong to these *sŏng* and *pon* created by the influx of Chinese during this era.[85] However, some historians are skeptical about the reliability of these statistics.[86]

During the Koryŏ dynastic period as Koryŏ adopted an open immigration policy, the largest numbers of foreigners in Korean history immigrated to

Korea and were naturalized. According to Kim Chŏng-ho, during this period a total number of 87 *sŏng* with 143 *pon* were naturalized. Today the descendants of immigrants number 2,826,111 among contemporary Koreans.[87] However, there were remarkable disparities in the number and kind of immigrants in the early period (919–1148) and later period (since 1170) of the Koryŏ dynasty.

During the early period, the dynasty needed talented human resources to establish an ambitious new dynasty after unifying the later Three Kingdoms. The dynasty wanted to model itself after the cultural and political system of the Sung dynasty (960–1279) of China. For this reason, Koryŏ adopted a liberal policy in accepting foreign immigrants, including men of letters, writers, medicine men, musicians, translators, merchants, monks, and even fortune-tellers.[88] Koryŏ also embraced northern tribes, including Jurchens and Khitans, and refugees from Parhae. They were welcomed into the country for the defense of the northern border and for their skills and knowledge as workmen and artisans.[89] As it turned out, almost 83 percent of the immigration and naturalization that occurred during the entire Koryŏ dynasty took place in the early period.

In the later period, Koryŏ's immigration and naturalization policies came up against several internal and external obstacles. Military rule was imposed in 1170. The Mongolians invaded in 1206 and established in 1271 the Yüan dynasty (1279–1368). Consequently, while immigration from China was very limited, new groups of immigrants came to the peninsula, including Japanese (mostly prisoners of war), Mongolians, and Manchurians. Most of the immigrants came involuntarily as prisoners of war, spouses, chamberlains, and horse breeders from Mongolia (*mokhoin*).[90] The Mongols occupied Cheju Island and dispatched their mighty army to the island. Recognizing that the island had ideal conditions for breeding horses, beginning in 1276 the Mongols made Cheju a center for horse breeding. They occupied the island for one hundred years, a century that saw many social, cultural, and linguistic changes for the Cheju people.[91] During the Yüan domination of Koryŏ, only nine *sŏng* with nine *pon* were naturalized. Today, the descendents of these immigrants are estimated to be 15,533.[92]

During the Yüan period international marriages for Koryŏ princes and princesses were common. These international marriages between the two royal families of Yüan and Koryŏ were initiated by Koryŏ to strengthen the royal authority within Koryŏ and to bring reconciliation with Yüan. With permission from the Yüan emperor, Koryŏ's King Wŏnjong (1259–1274) arranged for his son (who later became King Ch'ungyŏl, 1274–1308) to wed a Yüan princess, a daughter of the Yüan emperor Shih Tasu (Kublai Khan). She later became King Ch'ungyŏl's queen.[93] Thereafter a succession of four

Koryŏ kings—Ch'ungsŏn (1308–1313), Ch'ungsuk (1313–1330, 1332–1339), Ch'unghye (1330–1332, 1339–1344), and Kongmin (1351–1374)—had princesses of the Yüan imperial house as their primary consorts, while sons born to these queens typically succeeded to the throne.[94] Such arranged marriages continued for a century. King Ch'ungsŏn is the first Korean king born to an internationally arranged cross-racial marriage (*honhyŏl wang*).

For a century when Yüan princesses came to Koryŏ they were accompanied by a host of chamberlains and aides-de-camp. Many of these attendants remained in Korea and eventually became naturalized Koreans. Kim Chŏng-ho estimates that they account for twenty *sŏng* and forty *pon,* and their descendants would amount to 429,012 contemporary Koreans.[95]

Unlike the Koryŏ period, during the early period of the Chosŏn dynasty from T'aejo (1392) to Injo (1627), major groups of immigrants were limited to Jurchens and Japanese (*waegu*). During the later period of the Chosŏn dynasty, there were virtually no new immigrants because Jurchens were the major immigrants groups incorporated in a new Jurchen–Manchu dynasty, Qing (1644–1911). After that time, Qing closed its border to Chosŏn and even demanded the return of persons who had earlier settled in Korea.[96] Consequently, during the 518 years of the Chosŏn dynasty, only 31 *sŏng* and 60 *pon* were introduced.[97] Nevertheless, there were some notable foreign immigrants who came to Chosŏn, including Jurchen's Yi Chi-ran (1331–1302), Japanese Kim Ch'ung-sŏn, and the first European, Pak Yŏn, who came from the Netherlands.

Since the time of the Japanese domination of Korea beginning in the late nineteenth century, there were virtually no immigrants coming into the country other than a large number of Japanese colonists. Toward the end of the Chosŏn dynasty, the third son of Kojong (1864–1907), a stepbrother of the last king Sunjong (1907–1910), was designated as the king in 1900. This heir-apparent Yi Ŭn (King Yŏngch'in) was forced by Japanese authorities to marry a Japanese woman. In December 1907, two years after the signing of the Protectorate Treaty and three years before formal annexation of Korea in 1910, Itō Hirobumi, the principal architect of Japan's act of aggression against Korea, forced a symbolically significant international marriage. Taking Yi Ŭn, who was then eleven years old, to Japan, he arranged for him to marry Masako, daughter of Nashimoto Nomiya, a member of the Japanese royal family. Yi returned to Korea in November 1963, fifty-six years after he had left Korea. He lived in Korea with his wife for seven years until he died. His wife remained in Korea after the death of her husband, until she died. They had a son, Yi Ku, who was born in Japan, educated at MIT, and married to a Ukrainian American. He later divorced her without leaving any offspring.[98]

Parenthetically, after the end of the Chosŏn dynasty and the period of Japanese rule of some thirty-six years (1910–1945), the first republic was born in 1948, three years after World War II had ended in 1945. Syngman Rhee [Yi Sŭng-man, 1875–1965] became the first president of the first republic. Rhee himself belonged to the Chŏnju Yi lineage (*pon*), which includes all the kings of the Chosŏn dynasty and their royal families. In his second marriage, the fifty-nine-year-old Syngman Rhee married a thirty-four-year-old Austrian American, Francesca Donner. Francesca had been a lifelong companion, supporter, and nurse during Syngman Rhee's years of fighting for Korea's independence. Donner chose to remain in Korea after her husband's death and was later buried there.

Since then, many Koreans, men and women, have married foreigners. Without question, international marriage among Koreans is not new, rooted in ancient times and extending through the marriage of Kaya's King Kim Suro through five successive kings of Koryŏ to President Syngman Rhee. Today, over 181,671 Koreans (161,999 men and 19,672 women) have foreign-born spouses.

THE CONTRIBUTIONS OF IMMIGRANTS TO KOREA

Because of the scarcity of written documents on ordinary immigrants, most of the available detailed information is about the most prominent among them.[99] Also, some members of *sŏng* and *pon* are reluctant to reveal their origins publicly unless their origins are connected to China, because Koreans were long adulated in the tradition of *mohwa sasang*—the doctrine of serving China as honorable.[100] Therefore, the cases described here are among the most widely known and have verifiable genealogies. Descriptions follow in chronological order.

Hŏ Hwang-ok (Yellow Jade)

According to a legendary story written in the *Samguk yusa* (*Memorabilia of the Three Kingdoms*) by the monk Iryŏn (1206–1289)[101] in AD 48, Hŏ Hwang-ok (Yellow Jade), the princess of an old Indian kingdom, Kosala, known as Ayuta (or Ayodhya), married Kim Suro, the first king of the Kaya kingdom. She became queen of the Kaya kingdom, the first "first lady" in Korean history, and it is the first international marriage known to have occurred. Hŏ's legendary stories will be told in the next chapter as a part of Kim Byung-mo's epic journey.[102]

Ssang'gi (Shuang Chi)

A very prominent Chinese scholar and man of letters, Shuang Chi (Koreans call him Ssang'gi) was the son of Ssang Ch'ŏl of the Late Chou (951–960), the last kingdom of the Five Dynasties in China. He came to Korea in 956 accompanying the diplomat Sŏl Mun-u and stayed in Korea because of an illness. Koryŏ king Kwangjong (1211–1213) recognized his knowledge and talent and asked the Chou court if Shuang Chi could stay in Korea. Permission was promptly given.

In 959, Shuang Chi proposed a civil service examination to King Kwangjong that emulated the system of T'ang China. The Koryŏ court adopted the civil service examination, which was administered throughout the Chosŏn dynasties. The enactment of the "civil service examination system constituted a fundamental effort at establishing a new bureaucratic structure that would serve to strengthen royal authority."[103] Shuang Chi's case is an example of the Koryŏ dynasty's active recruiting of talented foreigners. Further information about his family and descendants is unavailable.

Vietnamese Yi Yong-sang

Yi Yong-sang was a descendant of T'ang Vietnamese and the second son of the sixth King Lý Thiên Tô of the Lý Kingdom in Vietnam. He was commonly called a prince. As Lý's royal family members in Vietnam were hunted down, Lý escaped the country with some chamberlains. In 1226, voyaging across the Yellow Sea, Lý landed at Hwasan-dong, Kŭmch'on-gun, in Hwanghae province, near the Ongjin peninsula. Upon his arrival, he joined his new countrymen in defending against sporadic raids from Japanese pirates (*waegu*). Grateful for his successful defense, the magistrate of the Ongjin district recommended that the Koryŏ court reward him. Later in 1253, during the Mongolian attack, he fought against the Mongolian army successfully. In 1226, recognizing Lý's contribution, the Koryŏ court gave him the *sŏng* Yi and the *pon* Hwasan, named for the village where he first settled. His sons had careers of distinction in high office. One branch of the lineage, Yi Chang-bal, created another *pon* of Chŏngsŏn Yi. Hwasan Yi has 1,775 descendants, and Chŏngsŏn Yi has 3,657 among contemporary Koreans.[104]

Parenthetically, knowing that the progenitor of Hwasan Yi was prince of the Lý dynasty of Vietnam, the representatives of the lineage visited Vietnam in 1995, where they were welcomed with a reception attended by dignitaries of the Vietnamese government. They were treated as though they were members of royal families. The plan now is for the representatives of the lineage to make an annual visit to Vietnam every March 15 on the founding day of the Lý dynasty. A professor at Ch'ungnam University tested the DNA of

Lý's descendants in Vietnam, as compared to his descendants in Korea, and found that the Hwasan Yi lineage in Korea was a closer genetic match to Lý than those among them in Vietnam. Interestingly, members of the Hasan Yi lineage state that members of the Lý lineage lived as a racially mixed group, yet they did not believe they have been discriminated against because of it.[105]

Chamberlain Chang Sun-ryong

Chang Sun-ryong, whose original name was Samga (or Samko, as the name is pronounced in Chinese), lived in Yüan but came to Koryŏ in 1274 as a chamberlain. He came as a member of the entourage of the Mongolian Princess Cheguk-daejang-gongju (Holdrogerni-misil), daughter of Sejo, the fifth emperor of the Yüan dynasty. Once the princess moved to Korea, she never left. Because of his own merit and with some help from the Mongolian princess, Chang was appointed to various high governmental positions. He was elevated to a front rank of the fourth degree and enjoyed special privileges, including tax exemption as a reward for his service and merit.[106] He became the progenitor of the Tŏksu Chang lineage, whose descendants account for some 21,006 contemporary Koreans.[107] A later branch of his lineage created the line of P'ungdŏk Chang.

Chang Sun-ryong's origin remains a subject of much debate. Was he an Arab, Uighur, or Muslim? While Ch'oe Sang-su suggests he was an Arab,[108] Park Ok-kol identifies him as *saekmok-in* (people who have colored eyes).[109] The genealogy of the Tŏksu Chang lineage indicates that he was *hwoe'hwoe-in,* meaning "Muslim."[110] Still others believe that he must have been a Uighur (*Wérwú'er* or *Weiwu'er* in the Chinese pronunciation).[111]

Chang and his descendants made some contributions in Koryŏ that continued into the Chosŏn dynasty. Among Chang's descendants, Chang Yu was the most notable. He became Chief Justice of the Supreme Court and Chief Professor of the Confucian College in 1623 during the Chosŏn dynasty. One of Chang Yu's descendents became father-in-law to King Hyojong (1649–1659), whose son became King Hyŏnjong (1659–1674) by the Chosŏn dynasty.

Sŏl Chang-su, a Diplomat and Translator

Toward the end of the Koryŏ dynasty in 1359, Sŏl Chang-su, whose origin was known to be a Uighur, came to Korea with his father and was eventually naturalized. He was an intimate friend of King Kongmin (1351–1374) before he became king during his stay in Yüan. When he was naturalized, the Koryŏ court allocated farmland for him in the Koch'ang district in south Chŏlla province. As a distinguished man of letters, he was a writer and poet. In 1362 he passed the civil service examination with distinction. He was instrumental in establishing the Chosŏn dynasty by assisting Yi Sŏng-gye, founder of Chosŏn. In 1398 when Chŏngjong (1398–1400) became king, Sŏl Ch'ang-su played a major diplomatic role in negotiating with the Ming dynasty (1368–1644) of China. Because he was fluent in four languages, he was an important diplomat and translator. He became the progenitor of Kyŏngju Sŏl, as his *pon* was established as Kerim (Kyŏngju) and his descendants include some 6,060 persons among contemporary Koreans.[112]

Yi Chi-ran, an Intimate Friend of the Chosŏn Founding Father

Yi Chi-ran (1331–1402) was a Jurchen immigrant whose original name was Kurant'urant'imur, but he is often called Tonan, Turan, or Tungduran. Technically, one might argue that he was not an immigrant because his hometown was Pukch'ŏng, in south Hamkyŏng province of Korea. It was originally the territory of Koguryŏ, but after Koguryŏ's fall, Parhae occupied the territory. Jurchens still resided in that territory at the fall of Parhae. In 1073, it became a part of Koryŏ, but Yüan controlled the region as they invaded Koryŏ. When Yüan was losing its strength, King Kongmin in 1356 recovered the territory again as part of Koryŏ's domain. In 1371, Yi became a Koryŏ subject along with thousands of his subordinates.[113]

Although Yi was naturalized in the Koryŏ dynasty,[114] he played his most significant role in founding the Chosŏn dynasty. He was a first-ranking, able retainer who assisted Yi Sŏng-gye (T'aejo), who later became the progenitor of the Chosŏn dynasty. Yi Chi-ran first met T'aejo when they were young, and the two became lifelong friends. Yi Chi-ran played a key role in fighting the Japanese and assisted T'aejo in implementing Jurchen policy. At Yi Chi-ran's recommendation, T'aejo allowed Jurchens to marry Koreans and did not discriminate against them in taxation. In so doing T'aejo adopted an open policy for Jurchens to become naturalized Koreans.[115] Yi Chi-ran distinguished himself in the Chosŏn court, and his four sons also excelled, all eventually occupying high administrative positions. He became the progenitor of the Ch'ŏnghae Yi lineage, named after his original hometown of Ch'ŏnghae. His descendents numbered 12,002 Koreans by the year 2000.[116] The genealogy of Ch'ŏnghae Yi lineage corroborates these facts.[117]

Yi Wŏn, the One Who Introduced Gunpowder

Most Koreans know that Ch'oe Mu-sŏn was the manufacturer of gunpowder, but they do not know that Yi Wŏn played an instrumental role in helping

Ch'oe formulate gunpowder. As a lesser-known Yüan artisan, Yi came to Koryŏ seeking refuge, fleeing the political turmoil of the Yüan dynasty.[118] Later, Yi instructed Ch'oe and urged him to manufacture powerful and effective gunpowder. According to Ki-baik Lee, "Eventually learning its secret from a Yüan Chinese soldier, Ch'oe persuaded the Koryŏ court to establish the Superintendency for Gunpowder Weapons (1377) where cannons of various kinds could be made and gunpowder employed on other weaponry as well. He also equipped the navy with newly built ships, which with their cannon, achieved major success in repulsing the Japanese marauders."[119] Since Yi was not viewed as a prominent immigrant, there is not extensive documentation about him.

Chang Yŏng-sil, Genius Inventor

Chang Yŏng-sil was not a first-generation immigrant, but he was the son of a Yüan immigrant father and a *kisaeng* (a young female singer who performed at male drinking parties) mother, and thus he was classified as a *ch'ŏnmin* (the lowest class of four social classes in the Chosŏn dynasty). Because he was a *ch'ŏnmin* and a slave, the dates of his birth and death are not known for certain.[120] In the final years of the Koryŏ dynasty, Chang Yŏng-sil was classified as a slave. Despite his lowly background, he possessed extraordinary talent as a skilled artisan, which drew the attention and patronage of King T'aejong (1400–1418). Later, because of his extraordinary talent, King Sejong (1418–1450) promoted him to the third rank in the front row of the Chosŏn court despite vehement opposition from *yangban* bureaucrats.[121] At the request of King Sejong, Chang invented various kinds of astronomical clocks, sundials, and clepsydras (water clocks).[122]

Kim Ch'ung-sŏn, Former Japanese Field Commander

In the ranks of prominent military personnel, Kim Ch'ung-sŏn is notable. Kim was a field commander during the Toyotomi Hideyoshi's invasion (1592–1598), but in 1592 he surrendered to the Korean army and fought against his native Japanese army. Kim was known to be "Sayaga" in Korean, or "Saika" in Japanese.[123] Whatever his real identity may have been, Kim introduced Japanese matchlocks and a technique of making gunpowder to the Chosŏn army. He played a major role in fighting back the Hideyoshi invasion, particularly during the second wave of the invasion (1597–1598).

He also fought against the Manchurian invasion (*pyŏngja horan*) of 1636. He served eight years in the Korean military. Recognizing him for his services to Chosŏn, King Sŏnjo (1567–1608) gave him the *sŏng* of Kim and the *pon* of Kimhae. The king also named him Ch'ung-sŏn and appointed him to a high position, a front rank of the second degree.[124] He married a daughter of the district magistrate of Chinju, retired, and settled in the village of Urok, Talsŏng-gun, in north Kyŏngsang province in the vicinity of Taegu.

Currently, some fifty members of Kim's lineage are living in Urok, making his line a dominant one in the village. There are some four thousand of Kim's descendants living in Korea as of 2000. Kim wrote a memoir entitled *Mohadangmunjip.*[125]

Pak Yŏn, the First European Immigrant

J. J. Weltevree (1595–?) of the Netherlands was the first European immigrant to come to Korea. In 1627, Weltevree came to Cheju Island when his ship wrecked on his way to Japan. He and two other crew members were captured by Cheju officials. After he was taken to the nation's capital, the Chosŏn court assigned him to work in Military Training Command, as Weltevree possessed the skill to improve the cannon. During the Manchurian invasion of 1636, he fought for Chosŏn, but two of his countrymen were killed in the war. During his stay at the Military Training Command (*Hullyŏn Togam*), he taught soldiers how to use the cannon and oversaw the importation of cannons manufactured in Ming China.[126] After the war, he decided to remain in Korea, where he was naturalized and given the Korean name Pak Yŏn. In 1653 when Hendrick Hamel and his thirty-five crew members came to Cheju Island after their ship wrecked, Pak Yŏn went to Cheju and translated for his countrymen.[127] Pak Yŏn married a Korean woman and had a son and daughter. Since the children knew the Korean language and some European languages, they served as translators for the Chosŏn court.[128] Unfortunately, detailed information about the family's subsequent history is unavailable.

Other Immigrants Who Helped Defend the Country

As noted earlier, information regarding the lives of many ordinary foreigners, particularly northern tribes who entered the peninsula, is scanty. The number of Jurchens who came to Koryŏ is estimated at over 30,000, and the number of Khitans was 2,600 at one time.[129] From the reign of T'aejo (918–943) to Mokchong (997–1009), some 22,653 Parhae immigrants came to Koryŏ.[130] Since Parhae was founded by a Koguryŏ general and adopted Koguryŏ culture, Parhae was called a "Lesser Koguryŏ" at times.[131] Because of such ties, Koryŏ perceived Parhae people as if they were "brethren," even though they belonged to two separate kingdoms.[132] Knowing the talent and navigational skill of the Parhae people, T'aejo of Koryŏ, located in Tae Kwang-hyŏn, and his followers from Parhae went to Paekchu, a strategically important naval port from which to defend against possible attacks by sea from Khitan.[133]

Foreigners Recruited in Response to Population Loss

Koryŏ found it convenient at times to use foreign immigrants to make up for a shortage in manpower. They did this in 1254 during the Mongols' invasion of Korea. As mentioned, the Mongols captured some 206,800 Koryŏ people and took them to Mongolia. With an estimated total population of Koryŏ at around 2.1 million at the time, Koryŏ lost about 10 percent of its people. In order to compensate for such a huge loss, Koryŏ recruited foreign immigrants. Koryŏ offered food and living arrangements to attract immigrants. Such an effort appeared to be successful, as the total number of recruits totaled over 2,300 households around 1259.[134] The population crisis that led Koryŏ to recruit foreign immigrants is similar to what contemporary Korea is experiencing. The critical shortage of marriageable women in rural farming and fishing villages has led Korea to invite foreign women to wed Korean men, in some ways replicating the strategy of the Koryŏ.

The Lives of Ordinary Immigrants

For upper-class immigrants, mostly those from China, life in Korea was generally comfortable, relaxed, and even luxurious. On the other hand, little information about the lower echelon of commoners exists in the historical records. Despite this dearth of information about the lives of ordinary immigrants, Lhim Hag Seong has reconstructed the lives of fifty northern Jurchen immigrants in the first half of the seventeenth century by analyzing two census registers, one in Ulsan (1609) in south Kyŏngsang province and the other in Haenam (1639) in south Chŏlla province. According to Lhim's description, in these registers all naturalized Jurchens and their descendants were identified as Jurchens in their origin, their naturalization statuses, their economic statuses, size of families, and marital status.[135] All of them retained common Korean *sŏng* such as Kim, Yi, or Pak, and most of them adopted common Korean names such as Mun-san, Yun-hak, Ok-ch'ŭn, etc. However, others used common Korean *sŏng* but retained their original Jurchen names, such as P'yŏng'ŭlrangi, Anaeunsŏk, Asongajŏk, Abugi, etc.[136] Jurchens made a subsistence living by fishing, farming, and hunting. Among them, only one family was rich enough to own a slave. The authorities allowed them to own slaves if they could afford to do so.[137] Many of them served in the army as soldiers and were distinguished in the war against the Japanese during Hideyoshi's invasion in the sixteenth century. All of the descendants of first-generation immigrants were able to serve in the army without any discrimination based on their ethnic origin.[138]

The Chosŏn dynasty encouraged them to marry Koreans and settle down. Jurchen men were favored by marrying daughters of Korean commoners. Nonetheless, the first generation of Jurchen appeared to have practiced tribal endogamy by marrying within their ethnic group (91 percent). Only 16 percent of them married Koreans. Even their descendants tended to marry within the group (62 percent). Jurchens' marriages with Koreans increased after the sixteenth century as their Jurchen identity grew weaker.[139] The average family size was 2.4, as the average number of children per family was only 0.45. Many Jurchen couples did not have any children (43 percent).[140] Their fertility rate was apparently very low, much lower than the contemporary Korean fertility rate of 1.2, which was the lowest fertility rate among 193 countries surveyed in 2008.[141]

Although their numbers were small (less than 2 percent of the population of the two surveyed areas), they formed their own enclave. Despite a government effort to upgrade their lifestyle, their economic condition was apparently worse than it was for average Koreans. Also, on account of their enclaves, Jurchens did not assimilate into Korean life as easily as others did. In fact, in 1609, four Jurchens out of forty-one (about 10 percent) left Chosŏn.[142] They thought that they might not be able to fulfill the "Chosŏn dream," so to speak.

Also, there are some records of Khitan immigrants who lived the hard life of butchers,[143] an occupation plied by *ch'ŏnmin,* the lowest social class. This was also the class of shamans, singing girls, and performers. It was similar to the "untouchables" in the traditional caste system of India.[144] According to Yi Hŭi-kŭn, a larger number of Khitans came to the Korean peninsula than one can accurately estimate during a quarter of a century of war from 998 to 1018.[145] Since they did not possess many skills (with few exceptions), most turned to butchering. Butchering was a skill that almost all nomadic people had, while most Koreans did not.[146]

While butchering was legal, and the occupation of butchering was not so despised in Koryŏ, the Chosŏn dynasty, from the outset, made slaughtering cows illegal. The government persuaded and forced butchers to become farmers and cultivate farmland. But their efforts were unsuccessful. Eventually butchers pursued their work clandestinely and produced fine leather to make all sorts of items such as shoes and bags. Since those butchers were slaughtering cows illegally, however, a good many of them were classed as criminals. Yi Hŭi-kŭn estimates that the number of butchers increased to nearly one-quarter of the total population of the early Chosŏn dynasty.[147] Illegal butchering changed Koreans' diet from one of mostly vegetables to one that included much meat. Until then, only a limited number of elite yangban and royal family members ate meat.[148]

In summing up, prehistoric evidence and historical documents indicate that there is no shred of evidence that Korea is the homeland of a single ethnic group descended from a common ancestor. The figures on "naturalized Koreans" who came from elsewhere might be exaggerated here or there, but the wealth of evidence from diverse sources makes it clear that the idea of Korea as a single ethnic nation is at best a political myth.

2

The Epic Journey of an Archaeologist in Search of His Ancestress

I was pleasantly surprised recently when I came across an article in the Ŭisŏng Kim clan's quarterly newspaper, the *Ŭisŏng Kim-ssi Chongbo*. The article, dated April 1, 2009,[1] was titled "Are We the Descendants of the Nomadic Northern Tribe of Hyungno (*Xiongnu* in Chinese)?"[2] As a member of that clan myself, it was an amazing discovery to see such a question raised in the clan's official bulletin. To this point, the clan has claimed that its progenitor, Sŏk, was the prince of King Kyŏngsun (927–936) of the Silla dynasty.[3] This is a clear manifestation of contemporary Koreans' century-old notion of a single ethnic nationalism being replaced by a new and fashionable multiculturalism. This is largely due to a trend in Korea toward accepting the multiculturalism of its people.

In fact, before the twenty-first century, according to Kim Chŏng-ho, author of *Han'guk-ŭi kwihwa sŏngssi* (*The Naturalized Korean Surname Groups*), some Korean clan members were sensitive and reluctant about revealing their ethnic and racial identities, particularly those whose ancestors had foreign origins. The author has bitter memories of when he innocently identified some Korean *sŏng* and *pon* as having foreign origins in a newspaper series. He found himself charged with four libel suits.[4] Today, however, there is less of a stigma attached with foreign ethnic origins, and a growing number of Koreans are interested in inquiring into their ethnical and racial roots and genealogies. This new interest is not unlike the interest that was generated among African Americans after the publication of Alex Haley's *Roots*.[5]

Before multiculturalism became a popular topic of public discourse after 2000, Kim Byung-mo began in the 1960s tracing the origin of his remote ancestress, the wife of King Kim Suro of the Kaya kingdom. In this chapter, I narrate Kim Byung-mo's epic journey to demonstrate Koreans' interest in searching for their ancestral roots and in recognizing the history of international marriage in Korea. I also relate Kim Byung-mo's work to discover the details of his roots in appreciation of the contributions that archaeology, ethnology, and ethnohistory have made in documenting Korea's multicultural legacy.

The epic journey of Kim Byung-mo to trace his ancestral roots is a fascinating story. His books that describe this journey are so intriguing that readers have a difficult time putting them down once they begin reading.[6] Even before I read Kim's books, I had run into him on several occasions but had never actually met him. To understand from a more personal perspective the effort to trace his roots, I set out to meet with him.

In March 2009, armed with the knowledge that he was the brother-in-law of my college mentor, I made a visit to his office at the Korea Institute of Heritage (*Koryŏ Munhwajae Yŏnguwŏn*). At the time, he was chairman of the Institute. In the entrance to his office, I noticed an engraved figure of a pair of carp, called *ssangŏ,* or "twin-fish" (hereafter called twin-fish) on a wooden board mounted above his office door. Since both of us belong to a same "fraternity" of anthropology, we are able to speak the field's jargon. When I asked his permission to retell his epic journey as "an enthnography of an archaeologist" as a chapter of my book, he willingly approved. During our long conversations and discussions over lunch, I learned that his curiosity and desire to pursue his origin had started some thirty years ago before he knew anything about anthropology, and archaeology in particular.

ENCOUNTER WITH REMOTE KIN AND THE "INCEST TABOO"

Visiting the Tombs and Shrines

Kim Byung-mo's story began when he dated a beautiful college student, Hŏ Mi-kyŏng,[7] who was part of a student volunteer service work group during the summer of 1961. When the summer work was completed, most of the team members left the service site of Sunch'ŏn, a coastal city of south Chŏlla province, for Seoul, and some of them wanted to tour Pusan, a harbor and the second-largest city in Korea. They decided to take a boat ride in the harbor. It was a lovely and romantic cruise, leaving the port of Yŏsu and sailing through the calm, beautiful, and shallow southern coastal sea called Tadohae, meaning "the sea that has many islets." Whether it was a sheer luck or carefully planned, Kim managed to talk to Hŏ on the deck of the ship during the cruise. Although they knew each other from campus and had worked together during the summer, it was the first time the two of them were alone, talking to each other in such a romantic setting.

After they landed at Pusan, Kim told Hŏ that he was going to visit and pay tribute to the tombs of his remote ancestors, the progenitor of his lineage, the first king of Kaya kingdom and his wife Hŏ Hwang-ok. He was also going to visit the shrines dedicated to the couple in Kimhae, a suburban county of Pusan and home to the airport that serves passengers flying in and out of Pusan. When Kim told Hŏ about his plan to visit the shrines and the royal tombs, Hŏ told him that she would like to join him. Without knowing Hŏ's background and her relationship to the tombs and the shrines, Kim thought she might have taken an interest in him. So, together they walked to the site in Kimhae. As they passed the gateway to the shrines, walking past several stone statues, they found the royal tomb. Apparently, however, Kim was not very impressed with the size and scale of the tomb as a royal tomb of the Kaya kingdom.

The security around the tombs was lax, and virtually no one was around. Standing before the tomb, Kim did not know what to do in terms of protocol and what rites to perform to pay respect to his two-thousand-year-old ancestor and ancestress. Knowing that by and large women are excluded from officiating the rites of ancestor worship,[8] Kim told Hŏ, "Why don't you stay on the other side while I pay my respect to my ancestor, King Kim Suro!" Surprisingly, Hŏ told Kim that she would like to do the same because she, too, claimed to be one of the descendants. Also Hŏ Hwang-ok's tomb was not far away from her husband's tomb, located within walking distance by simply going though an adjacent gate. Hŏ Hwang-ok's tomb was engraved "Tomb of Hŏ, the Empress Dowager of Poju (*Puzhou Taihou* in Chinese pronunciation) and Queen of King Kim Suro of the Kaya Kingdom (*Karak-kuk Surowangbi Pojut'aehu Hŏ-ssi Nŭng*)." At that time Kim did not realize the significance of Poju (Puzhou).

Kim and Hŏ took some pictures and went down to the office of the manager of the site to learn more about the tombs. Kim was curious about the engraving of twin-fish (*ssang-ŏ*) over the gate leading to the tomb and about the red-colored stones stacked up right beside Hŏ's tomb. The manager explained to them that twin-fish symbolize a "twin-fish-god" (*ssang-ŏ sin* in Korean). The manager confessed that he could not explain anything further about the symbol, but it was thought to be so important that, when the main gate had been repaired, the twin-fish had been restored and replaced. As for the red stones, the manager said they were remnants of a pagoda that Hŏ carried with her when she came to Kaya. A legendary story had it that, when Hŏ was sailing from India, her ship was so small that it threatened to roll over. So to keep the ship upright in the wind, Hŏ's father gave her a pagoda as ballast.

Although the young visitors to the tomb were kin, they had different *sŏng*; Kim was a member of the Kimhae Kim clan, and Hŏ was a member of the

Kimhae Hŏ clan. They did belong to the same *pon'gwan, ponhyang,* or *pon* (clan-seat). The manager in the office told them that "since members of Kimhae Kim, Kimhae Hŏ, and Inch'ŏn Yi are descendants of the same Kim Suro and Hŏ Hwang-ok, they cannot marry among themselves." Indeed, this was the norm in Korean culture in general. If they chose to get involved, they would violate the incest taboo, which prohibited a sexual and/or marital relationship between individuals who were in a real, assumed, or artificial bond of kinship.[9]

The Root of the Incest Taboo in Korea

Historically, most Korean dynasties imposed the incest taboo. In Koguryŏ (37 BC to AD 668) and Paekche (18 BC to AD 660), marriage within the same lineage (or clan) was prohibited, while Silla (57 BC to AD 935) encouraged close kin marriages beyond the third degree of relationship (beyond uncle and aunt)[10] and with members of the same clan, especially among royal and upper-class families.[11] In the early dynastic period, Koguryŏ followed the Silla system, allowing close kin marriage even within a two-degree relationship (even brother and sister, if the mothers were different) in royal families as an effort to maintain the "same blood" and protect the purity of the royal blood line.[12] In fact, King T'aejo of the Koguryŏ dynasty encouraged close-kin marriage.[13]

The prohibition of marriage between members of the same lineage or clan was one that technically would limit the seriousness of the relationship of Kim Byung-mo and Hŏ Mi-kyŏng. This taboo rule had come into being in the Chosŏn dynasty after the adoption of *Ta Ming Lü* (Law of the Great Ming), the comprehensive body of administrative and criminal law of the Ming dynasty (1368–1644) of China.[14] Nevertheless, *yangban* in many cases ignored the rule and continued to marry matrilineal cousins (siblings of a mother's sisters and father's sisters).[15]

In Korea, unlike China, several different clans may share one *sŏng,* and clans with different surnames may share a *pon,* in which case the rule of clan exogamy is applied. Kim and Hŏ would run up against this taboo were they to think seriously about getting married. Under this rule, some clans with millions of members have been prohibited from intermarrying. As Kim has alluded to in his publications, both he and his friend Hŏ were disappointed by this realization. The rule meant they could not and should not fall in love as a man and a woman because they would be committing incest by violating the Korean rule of clan-seat exogamy. There have been many heartbreaking stories of people who fell in love without knowing they were members of the same clan and thus could not marry. In a sense, Kim and Hŏ were lucky to know that they belonged to the same clan-seat before their relationship became serious.[16]

DARK SKIN PIGMENTATION AND
THE SUPPOSITION OF INDIAN ORIGIN

While Kim and Hŏ were riding the train home, they were talking about their hometowns and birthplaces. Since it was going to be a long ride, Kim entertained an episode about his birth to Hŏ:

> Our family used to live in Nakwŏndong, Chongno. But I was born in a small obstetrics and gynecology hospital (predecessor to the medical school of Ewha Womans University) in Tongdaemun. By riding an *illyŏk'kŏ* (a rickshaw), my grandmother came to the hospital to see me, expecting that her grandson would be good-looking with light skin. To her disappointment, her grandson had unusually dark skin with a projected nose, not like other light-skinned babies. She remembered that when his son (Kim's father) was born, he had light skin, even looked almost Caucasian and was good-looking. My grandmother as an elderly woman could hardly understand the hospital system. Nevertheless, she thought that accidentally I had been swapped with another baby. She insisted that the bloodline had to be investigated. My grandmother began to recognize me later when I did well in school and was elected class president. I was shocked when I heard my grandmother's "swapping conspiracy" when I became a teenager. During puberty and my adolescent years, I agonized as to whether I had different genes from my siblings or whether I really had been swapped when I was born because my skin color was dark. Whenever I looked at a mirror I tended to think about my grandmother's swap thesis.[17]

Hŏ listened to Kim's tales with a great interest and curiosity, and she commented casually that "it wouldn't be a big deal for a man whose skin is a little bit dark."

Kim continued telling his story to Hŏ, saying that his agony and curiosity had been answered partially when he was in high school. "Once in class when students were laughing, talking, and fidgeting without concentrating on the lesson, the history teacher decided to recount a legendary story to draw the students' attention. He was telling students the story of a king's love and the first international marriage. The teacher began to ask students, 'Do any of you in this class have the surname (*sŏng*) with the clan-seat (*pon*) of Kimhae Kim?' While most were hesitant, some raised their hands." Kim was one of them who raised his hand. The teacher began to tell the story. He said that among Korean *sŏng* and *pon*, Kimhae Kim is the most frequent in the population, their members numbering in the millions. "Does anyone know the progenitor of Kimhae Kim?" Most students answered that it was King Kim Suro. The teacher said, "You are right. But, does anyone know whom the king married?" No one seemed to know the answer. Later, though, one student answered, "A princess of India," but it was not Kim.

The history teacher became enthusiastic about telling his story to the students, as they paid a great deal of attention and showed interest. The teacher asked the pupils, "Does anyone know what her name is?" Only one student knew that her surname was Hŏ. The history teacher told the students that the princess's full name was Hŏ Hwang-ok and that she had come from India and married Kim Suro. After they married, they had several children. While some of the sons inherited the father's surname, two others were given the surname Hŏ. The teacher told the students that this was the reason that the Kimhae Kim clan and the Kimhae Hŏ clan could not get married. If your *pon* is Kimhae Kim, you have to avoid falling in love with Kimhae Hŏ; otherwise you become incestuous. After hearing the teacher's story, Kim realized that, even if his relationship to his progenitor was remote, he was the descendant of an Indian princess and a Kaya king—a sort of royal family he could be proud of. Furthermore, since the skin of Indians is dark, his own skin was a natural consequence of his ancestry.[18]

After his visit to King Kim Suro and Hŏ Hwang-ok's tombs and shrines, Kim's desire to know more about his ancestor intensified: if any Kimhae Kim or Kimhae Hŏ have darker skin, would they preserve this gene more than the others? What did Hŏ Hwang-ok look like? Kim decided to pursue the tracing of the root and route of Hŏ Hwang-ok's marriage archaeologically. The legendary story of Hŏ Hwang-ok's marriage to King Kim Suro was mainly based on the writing of *Samguk yusa*.[19]

THE KAYA KINGDOM (AD 42–532) AND
THE LEGENDARY STORY OF THE KIMHAE KIM CLAN

Description of *Samguk yusa*

Kaya or Karak was a confederation of related city-states located on the south coast of the Korean peninsula, along the Naktong River, in a region called Pyŏnhan in early Chinese documents. Kaya existed only in the early centuries, for the cities were conquered one by one by Silla, and by AD 512. the entire Kaya territory was conquered and annexed by Silla and became part of its domain.[20] By reason of Silla domination, or perhaps some other reasons, information regarding Kaya is sketchy, other than some lengthy descriptions in *Samguk yusa* by the monk Ilyon [Iryŏn].[21] Despite the paucity of the historical record, "the Kaya region is now the focus of intensive archaeological exploration, and many new finds demand reassessment of Kaya's role in southern Korea."[22] Perhaps in the future more archaeological remains may reveal more about Kaya than we know now.[23]

Section 58 of book 2 of *Samguk yusa* relates the legendary story of the origin of the Kaya king, Kim Suro. Just like other mythic stories of kingdom founders, the Kaya legend is no exception. According to the *Samguk yusa,* "Since the creation of heaven and earth there had been no national name and no king of the people of the Kimhae region (north of the Naktong River delta). The nine chiefs . . . ruled over 75,000 natives, who plowed their fields and sank wells to support their simple lives."[24] On the day of the spring festival in AD 42 (during the year of the tiger in Emperor Kuang Wu's reign) villagers in the Bathing Valley heard a strange-sounding voice. The heavens opened up and a purple rope descended to the earth. Tied to it was a wrapped golden bowl, which held six golden eggs. The eggs later hatched into six boys of noble and handsome appearance. One of the six boys was crowned king, with the title "Suro."[25] He named his kingdom Karak-kuk (or Kayakuk), and the other five men became the rulers of the five neighboring Kaya tribes. Suro became a powerful king.[26] *Samguk yusa* reports that "the King adopted the official organization of Kerim (Silla), creating peers with titles such as Kakkan, Ajikkan and Kupkan and reforming his government on the models of the Chou and Han dynasties of China. He loved his people like his own children and benevolently taught them the arts of civilized life."[27]

Nine chief courtiers of King Suro said that "it is not good for the King to be alone. . . . Let Your Majesty choose the most beautiful and virtuous maiden from among the girls whom we shall bring to the palace and make your queen." The king replied, "I was sent down from heaven to rule this land, and so my spouse will also descend from heaven at divine command. Sail toward Mangsan-do (Mountain-viewing Island) in the south and see what happens." In the meanwhile, as the courtiers obeyed, *Samguk yusa* reports that

> far out at sea, a ship with a red sail and flying a red flag appeared on the horizon, darting toward the north like an arrow. The Kaya sailors waved torches and made signs for the mysterious ship to come near. When it did so, they found that a beautiful princess was on board. The sailors escorted her to the shore, where a courier mounted a swift steed and galloped off to convey the news to the King. The King was exceedingly glad. He commanded the nine senior courtiers to meet the princess on the seashore and conduct her to the palace.[28]

Samguk yusa then relates that the courtiers of the king proceeded to the coast and encountered the princess:

> "Welcome, princess!" they said. "The King desires you to enter the palace and be received in audience immediately."

"You are strangers," the princess modestly replied. "I cannot follow you, nor can I be so unmaidenly as to enter the palace without due ceremony."

The courtiers conveyed the princess's words to the King, and he was struck by her virgin modestly and queenly dignity. He ordered a tent pitched in front of his detached palace on a hill sixty feet southwest of the royal residence and awaited her arrival. The princess left her ship with her suite, which consisted of the two courtiers Sin Po and Cho Kuang, their wives Mojŏng and Moryang, and twenty slaves who carried gold, silver, jewels, silk brocade and tableware in countless boxes as her trousseau. When she reached the top of the hill she changed her brocade trousers and offered them as a gift to the mountain spirit. Then she approached the tent and the King rose to meet her. The King bestowed native costumes and jewels upon the suite and bade them rest on beds covered with embroidered quilts and pillows. Then he and the princess entered the sleeping chamber.[29]

The princess told the King and others, "I am a princess of Ayuta (in India). My family name is Hŏ, my given name is Hwang-ok (Yellow Jade), and I am sixteen years old. In May this year my royal father and mother said to me, 'Last night we had a dream, and in our dream we saw a god who said, I have sent down Suro to be King of Karak, and Suro is a holy man. He is not yet married, so send your daughter to become his Queen. Then he ascended to heaven. It is the command of the god, and his words are still ringing in our ears. My daughter, bid farewell to your parents and go.' So I started on my long voyage, with steamed dates of the sea and fairy peaches of heaven for my provisions. Now I blush to stand in your noble presence." In response to that, the king told the princess, "I knew that you were coming, so I refused all the maidens whom my courtiers recommended as my spouse. Now my heart leaps with joy to receive a most beautiful and virtuous princess as my Queen."[30]

Samguk yusa goes on to say:

[T]he King passed two nights and one day with the princess from India. When it was time for her escort to return home he gave each person thirty rolls (one roll is forty yards) of hempen cloth and ten large bags of rice to sustain them on their voyage. On the first day of the eighth month the King and his Queen entered the royal palace in colorful palanquins, accompanied by courtiers in carriages and on horseback and followed by a long train of wagons laden with the trousseau which the princess had brought with her from India. She was escorted into the inner palace, and the two courtiers and their wives who had accompanied her from India were accommodated in separate apartments. The rest of her suite were given a guest house of twenty rooms and given food and drink, and her household articles and precious jewels were put in a store-room for her use at all times. . . . The royal couple lived happily for many years. In due time they both dreamed of seeing a bear, and sure enough the Queen conceived and bore a son. This was Crown Prince Kŏdŭng.[31]

Samguk yusa does not specify the exact number of princes and princesses and their names. In fact, they were identified by Kim Byung-mo's research, which will be related in a later section.[32]

The Credibility of Samguk yusa

Along with *Samguk sagi* (*History of the Three Kingdoms*) by Kim Pu-sik, *Samguk yusa*, assisted by eleven historians, is one of the few remaining written documents about the Three Kingdoms period on the Korean peninsula. While *Samguk sagi* was written in 1145 by eleven historians led by Kim Pu-sik (1075–1151), *Samguk yusa* was written by a monk named Ilyon [Iryŏn] (1206–1289) more than one century after *Samguk sagi,* circa 1281 to 1283. Owing to the qualifications, training, and background of its authors, *Samguk sagi* tends to be regarded as an official history of the Three Kingdoms period; *Samguk yusa,* on the other hand, has been regarded as an unofficial history. Apparently, though, both of these books have some inherent biases and errors. As Sarah Nelson has pointed out, "I have noted differences of reading when relating the ancient writings to the archaeological record."[33] For most historians, however, these two books have served as precious sources that complement archaeological findings and mythical and legendary stories.[34]

Regarding the credibility of these two history books, Nelson sums it up this way:

> The Korean *Samguk Sagi* (History of the Three Kingdoms) and *Samguk Yusa* (Memorabilia of the Three Kingdoms) were written in their present form much later than the events they record, although it is thought that they are based on early documents no longer extant. Each of these documents views Korean history through its own distorting lens, either Confucian or Buddhist, presenting mythic founding legends and detailed historical events as equally credible. Japanese sources, more nearly contemporaneous with the Three Kingdoms, tend to ascribe a secondary status to Korea, a stance which may have arisen from motives other than historical accuracy.[35]

It has been observed that *Samguk sagi* was written from a Confucian ideological orientation, influenced by the "doctrine of serving the great (*sadaejuŭi*)."[36] By contrast, *Samguk yusa* was influenced by Buddhism, as the author was a Buddhist monk. Others have pointed out that, since Iryŏn was from the Kyŏngsang region, his perspective on the Three Kingdoms was parochially associated with the Kyŏnsang province and he overlooked the northern region of the peninsula.

Despite such biases and errors, Nelson has pointed out that both documents are thought to be based on histories of the Three Kingdoms (including Kaya) that are now lost.[37] Also, in his recent book about the images of things "foreign" in Korean literature and culture, John M. Frankl has pointed out that "while most descriptions on *Samguk yusa* are not received as historical facts, the portion on Karak-kuk are very detailed and lengthy descriptions, more so than any other subjects treated; thus this is a sign that the tales are likely true. Karak-kuk was located in current Kimhae, and even at present Kimhae Kim and Kimhae Hŏ members of lineages do not marry with each other. As such ethnographic evidence indicates, the descriptions in *Samguk yusa* are not simple legendary stories."[38] Frankl suggests that some further studies of the Hŏ Hwang-ok marriage—studies archaeological, ethnographical, folkloric, and religious—should be undertaken.

Kim Byung-mo was determined to study the marriage of King Kim Suro and Hŏ Hwang-ok using every available research method—archaeological and ethnographic. He wanted to understand the belief system symbolized by the twin-fish.

SEARCH FOR HO HWANG-OK'S ROOTS

Where Is Ayodia?

Kim Byung-mo's study of Hŏ Hwang-ok's marriage to King Kim Suro began with his examining the descriptions in *Samguk yusa* to find the exact location of Ayuta. Kim obtained a detailed map of India and searched for Ayuta, using all possible place names similar to Ayuta phonetically, including Ayuda, Ayoda, Ŏyuta, Ŏyuda, Ŏyota, etc. Kim made inquiries to the Indian embassy, which had established the office of the Consulate General in Korea in 1973, and he was able to talk to a consul. He explained to the consul who he was and that he wanted to identify the name of a place in India, which would be similar to "Ayodia" phonetically. The consul told Kim that Ayodhia[39] was an old city located near Lucknow, the capital city of the state of Uttar Pradesh (also known to be the birthplace of Rāma).[40] It is located in northeastern India, and it is in the center of Hindu and Islamic cultures. Kim assumed that Ayodhia or Ayodhya must be the territory of the old Kosala kingdom. Although Kim was able to locate Ayodhya, his research stalled for a few years as he was engaged in other research.

Children of Kim Suro and Hŏ Hwang-ok

Samguk yusa does not give an account of the children of the royal couple other than the crown prince Kŏdŭng, who inherited the kingship of Kaya. However, one of Kim Byung-mo's students who had participated in Kim's seminar on the belief system of the twin-fish became so interested in Hŏ's marriage route that he eventually wrote his master's thesis on the subject. Also, he was working at the National Research Institute of Cultural Heritage in Ch'angwŏn (*Ch'angwŏn Munhwajae Yŏn'guso*), which is in the heartland of the old Kaya territory. One day, Kim's former student called and told him that he had found a document about the seven sons of Kim Suro and Hŏ Hwang-ok when he went to Ch'ilburam (the monks' hermitage of Ch'ilbul) at Ssanggyesa (Ssangye Buddhist temple) at Hadong, in south Kyŏngsang province, near the Kaya's border with Paekche (18 BC to AD 660), one of the Three Kingdoms. Kim remembered that in his seminar he had told his students that Ssanggyesa was the temple where King Kim Suro's seven sons became Buddhist monks; thus one might be able to learn their names there. As it turned out, one of his students had remembered that lecture of long ago.

The document of reminiscences (*yusa* of Ch'ilburam) found by Kim's former student was originally written in Chinese characters in the form of a hanging board (*hyŏnp'an*). It reads:

Before Kim Suro was sworn in as king, a Buddhist priest Po-ok-sŏnsa from Wŏljiguk foresaw that his sister, Hŏ Hwang-ok's would-be husband would be in the East, the priest took his sister with him to Kaya, and let her marry Kim Suro. They had ten sons. Of the ten, the eldest son, Kŏdŭng, became the crown prince, and two other sons inherited their mother's surname, Hŏ. The remaining seven sons followed their maternal uncle Po-ok-sŏnsa for Pangjang-san [a mountain], built a humble hut, and devoted themselves to Buddhist meditation. Eventually, all of them reached the state of Nirvana. . . . Their names were Hyejin, Kakch'o, Chigam, Tŭngyŏn, Tumu, Chŏnghŭng, and Kyejang was the last of the seven. This was the sixty-second year (AD 103) of the Kaya kingdom. They build Ch'ilburam [*Ch'il* means "seven" in Korean; thus the literal name is the hermitage of seven monks], which is located about twenty *ri* [about 8 kilometers] northward from Ssanggyesa, Hadong, south Kyŏngsang province.[41]

Besides these names, they all had Buddhist-style names suffixed with *bul*, meaning Buddha or Buddhist.[42]

The information written in the Ch'ilburam reminiscences concurs with general descriptions of *Samguk yusa*—a princess from an old kingdom in India had an international marriage with the Kaya king and had several children. Nonetheless, there are some discrepancies between the two documents. *Samguk yusa* states that when Hŏ Hwang-ok came to Kaya, she was accompanied by the two courtiers Sin Po and Cho Kuang, their wives, and twenty slaves. No mention is made of her older brother, a Buddhist priest named Po-ok-sŏnsa.[43] Also, the Ch'ilburam document states that Hŏ's brother was not from India, but Wŏljiguk, which was a nomadic tribal nation in the west of China during the Ch'in and Han dynastic periods. Later the people of Wŏljiguk moved westward.[44]

Although the document names the nine sons of Kim and Hŏ's royal family, the rest of them were not identified in either *Samguk yusa* or in the Ch'ilburam reminiscences. Through his own research, Kim Byung-mo was able to find the name of the remaining one son with Sŏn-kyŏn, and he believes there were two daughters. Of two daughters, one is P'yŏnnyŏn, who became the daughter-in-law of Sŏkt'arhae Isagŭm of Silla.[45] The other daughter is assumed to be Sinnyŏ, meaning "god-woman," who left the Kaya with her brother Sŏn-kyŏn. The myth of Sinnyŏ was not known. It is apparent that Kim and Hŏ had many children. Furthermore, the two courtiers Sin Po and Cho Kuang, who accompanied Hŏ Hwang-ok, also had several children. Sin Po's daughter became the queen of the second king, Kŏdŭng, and Cho Kuang's granddaughter became the queen of the third king, Map'um of the Kaya kingdom. This means that three queens of the early period of Kaya were of foreign origins. A combination of the cultures of Ayodia (Ayodhya) and the native Kaya upgraded the native culture into a higher one.[46]

A Clue about the Twin-fish (*ssang-ŏ*)

Meanwhile, Kim Byung-mo was reading a travelogue by an expert on children's literature, Yi Chong-gi, who traveled to Ayodhya[47] to attend meetings of the international pen club in India. He had written a lengthy travelogue titled "The Exploration of Krak-kuk." In that travelogue, Yi wrote that "in numerous buildings in Ayodhya, the figures of twin-fish had been carved. They looked identical in design—a pair of carp facing each other with a flower-like object between them," which were like the fish Kim Byung-mo had seen at the tomb of King Kim Suro in Kimhae.[48] Kim had thought from the time of college that the twin-fish would be an important symbol for tracing the roots of Hŏ Hwang-ok. Now, reading the travelogue, he had a "Eureka!" moment. The figure of the twin-fish strongly suggested that Ayodhya had been Hŏ's place of birth. Kim thought that if he had an opportunity to go to India, he was certain that he would be able to find some historical record of Hŏ and her family origin, along with the history of Ayodhya and the kingdom of Kosala.[49] Kim was determined to pursue his long-awaited project and wished to start his fieldwork in Ayodhya. In the early 1980s, however, it was a dream for a Korean archaeologist to conduct fieldwork with no external funding.[50]

While he was waiting for such an opportunity, in spring 1985 Kim Byung-mo received a phone call from a producer of the Korean Broadcasting System (KBS), who asked him to participate as a narrator and commentator for a television program, a documentary film on Pakistan. In his plans to produce this TV program, Kim Byung-mo was successful in including Ayodhya in his itinerary.[51] It was almost like a dream for Kim to go to India and observe the carvings of the twin-fish. The scheduled film included a large area—Karachi, Mohenjo-Daro, Islamabad, Taxila, and Peshawar—ranging from the downstream region of the Indus River all the way to the Hindu Kush mountain ranges.[52]

During his field trip to Mohenjo-Daro,[53] Kim Byung-mo was unable to find any carved or drawn figure of the twin-fish anywhere. From Mohenjo-Daro, Kim and the TV film crew drove to Peshawar, on the northwest frontier of Pakistan, where Kim was able to see a drawing of the twin-fish on the cover of a pickup truck. After Kim took a number of photographs of the drawing, he discovered an identical drawing on the other side of the pickup truck. While he was busy taking pictures, Kim found another representation of the twin-fish on the head of a rickshaw's driver; this one was made out of silver-colored sheet iron. Soon after, Kim noticed more twin-fish emblems decorating almost all small vehicles. Although the color and shape of twin-fish varied slightly, their basic form looked identical to the twin-fish he had seen at the tomb of King Kim Suro in Kimhae. Kim asked several renowned scholars in Pakistan and India about the origins of the twin-fish, yet no one was able to tell him. He assumed that the twin-fish symbol might not be native to Pakistan or even a part of Islamic culture. Perhaps it was not associated with any established widespread religion but to an indigenous belief system.[54]

When it came time, Kim Byung-mo was excited to visit the long-anticipated place, Ayodhya, near Lucknow, Uttar Pradesh. It took only forty-five minutes to travel from New Delhi to Lucknow by airplane, but it took another half a day to travel over ground from Lucknow to Ayodhya, even though it was only 150 kilometers (about 93.75 miles). The road was rough and narrow. Inhabitants numbered about one hundred thousand, but the city had more than one thousand Hindu temples, as Ayodhya was the birthplace of Rāma. To Kim's surprise, each and every temple was decorated with the twin-fish, either carved in the temple stone or rendered as a painting. Kim felt almost like he was hallucinating, as the twin-fish of Ayodhya reminded him so much of Kimhae. Kim became certain that the twin-fish would prove there was a connection between Ayodhya and Kimhae and thus would serve as a major clue in discovering Hŏ Hwang-ok's origin and route to Korea. Kim was so certain that Hŏ's original home had to be in India that he surmised that some Koreans might have more projected noses and darker skin pigmentation than the Chinese and Japanese.[55] Although he was yet unable to ascertain any definitive historical evidence, either any written documents or any informants (scholars in this case) who knew anything about Hŏ's marriage route to Korea, he had seen the twin-fish he had wished to see.

On his way back home from Ayodhya, he stopped in Bangkok, Thailand, where he learned of a city there named Ayuthia, a city-state that was created in the thirteenth century.[56] Despite a phonetic similarity, there is a disjuncture in time between the existence of the city-state and Hŏ Hwang-ok's life, which spanned part of the first and second centuries. The disjuncture is too great to support any connection. Nevertheless, Kim's trip to India and stopover in Thailand had led to a major breakthrough.[57]

Painting of Twin-fish at the *Ŭnha-sa* in Sinŏ-san

Kim Byung-mo visited the Pŏmŏ-sa in Tongrae, near Pusan, to see whether the temple had any drawings or paintings of the twin-fish since the literal translation of the temple's middle name (*ŏ* in Chinese script) refers to fish. Unable to find any and frustrated, he visited his acquaintance Hŏ Myŏng-ch'ŏl of Kimhae, who shares the same *pon* with Kim and is also a descendant of Hŏ Hwang-ok. Although Hŏ was a physician, he was interested in local history and the founder of the Kaya Cultural Center (*Kayamunhwa Yŏn'guso*), which published a journal on Kaya studies. Over a humble supper table, they were discussing a possible introduction of Buddhism in Korea around AD 48. This is when Hŏ Hwang-ok came to Korea from the Buddhist country of India. An earlier introduction would go against the conventional view that Buddhism was introduced to Korea in 372 during the reign of King Sosurim (371–384) of Koguryŏ.[58]

After learning that Kim Byung-mo had seen no twin-fish in Pŏmŏsa, the physician suggested that he visit the Buddhist temple of Ŭnha-sa, located on a small mountain, the Sinŏ Mountain. (A literal translation of Sinŏsan in Chinese characters would be roughly "the mountain of God of fish" or "fish God.") The physician also lent Kim his Jeep and a driver. Kim decided to make his field trip the next day. As Kim arrived at the small Buddhist temple of Ŭnha-sa, it looked as if the temple was deserted. Kim looked around, yet he was unable to find any likeness of a fish. Just as he was about ready to give up his search, a monk named Kim Tae-sŏng, the resident head monk (*chuji*) of the temple, returned from his daily walk.

Kim explained that the purpose of his trip was to look for any evidence of twin-fish. Recognizing that Kim was an archaeology professor at a university in Seoul, the head monk was cordial and helpful to Kim. The head monk asked Kim whether he saw the drawing of several paired fishes painted on the front side of the *sumidan,* a platform, about knee-high, for displaying a statue of Buddha. Sure enough, Kim saw many drawings of twin-fish on the platform, ones like those he had seen at the tombs of Kim

Suro and Hŏ Hwang-ok. The head monk told Kim that they are called *Sinŏ* (God fish), the same name given to the mountain. It was a moment just as exciting for Kim as had been his discovery in Ayodhya. The head monk also brought out two old wooden hanging-boards (*hyŏnp'an*), which were records of the remodeling of a building known as Ch'wiŭnru of Ŭnha-sa. The handing-boards were written in Chinese characters, and they read, "It has been told that Queen of the Kaya kingdom, Hŏ Hwang-ok came from India, and her older brother Changyuhwasang built Sŏrim-sa (old name of the Ŭnha-sa)."[59]

The most surprising revelation was the name of Hŏ Hawang-ok's older brother. The Ch'ilburam reminiscences had named Hŏ Hwang-ok's older brother Po-ok-sŏnsa, but the wooden hanging-board called him Changyuh-wasang. What they had in common, regardless of their actual names, was that they were known to be Buddhist priests. It is still puzzling as to whether Hŏ Hwang-ok had two brothers, both of whom came to Kaya when she was going off to marry, or one brother who came only after Hŏ had become queen of Kaya. What made this new information more puzzling was that it was not mentioned in *Samguk yusa*. Nonetheless, Kim was excited about his find, but it was too dark to take any pictures. Most of all, the flash in Kim's camera had run out. Instead of taking pictures, he decided to make a woodblock print by the intaglio method since he had black ink in his bag. He was able to make the print.[60] His fieldwork in Ŭnha-sa was most productive.

The presence of the twin-fish images in the old Kaya regions led Kim to investigate the origin and distribution of twin-fish further, as that would serve to be an indispensable clue in tracing Hŏ Hwang-ok's route to Korea. Thus far, Kim was able to conclude that the presence of twin-fish in Buddhist temples and in tombs on the Korean peninsula was limited to the Kaya region, and they likely dated from the Kaya and Silla periods. This evidence allowed Kim to postulate that twin-fish, and the belief system they symbolized, might have been spread by an elite group of foreign immigrants who emigrated from wherever the belief system had taken root. One possible route was from Mesopotamia, via India and south China, to Kaya.[61] Perhaps the twin-fish and their mythology had made it to Mongolia and the Lake Baikal region because during a field trip there Kim witnessed plenty of evidence of twin-fish in log cabins near Lake Baikal.[62] Parenthetically, the "Kaya-san" (Kaya Mountain), where a famous Haeinsa is located, has the same phonetic similarity with the "Gaya" Castle (meaning "head of cow") that is located in Buddha Gaya in India.[63] The Haein Buddhist Temple was built in the time of King Aejang of Silla (800–809). Before the temple was built, it was told that Kayasan was called Udusan by local people, which also means "head of a cow."

HŎ HWANG-OK IS FROM SICHUAN SHENG, CHINA

Sichuan as a Possible Site

Nearly twenty years after his first visit to the tombs of King Kim Suro and his wife in Kimhae, Kim Byung-mo went to the tombs with students for an archaeological field trip. Kim asked the students to read the engraving on the stone in front of Hŏ's tomb. It read: "Tomb of Hŏ, the Empress Dowager of Poju (*Puzhou Taihou* in Chinese pronunciation) and Queen of King Kim Suro of the Kaya kingdom (*Karak-kuk Surowangbi Pojut'aehu Hŏ-ssi nŭng* in Korean pronunciation)." Although it was erected in 1647 during the reign of Injo (1623–1649) of the Chosŏn dynasty, the engraved words were based on an oral history of Kaya, which is mostly as accurate as written history. When students asked Kim what *Poju* meant, Kim was unable to answer promptly because during his first visit he had overlooked the word in his preoccupation with the twin-fish.[64]

Kim's search to identify Poju (Puzhou) began as soon as he returned from his field trip. Since the mausoleum inscription was written in Chinese characters, he focused his search on China. He assigned graduate students in his seminar class to find the location, but no one was able to identify it on any map of China. Almost accidentally, however, while he was searching a 1931 edition of an old dictionary of place names, *Chungguk Kogŭmjimyŏng Taesajŏn (Gujindimingdacidian)*, he was able to find Poju, which is the old name of Anyuexian in Sichuan Sheng. The city went by the old name from the Zhou dynasty (1027–771 BC) to the Song (960–1279) dynasty.[65] He started to study the history of the Late Han dynastic period.

According to a detailed history of the Late Han, in AD 47, one year before Hŏ Hwang-ok came to Kaya, there was a people's rebellion against an unfair taxation system, and again in AD 101, a second rebellion took place. The rebellion was led by a person named Hŏ Sŏng (Xu Cheng in Chinese pronunciation). Afterward, people who took part in the rebellion were relocated to Wuhan in central China. Knowing that in Poju in Sichuan province there was a person whose name was Hŏ (Xu in Chinese pronunciation),[66] Kim searched for evidence of twin-fish. By carefully examining his archaeological books on China, he was able to find ample evidence of twin-fish figures on props of dishes in the Sichuan region and engraved on bricks and utensils that were made by copper in Yunnan province. There was indeed evidence that people who found significance in the twin-fish symbol once lived around the basin of the River of Yangzijiang (now called Changjiang). This was shaping up into a classic case where historical documents and archaeological evidence are in agreement.[67]

An Effort to Make a Field Trip to Puzhau (Poju in Korean) in Sichuan, China

In summer 1990 on his way back from his field trip to Mongolia, which has been supported by the *Chosun Ilbo,* a major daily Korean newspaper, Kim Byung-mo made a side trip to Beijing, China, in order to visit Puzhau. He was looking for evidence that Puzhau had been the hometown of Hŏ Hwang-ok (Xu Huangyu in Chinese pronunciation).[68] Kim asked for help from Luo Zhewen,[69] vice chairman of the Chinese National Institute of Culture and People (CNICP, *Zhongguo Wenwuyanjinsuo*). Luo told Kim, "Since Any-uexian (formerly Puzhau) is located in the remote countryside, it would be difficult to travel there, even if you can get to Chengdu. Also, the region is a restricted area, where foreigners cannot travel." Nonetheless, Kim could not easily give up his wish to visit Anyuexian because he had waited so long to go there.[70] He had overcome so many obstacles to visit China. At that time it was difficult for any Korean to get permission to visit China because the two countries did not establish formal diplomatic ties until 1992. Kim thought he had to go there and decided to try. However, owing to unexpected, acute stomach cramps, Kim had to cancel his trip and return to Korea.

Kim Byung-mo was unable to visit Puzhau in 1990, but in January 1991 he had another opportunity to revisit Ayodhya and learned from a local historian that Ayodhya had been invaded by Kosala, and elite groups including priests and royal families of Ayodhya were ostracized. Later, during the first century BC, they had faced the attack from the Kushan. During the Kushan attack, Kim postulated that, if the Ayodhyans wanted to seek their own safety, they would have gone to the opposite directions of the Kushan's attack. Since the Kushans came from the west and north, Ayodhyans had to go either east or south.[71] The local history of Ayodhya suggested to Kim that Hŏ families in India who became refugees from the Kushan's attack might have gone to Anyuexian (Puzhau). Kim felt that a trip to Anyuexian of Sichuan Sheng was absolutely necessary.

In June 1991, Kim Byung-mo was invited to attend an academic conference. Capitalizing on his opportunity to go to China, Kim decided to make his epic journey to Anyuexian via Chengdu, capital of Sichuan province, the gateway to enter Tibet. In Chengdu, through a personal network in Beijing, he was introduced to a Chinese Korean woman, Pak Myŏng-sil, who held a powerful position in Sichuan Sheng as vice-head of the division for external security of the province. As soon as they met, he explained to her his reasons for wishing to visit to Anyuexian (Poju). Kim told her that he postulated that Hŏ's (Xu's) families in Ayodhya sought refuge in Anyuexian and later relocated to Wuhan and the Yangzijiang River basin, and then went to Shanghai.

From there, Hŏ Hwang-ok (Xu Huangyu) and her courtiers might have set sail through the Yellow Sea, finally reaching Kaya.[72]

For the field trip to Anyuexian, Pak made arrangements for Kim, including a Jeep, a driver, and a translator who spoke both Korean and Chinese. Not only was Kim's field trip endorsed by the vice-head of the external security division, but also, in 1991 a ban restricting foreign travelers from Anyuexian had been lifted. The distance from Chengdu to Anyuexian was only 150 kilometers (about 93.75 miles), but because of poor road conditions, Kim learned it would take long hours. In fact, Kim and his party left the hotel at seven o'clock in the early morning but didn't arrive until around two-thirty in the afternoon, seven and half hours later under a blazing sun and in heat of forty degrees Celsius. Puzhou was a small and quiet town, located in a valley. Kim's party visited the editorial office of a publisher of local history on the Anyuexian district. Although Kim was unable to find any historical documents on the Hŏ (Xu) clan, the chairman of the editorial committee introduced the principal of a local middle school, whose name was Hŏ P'yo-byŏng (Xu Biaobing in Chinese pronunciation). Kim recognized instantly, of course, that the principal's surname was Hŏ (Xu). Kim was able to arrange to meet Hŏ at the hotel that evening.[73]

After Kim took a shower in his hotel room, he found the words *Puzhou Hotel* in red letters on the bathroom towel. Kim was so excited that people still opted to use the town's old name: *Puzhou*. He went outside the hotel, walked around the streets, and found quite a few stores and photography shops that carried names prefixed with the name of Puzhou. Kim trusted that he had come to the right place and knew that this was the town he had been looking for, for so many years. Late that evening, around ten thirty, Xu (Hŏ) Biaobing came by Kim's hotel. Sipping a few glasses of whisky together, Kim explained his study to Xu and the purpose of his visit to Puzhou.[74] The principal related quite valuable information to Kim. According to him, "In the city of Anyuexian, there are some 1,000 citizens whose surnames are Xu, most of whom are either farmers or petty storeowners." None of whom is a scholar from whom Kim can learn the local history of Xu families. However, some distance from the city, there is a consanguineous village of Xu clan members. Currently, the village is named Minzhuxiang (*Minjuhyang* in Korean pronun-ciation), meaning the "village of democracy." However, it used to be called either Xu (Hŏ)-jiabei or Xu (Hŏ)-jiayayuan.[75] Kim was intrigued and thought the village might have been the home village of Xu Huang-yu (Hŏ Hwang-ok).

The principal Xu spoke further, "Although I heard about the village, I have never been there myself." Kim importuned him as to whether he knew anyone who could guide the way. Then Xu said, "My uncle goes to the village every now and then. He is only one who knows the way. Also, the village is so remote and the road is in such poor condition that no one can drive a vehicle there. You must walk." Kim told him that he would not mind walking no matter how far away the village would be. As Kim was so persistent, the principal finally agreed to bring his uncle with him the next morning. And he said, "If my uncle cannot go with us, I will try to find someone in the village by asking around." The principal also asked him to bring his rented Jeep so that they could drive the car as much of the distance as they could. About six o'clock in the early next morning, the principal came to the hotel with his uncle. The Jeep took them about twenty minutes of the way, to a place called Changghe, but it could not proceed any further owing to the rough, narrow road. They left the Jeep at Changghe and went by foot toward the village. They walked along a muddy road, which was at times wide but mostly very narrow. Enduring these difficult road conditions, they eventually reached the village.[76]

The village Xujiabei (or Xujiayayuan) was located at the edge of a low mountain and consisted of some twenty houses scattered around. The scene reminded Kim of a Korean farming village with a rice paddy and a cornfield. Upon seeing the mulberry trees, he thought of *Samguk yusa*'s describing Hŏ Hwang-ok as having brought "silk brocade"[77] along with other gifts when she first came to Kaya.[78]

The son of a village elder, Xu Taixun, told Kim that about eighty villagers from twenty households had surnames with Xu, except those spouses of men who married outside the village. The village was known to be Xu-jiabei (Hŏ Ka-p'ae in Korean pronunciation), a classic example of a consanguineous village. There was a ruin of an old ancestral shrine of Xu. According to Xu Taixun, whose skin color looked darker (maybe because of distant Indian kin), there were more families named Xu only thirty or forty years ago. However, during the Cultural Revolution (1966–1976) led by Mao Zedong with his Red Guards, most consanguineous villages had been disbanded. Ancestral shrines were destroyed, burnt, the villagers banished and relocated elsewhere. Xu Taixun took Kim to the mountain behind the village; there were so many small and large ill-kept graveyards. Kim found one large piece of stone in the jumble that turned out to be a tombstone engraved "the grave of Xu Yingfen." Kim was certain that the mountain was the main graveyard of the Xu clan in China and Xu Huang-yu's (Hŏ Hwang-ok) home village. It is a historical irony that this clan became world wanderers: During the Kushan's attack, they ended up coming to China, and because of a rebellion, they were relocated again in Wuhan and the Yangzijiang. Even in modern times, because of the Cultural Revolution in China, they were ostracized once again and relocated elsewhere.[79] The clan had experienced diaspora from an earlier time.

At the graveyard of Xu clan members, Kim gave a short summary of the ancient history of the Xu families' ordeal based on the history book titled

The History of the Late Han (Hou Han), which he had studied thoroughly. He explained about the rebellion by the Xu clan members against unfair taxation system in AD 47, after which they were relocated to Puzhou in AD 101. And, when Kim was about to take a picture of the ruined tombstone of Xu Yingfen, Xu Taixun took him by the sleeve and asked him to refrain from taking any photos; he then turned the tombstone upside down as it had been before. He explained that he was afraid of any possible repercussions from the Chinese authorities, even though the Cultural Revolution was long over. Xu Taixun explained to Kim that during the Red Guard's tyranny they had barely survived by promising not to rebuild the shrine and other ruins. In order to survive, they had left them alone without restoring them. Also, before the revolution, on Qingming,[80] Xu clan members had gathered together to observe rites in honor of their dead ancestors at the clan shrine, but they could not do that anymore.

As Kim inquired about any genealogy of the Xu clan, Xu Taixun told Kim that there was no written document, including no genealogy. Instead of writing down anything that could be viewed as a revival of the clan, they tried to memorize everything, including the names of their ancestors in the form of oral history. As demonstration of such an ability, Xu Taixun wrote in Kim's notebook all the generation names[81] extending back thirty generations. Thirty generations amounts to roughly one thousand years. The preservative power and accuracy of oral history, particularly in preliterate societies, is on par with written documents. Kim reminded Xu Taixun that someday, when he became head of the consanguineous village, he might be able to restore the ruins. Kim also told him that knowing this is Hŏ Hwang-ok's natal home, some Kimhae Kim Koreans might pay homage the village and some might offer some aid. That's because some Kimhae Kim clan members are rich and powerful enough to assist in restoring the village.[82]

HŎ HWANG-OK'S NAME ENGRAVED IN SHENJING

After he published a single volume narrating his epic journey to trace the roots of Hŏ Hwang-ok in 1994, Kim Byung-mo became an instant celebrity.[83] Published by the *Chosun Ilbo*, the book was so entertaining that it drew the attention of the general public, particularly the descendants of the Kimhae Kim, Kimhae Hŏ, and Inch'ŏn Yi clans. In 2002, leaders in Anyuexian organized a research association (*Puzhou Taihou Yanjiuhui*) to study Hŏ Hwang-ok, and they invited Kim Byung-mo to serve as the honorary chairman of the organization. Soon after the appointment, six city officials from Anyuexian and local historians came to Korea to pay homage to the tombs of Kim Suro and Hŏ Hwang-ok. In response to this public interest, during the 2002 Asian Games at Pusan, the wedding ceremony of Kim Suro and Hŏ Hwang-ok was reenacted as an entertaining event.[84]

In July 2003, Kim Byung-mo joined a field trip to Sichuan, organized by Cho Hŭng-yun for the Association of Historical Studies for Sichuan [*Sach'on-sa yŏn'guhoe*]. Unlike his earlier trip in 1991, Kim received a warm welcome from citizens, particularly from those who had been to Korea. He had an opportunity to visit the consanguineous village of Ruiyunxiang (*Sŏunhyang* in Korean pronunciation), where there were more Xu clan members than lived in the village of Puzhou (Poju). Unlike Puzhou, in Ruiyunxiang, clan memorials were well preserved. Hundreds of people gathered to welcome the visitors. At the center of the Xu lineage shrine, there was a portrait of Xu Changshu, tenth head of the lineage. Most notably, in front of the entrance gate was an old and faded, yet clearly engraved, figure of the twin-fish. No one could miss them. According to Xu Ping, in the district of Anyuexian, there are fourteen consanguineous villages with Xu clan, and the total population of Xu would be 150,000 people.[85]

As Kim climbed up a mountain behind the village of Ruiyunxiang, there was a tomb resembling a rock cabin behind a rock wall, which appeared to be built during the East Han (the Late Han, 45 BC to AD 23) period and already had been raided by treasure hunters. However, Kim was able to see an engraved figure of the twin-fish on the wall of the rock tomb. Here again, the village was associated with the twin-fish. Coming down from the mountain, he came across a "well" called Shenjing, meaning "God-well" beside a rock wall, and Kim noticed a figure of twin-fish engraved there, too, along with some words. Kim almost fainted when he recognized the name of Hŏ Hwang-ok engraved in the stone. Some characters were defaced by the action of erosion over all those years since the East Han, but Kim was able to read the name of Hŏ Hwang-ok. While Kim was trying to read the entire contents of the rock wall engraving, the guide was urging him to return to the village promptly. Kim took some photographs of it and rushed back to the village, asking an official of Sichuan to make a rubbing and send it to him later. The official agreed to do so.[86]

Later, an official from the city of Kimhae and Ch'oe In-ho, a Korean novelist, who returned from Sichuan, brought the rubbing with them. Although some portions were illegible, some words about Hŏ Hwang-ok were intact well enough to read. Among many other things, the two most important facts related to Kim's study were legible: First, during the early East (Late) Han period, there was a beautiful girl named Hŏ Hwang-ok; second, regarding the twin-fish, when Hŏ was born, because of a severe famine, most of her relatives left the village, but Hŏ's immediate family members, including Hŏ's great-grandparents, grandparents, and parents did not leave because Hŏ's mother was about to give birth to Hŏ. Since they were so poor that they nearly starved to death while they remained in the village, Hŏ's great-grandfather went to the God-well to pray for help. Then, in answer to his prayer, fishes swam up into the well. Using fishhooks fashioned from wood, he caught two fishes a day and made porridge enough out of them to keep the family from starving.[87] By reading the writings that were engraved in the rock wall beside the God-well, Hŏ Hwang-ok's name was clearly visible. The story is similar to the legendary story of Manu's ancestors of the Kosal kingdom who, during the great flood, followed fish to the highlands of Himalaya.[88] Perhaps such a legendary story prevailed in the Kosal time in northern India was carried by the Xu families when they were relocated to China. The presence of twin-fish in all those sites might be the missing links to the Hŏ clan's history of emigration from Ayodhya, India, to Puzhou, China.[89]

In conclusion, Kim Byung-mo postulates that Hŏ Hwang-ok's ancestors left Ayodhya as the consequence of an attack from Kushan and were relocated to the Puzhou area of the Anyuexian district of Sichuan province. By cross-checking the records of the history of Han, Hŏ Hwang-ok was assumed to be born in AD 32 in Puzhou, China. (Her grandfather was estimated to be born in 54 BC.) When the Xu clans immigrated to Wuhan and Yunnan province via Puzhou and Anyuexian, China, they carried with them the cultural tradition of the priestly Brahmans, the highest Hindu caste. They built Brahman-style temples and decorated them with figures of the twin-fish. Their cultural tradition was transmitted to following generations through the mechanism of oral tradition.[90]

In March 1993, when Kim Byung-mo had made his third field trip to Ayodhya, India, he was invited by Vimalendra Pratad Mohan Mishira, who was the main heir of the royal family of the Ayodhya kingdom, to the old palace of Raj Sadan for a chat over tea. Mishira listened to Kim's story about Hŏ Hwang-ok with great interest and gave Kim a copy of a history book on Ayodhya. In 1997, Mishira was invited by the Korean government at Kim's recommendation, but the invitation was retracted owing to Korea's financial woes—the shortage in a foreign currency reserve and a loan from the International Monetary Fund.

However, in April 1999, as the economic crisis eased up, Kim Chong-p'il, prime minister of Korea and also a member of the Kimhae Kim clan remotely related to King Kim Suro and Queen Hŏ Hwang-ok, invited Mishira to Kimhae, Korea, to meet with leaders of the Kim clan. In return, a growing number of Korean tourists have begun to visit Ayodhya, India. In 2001, the clan association of the Kim clan and some businessmen from Kimhae built a commemorative stone slab (*kinyŏmbi*) in memory of Hŏ Hwang-ok in Kimhae, Korea, carried it to India, and erected it in the city of Ayodhya.[91] Also, in the fall of 2005 when the city of Kimhae had an international cultural fair, Kimhae city invited Mishira, the main heir of the Ayodhya kingdom, and had an exhibit of Indian folk customs.[92]

Also, as a growing number of Korean tourists began visiting Anyuexian (Puzhou), China, the city government of Anyuexian provided a city directory that leads to the Puzhou Xu Clan Ancestral Hall written in three languages, Chinese, Korean, and English. There is also information in Ruiyunxiang about the engraving on the rock wall that had given Kim Byung-mo critical clues about Hŏ Hwang-ok.[93] Since then, an increasing number of Koreans have begun to visit Ayodhya, India, and Puzhou, China. The nearly thirty years of the epic journey of Kim Byung-mo to trace the roots of his remote ancestress proved that by and large the legendary descriptions in *Samguk yusa* concur with archaeological, ethnographic, and ethnohistorical evidence.[94] In addition to tracing the multicultural roots of one Korean's clan, Kim Byung-mo has helped bring about cultural exchanges among the several countries that he linked together through his long search.

3

The Emergence of the "Pure-Blood" Myth and Human Rights

XENOPHOBIA VS. "XENOUNEASINESS"

In the early 1970s, during my fieldwork studying workers harvesting pulp-wood in a small town in the American South, I had been addressed as "boy" by workers and often had my offer of a handshake refused. And when I was conducting my fieldwork on the Mississippi band of the Choctaw Indians in northeast central Mississippi, some whites in the vicinity of the Indian reservation again refused to shake hands with me. It felt unpleasant, awkward, and uneasy to conduct fieldwork among them.[1]

Had I myself behaved in this manner to any foreigner in Korea? Immediately after World War II, in 1945,[2] I met an American GI in a local post office. I was shocked to see his "odd features," those blue eyes and projecting nose. I had never seen any human being with such odd features. I ran to my friends and shouted about the stranger. The GI might have been embarrassed at seeing an astonished boy. In the mid-1960s, when I lived in the American South, there were hardly any Asians living in small Southern towns. So, whenever I went to any shopping mall or grocery store, small children followed me around in curiosity. I did not know what to do; again, it was uncomfortable.

Another time, when I was riding a train to Seoul soon after the cease-fire agreement that ended the Korean War in 1953, I found the train was over-crowded. There was only one vacant seat, right beside an American GI. Even if it meant standing for over twenty hours on the train, no one wanted to sit next to the GI. I, too, stood up the whole time instead of taking the seat because I did not feel comfortable sitting next to a foreigner.

I have even witnessed a similarly uneasy feeling exhibited by a dog. When I was a faculty member of a Southern university in northwest Tennessee, there was a Chinese American faculty member who had a big, aggressive dog. Whenever strangers passed near the fence, the dog grew furious and barked loudly. However, whenever I visited the house, even though only thin glass separated us, the dog never barked at me. Instead, he seemed quite friendly, wagging his tail. When I asked about it, the Chinese faculty member told me that the dog never barked at Asians because the dog was familiar with them.

Are these illustrations of uneasiness, discomfort, unpleasantness, or curiosity manifestations of xenophobia? The definition of xenophobia in anthropology means something different than it does in psychology, where it is thought of as a personal neurosis rather than a sociopsychological phenomenon. Anthropologists David Hunter and Phillip Whitten describe *xenophobia* as follows: "We talk of a certain society, for example, as harboring xenophobic tendencies—meaning that members of that society manifest a strong suspicion of other societies with which they have had little or no contact."[3] If a "strong suspicion" would be a necessary and sufficient requirement in the definition of xenophobia, I must admit that I have been xenophobic, as was the dog of my Chinese American colleague. Instead of labeling such ambivalent feelings and awkward behavior toward strangers and foreigners xenophobia, may I propose the neologism *xenouneasiness* as an alternative? Perhaps xenophobia has been used indiscriminately at times, but most hyperbolic uses are harmless.[4] It seems to me that in order to be labeled as xenophobia, there must be more than a strong suspicion; there has to be a systematic or institutionalized form of differential treatment—legally, socially, and otherwise—against foreigners and strangers. One example would be the institutionalized xenophobia against Chinese and Japanese living on the U.S. West Coast in the 1870s.[5] As farm laborers in cotton fields of the Mississippi Delta in the late 1860s, Chinese were targets of racial discrimination and barred from white schools, organizations, and other institutions until the 1940s.[6] Even during World War II, the U.S. federal government began to discriminate against some 120,000 Japanese American citizens. Harry H. L. Kintano, an authority on Japanese American studies and a prisoner in one of the Japanese internment camps, has written vividly of his experience.[7]

No matter how one defines xenophobia, the Chinese Exclusion Act in 1882 on the U.S. West Coast and the wartime internment of Japanese Americans went beyond "xenouneasiness." It was a clear manifestation of an extreme form of xenophobia, which was endorsed and initiated by the legislative and executive offices. The internment was carried out systematically and with public approval. According to contemporary ethics, it was a gross violation of human rights, even if an official apology was later made and payments were offered to compensate for inhumane acts of the past.

Korea's Xenophobia and Violation of Human Rights

Some foreign writers such as Michael Breen have commented that "what is profoundly disturbing is that Korean intellectuals become more xenophobic and nationalistic, and perpetrate the idea that all of Korea's problems are the result of wilfulness by foreigners."[8] It is worth remembering, though, that xenophobia is present in virtually every part of the world, including Breen's native country of Britain. Jürgen Habermas, professor of philosophy, wrote an extensive commentary on Charles Taylor's multiculturalism. He reports that "xenophobia is widespread these days in the European Community as well. It is more marked in some countries than in others, but the attitudes of the Germans do not differ substantially from those of the French and the *English*"[9] (emphasis mine).

Nevertheless, xenophobic sentiment, including prejudice and intolerance against foreigners or outsiders, may have been more prominent among scholars and intellectuals than among laypersons. According to Francis L. K. Hsu, in the United States, for instance, although segregation and discrimination have been outlawed in word and deed since the enactment of civil rights legislation in 1964, there has been residual xenophobic sentiment among anthropologists. Hsu reported, "White anthropologists find it most intolerable to accept theories about their White American culture by non-White anthropologists, especially if the theories contradict the ones White anthropologists have already held dear."[10] In 1974, when I presented a paper at the ninth annual meeting of the Southern Anthropological Society describing an off-reservation Choctaw Indian community in Northwest Tennessee, I got a cold reception.[11] As Robert Redfield has said, "Americans deny that any of themselves are or were peasant, in part, no doubt, because of their strong egalitarian and republican sentiments."[12] I learned that the word *peasant* is almost taboo to Americans. Arthur Raper learned so, too, when he used the term to refer to Americans; his use met with vehement opposition.[13]

Most recently, in a special report on Korea by the *Wall Street Journal* (dated November 8, 2010) on the occasion of Korea hosting the G-20 summit, Mike Weisbart, principal consultant to Tower Communications in Seoul, wrote,

> At the end of the day foreigners here [Korea] will always be foreigners. . . . My experience is that foreigners don't fit well in that hierarchy, especially if they are white. Too often, older team members don't know how to relate to foreigners. They may lack the linguistic skills, or simply feel that a foreigner can't be ordered around like they do their younger colleagues. In such an environment, a foreigner will tend to be marginalized or perhaps relegated to talking to a junior person on the team who happens to have lived in the U.S. but in

truth isn't privy to strategy or creative discussions. As a result, even foreigners who speak Korean well can feel underutilized and their skills unappreciated. . . . For people willing to make that investment, Seoul more often than not turns into a posting that people seek to extend.[14]

Weisbart's writing indicates that he seems to love Korea and likes certain elements of Korean culture. In 1995 he came to Korea not assuming to live there any longer than a year, but he eventually stayed five years; in 2003, he returned to Korea and lives there even now. Nevertheless, he cautiously alludes to Koreans' xenophobia. Perhaps Koreans he encountered were xenophobic toward him. However, uneasy feelings like being lonely and being excluded can occur in any strange place. In 1954, one year after the cease-fire of the Korean War, I, a timid country soul from a remote corner of the northeastern part of Kyŏngsang province, came to Seoul all by myself. My feelings upon arrival might have been worse than Weisbart's. Surely my time living in the American South from 1965 to 2001 included some experiences comparable to those Weisbart had in Seoul.[15] However, an old Korean saying is that "a virtuous man never feels lonely too long before attracting friends from all over (*tŏkpulgo, p'ilyuin*)." I assume that sooner or later Weisbart has or will draw the attention of many Korean friends.

As mentioned, throughout Korean history and prehistory, many foreign immigrants came to Korea. As late as 2009, a fifty-six-year-old German named Bernhard Quandt, who came to Korea in 1979 and was naturalized in 1986, was appointed by the Lee Myung-bak [Myŏng-pak Yi] government as president of the government-owned Korea Tourism Organization (*Han'guk kwan'gwang'gongsa*), which is the highest governmental position ever occupied by a foreign-born person. Bernhard Quandt, who goes by his Korean name Yi Ch'am, reminds Koreans that before him there were many foreigners who served Korea and thereby distinguished themselves. Among them was his countryman P. G. Möllendorff, who served as a special adviser to the Chosŏn court in 1884. In an essay published in a Korean newspaper, Yi Ch'am suggests that his government appointment owes to Korea's tradition of opening up high government offices to talented foreigners. To this he adds that his counterpart in "the Japanese government was impressed by the Korean move, and the Japanese official envied Korea's openness in appointing foreigners to such high governmental positions."[16]

There are occasions when foreigners enjoy their status as being foreigners. In the early 1960s, when I was conducting a nationwide study, I learned that foreigners would receive more help from the local people, who seemed uneasy talking to me and tried to hide if they could. While I was trying to reiterate the purpose of my research and ask for their assistance, a German

Catholic priest came to the village and got the attention of the people. Almost everyone followed the priest, and I was unable to secure the villagers' attention, even if (or perhaps because) I was a native Korean.[17] It is the same in Japan. Emiko Ohnuki-Tierney, a Japanese American anthropologist and a good friend of mine, may be correct when she says that, for fieldwork in Japan, foreign anthropologists have a tremendous advantage: "All foreigners, especially Westerners, usually receive the red-carpet treatment from the Japanese, who go out of their way to accommodate their visitors."[18]

Whatever the realities are, it seems to be that many foreigners who live in Korea, including foreign married immigrants, share the thought that a strong feeling of xenophobic sentiment is prevalent among contemporary Koreans. A survey conducted by the Corea [Korea] Image Communication Institute (CICI) provides some evidence of this. Of 213 foreign "opinion leaders"—including foreign companies' CEOs, diplomats, foreign professors, correspondents, branch managers of foreign banks, and business expatriates living in Korea—17.8 percent responded that Koreans are not open-minded and are xenophobic toward foreigners, and 10.2 percent responded that Koreans are not courteous toward foreigners.[19]

Regarding the suffering and challenges foreign brides have faced, Rowena Yoon, a married immigrant from the Philippines who is a member of the support network for foreign women (the International Spouses in Korea Association or ISKA) sums up possible sources of suffering for foreign brides. These forms of suffering may amount to direct or indirect violations of human rights. The major causes for suffering are as follows: a language barrier, domestic abuses from a spouse or in-laws, poor education of children, poverty, and social ostracism over visa issues.[20]

Yi Sŏng-mi, the former chief officer who dealt with the affairs of foreign brides in both the Ministry of Gender Equality and Family and the Ministry for Health, Welfare and Family Affairs compiled a list of minor cultural differences that foreign wives face in their daily activities living in Korea.[21] For instance, brides from Indonesia object to eating pork and *samgyŏp-sal* (grilled or roasted, thinly sliced pork belly), a favorite food of Koreans. Since most Indonesian brides are Muslim, eating pork is taboo. Brides from Mongolia long to eat meat, lamb in particular, but most Koreans prefer fish and vegetables over meat. In their native land, Mongolians seldom eat fish and vegetables. Most brides from Thailand are uneasy using chopsticks. For them, fingers are much handier for eating food. Wives from the Philippines use forks, chopsticks, and spoons, but many prefer to use their fingers at meals as well. Also, wives from the Philippines tend to arrive about fifteen minutes later than the appointed time because they consider punctuality discourteous. Vietnamese wives are asked to bow to their parents-in-law by kneeling down to the floor; however, in Vietnam they do such a bow only to dead persons. They are uneasy about the Korean custom. Also, most brides from Vietnam find it difficult not to take a nap during the day. Nearly all brides, regardless of their country of origin, encounter misunderstandings when it comes to the food they are to eat in the aftermath of childbirth. Yi Sŏng-mi describes the differences in her book.[22]

Behind many of the problems identified by Yi Sŏng-mi are two larger difficulties that foreign wives face: a language barrier and an unawareness of cultural differences. I discuss these difficulties in the following two sections.

Language Barrier

A language barrier is an unavoidable problem for any immigrant transplanted to an alien society who does not speak the language. I have a vivid memory of coping with a language handicap myself when I went to the United States. I knew that no one could help me other than myself. Nevertheless, in order to assist foreign brides in learning the Korean language, the Korean government, both central and local governments and various civic organizations, have instituted special language programs involving thousands of teachers and volunteers who provide one-on-one lessons to immigrants. These home visits take place twice a year, once between March and July and again between August and December. In all, an immigrant can receive no more than eighty total hours of instruction. Most married immigrants being served by this program have complained that eighty hours of instruction is insufficient to learn the Korean language.[23] Nevertheless, persons wishing to become naturalized Korean citizens must either pass a written examination demonstrating Korean language proficiency or take 220 hours of Korean language and culture training.

Most foreign wives with school-age children feel guilty about their inability to help with their children's homework. They are frustrated when they cannot read notes from school teachers that their children bring home. Most in-laws of foreign brides want to speak Korean at home, so interactions between mothers and children tend to be limited. A Vietnamese mother lamented that she was discouraged from speaking any Vietnamese at home: "I can only sing Vietnamese songs when the child is sick or just before the child falls asleep."[24] Such limited interaction between mothers and children leads to a mother's low visibility at home. In 2009, a psychological test administered by Min Sunghe [Sŏng-hye Min] at the CUK found that, out of 165 students tested, 25 were unable to draw portraits of their mothers at all. Even those who attempted to draw images of their mothers drew very rough sketches. Some drew figures with no ears, no eyes, no mouths, and no noses. When asked about their mothers' names, many answered that they did not know, and others answered that they could not pronounce the name because it was too long and too hard to pronounce. Min believes these results point to the limited interaction between children and mothers.[25]

For married immigrants, acquiring Korean language proficiency is essential to becoming a functioning member of Korean society. The necessity of learning language goes beyond communication.[26]

During my fieldwork I learned that foreign brides are widely dispersed throughout the country, often living in remote villages and on small islands. Their dispersal makes it difficult to assemble a large group of them at one time and place. To teach Korean language and culture to foreign brides, the traditional face-to-face instructional method of the classroom has presented a real problem. Since most of them are working full time and raising young children, they cannot find the time needed to study. With the various obstacles of the traditional method of education in mind, I implemented an alternative at the CUK—a distance-learning approach conducted over the Internet.[27]

Unawareness of Cultural Differences

Misunderstandings resulting from cultural differences are another source of discomfort for foreign wives. For instance, most Korean Chinese who were born in China and grew up in the home of Korean Chinese parents do not have a major language barrier, but they do have cultural misunderstandings. Unexpectedly, perhaps, the second highest incidence of divorce and separation is among Korean Chinese (14 percent) next to native Chinese (28 percent) among foreign immigrant groups.[28]

A language handicap may not be the primary cause leading to family squabbles, separation, and even divorce. Recognizing the seriousness of cross-cultural understanding, the CUK's Campaign urges multicultural families to be cognizant of the values and customs of their foreign-born family members. The Campaign offers classes on the language and culture of Vietnam, which is the birth country of the largest number of foreign brides, except for Korean Chinese and Han Chinese. These classes will be extended to cover other countries as well. Many Korean families who have Vietnamese brides have expressed their appreciation for such an opportunity to be acquainted with the other culture.

FAMILY SQUABBLES, DOMESTIC ABUSE, AND VIOLATIONS OF HUMAN RIGHTS

If a language barrier and an unawareness of culture lay behind many problems that foreign wives face, some of the more serious consequences include family squabbles and domestic abuse.

Domestic Squabbles and Abuse by Family Members

According to a report made by the Ministry of Health, Welfare and Family Affairs, based on a nationwide study of 945 international married couples, only 8 percent of them reported experiencing family squabbles and domestic violence once or twice a week, while 41 percent of the international marriage couples surveyed claimed not to have serious domestic squabbles.[29] Causes for squabbles are due to differences in personality (33.4 percent), cultural differences in lifestyle (22 percent), economic hardship (12 percent), and alcohol abuse (11 percent).[30] However, such statistics on the cases of family squabbles and domestic violence vary from study to study, ranging from 8 percent of the cases to 50 percent.[31] Since the results of each study vary so widely, any review of the studies may yield no reliable statistics.[32] Nevertheless, the reported forms of abuse were verbal abuse (31.1 percent), threats of a beating (18.4 percent), throwing of furniture and other household objects (23.7 percent), pushing down (13.9 percent), physical abuse with the hand or foot (13.5 percent), demands for unwanted sex (14.0 percent), and demands for sadistic sex (9.5 percent).[33]

For these reasons, the divorce rate is higher among multicultural couples than it is among native Koreans. The number of divorces for international couples surged to 30 percent (11,255 cases) in 2008, accounting for nearly 10 percent of marriage breakups. Nearly 83 percent of those couples who do get divorced do so less than five years after their marriage—a sharp increase from 15.9 percent in 2002.[34] The divorce rate for Korean husbands and foreign wives is higher than for couples where the husband is a foreigner. Such figures indicate that marriages between Korean men in rural areas and brides from other Asian countries are difficult to sustain. More Chinese wives divorced their Korean spouses than wives from any other country—5,398 cases—which accounted for 67.8 percent of divorces among international couples. Vietnamese brides placed second with 1,078, followed by Filipinas with 268 and Japanese brides with 205. Most of the divorced international couples did not have children. Nearly 90 percent of divorces between Korean husbands and foreign brides were between couples without children.[35] Parenthetically, however, the total number of divorces in Korea declined for the fifth consecutive year since 1998. For instance, in 2003, Korea had 116,660 divorces, while the total in 2008 was 116,500.[36]

If international marriages are less successful on average than domestic marriages in Korea, one may wonder what motivates foreign women to pursue these matches in the first place. The reasons why foreign brides marry Koreans are typically one of the following: the first reason is "economic" (41 percent), and the other is "fell in love" with the would-be husband (37 percent). In cases of marriage arranged by international marriage brokers, 73 percent of foreign brides said that they married for economic improvement. One out of every five (20 percent) brides indicated that most information about the grooms before marriage was inaccurate, and 44 percent of women who had a brokered marriage received some wrong information about the groom.[37] In fact, many of the problems faced by international couples can be traced back to the brokering of their marriage.

Economic Hardship

A good many foreign brides marry Korean men for economic betterment. An overwhelming majority (about 73 percent) of them who married through a broker did so to improve their economic situation, hoping to assist their natal families back home. Contrary to their expectations, however, most Korean men who seek foreign brides are not well-off economically. A good many Korean grooms live in economically underprivileged areas—farming and fishing villages. Most of them are unable to pay expensive fees for marriage arrangements or make trips to the countries where they hope to find prospective brides. In order to assist them, some local governments have taken a bold step by introducing local laws and city ordinances to accommodate international marriages. Kim Hyun Mee reports that

> single men aged 35 to 50 and working in the agricultural or fishing industries can apply for financial support ranging from 3 to 8 million Korean won (US $3,200 to 8,600) to assist them in finding a wife through international marriage. As of May 2007, 60 cities and local governments have implemented a similar act, with all the budget totaling 2.85 billion Korean won. Representatives of local governments are rushing rural men off into the international marriage market instead of making long-term policies that would help improve rural areas, which will experience even more difficulties after the Free Trade Agreement (FTA).[38]

Korea's local and municipal governments appear at times to be overzealous in their effort to facilitate international marriages. Often new policies and provisions are not well thought out and are executed too hastily, at times without clear goals and procedures. The major beneficiaries of these wasteful measures are the business-minded and unlicensed brokers.

Those not eligible to receive government funds for an international marriage have to pay for it themselves, mostly by taking out loans. Debts resulting from such marriage arrangements force brides and grooms to work harder than ever to pay them off, but for many these debts are too high to repay. In a training session during the CUK's Campaign, a social worker told me that a lady from Vietnam is working like a slave in a tiny hot pepper patch to pay back the outstanding loan for her marriage, estimated to be 1.5 million wŏn (about $1,250). It is reported that on average most married immigrants work 47.7 hours per week.[39] According to a survey conducted by the Ministry of Health and Social Welfare in 2005 (before it combined with the Ministry of Gender Equality to become the Ministry for Health, Welfare and Family Affairs), a majority (52.9 percent) of multicultural families belonged to an income bracket below minimum income level.[40] Because of poverty and a Korean language deficiency, as of 2005, only 27.5 percent of children in these multicultural families were enrolled in nursery schools and kindergartens, while 56.8 percent of native Korean families were able to do so for their children.[41]

Worse than the inability to send their children to preschool is the separation between parents and children. Since these parents are too poor to support their children, and since both parents work full time to earn a living, the result is family squabbles, separation, and divorce. This in turn leads to some children of multicultural families being sent to live with their overseas maternal grandparents.[42] On May 9, 2008, the *Chosun Ilbo* reported that currently in Vietnam a growing number of children born to a Korean man and a Vietnamese woman are being sent to live with their maternal grandparents in Vietnam.[43] These children are collectively called *raihankkwŏk* in the Vietnamese language, meaning "[persons] who come from Korea."

In 2003, for example, a forty-year-old Korean man who worked on a ship hired a marriage broker to arrange his marriage to a twenty-four-year-old Vietnamese woman from a small rural town of the Tai Nin district of southern Vietnam. They became parents to a daughter who was four years old in 2008. However, during the course of their marriage, they had constant fights over remitting money to her parents in Vietnam. Finally, her husband asked her to go back to Vietnam and stay there with the young daughter, Yŏng-ŭn (a pseudonym). The wife returned to Vietnam for a while but left her daughter with her parents in Vietnam when she came back to Korea. However, because her visa was not supported with an affidavit from her husband, she was detained under the custody of the Korean Immigration and Naturalization Services and later released.

Nonetheless, this Vietnamese bride works various odd jobs as an illegal worker. In the meantime, Yŏng-ŭn, as a Korean citizen in Vietnam, was unable to have her visa extended in Vietnam because her mother took her Korean passport with her when she left Vietnam. Now Yŏng-ŭn is staying in Vietnam illegally. By now she has forgotten the Korean language, except for the single word *appa*, meaning "daddy." She is unable to attend nursery school and kindergarten because of her illegal status in Vietnam. Yŏng-ŭn's maternal grandfather lamented to the reporter that he could not afford to send Yŏng-ŭn to a Korean school in Vietnam because it is too expensive for the family's income. Her grandfather's daily earnings are reported to be 50,000 dong (about $2.50).[44]

There are no accurate statistics on cases such as Yŏng-ŭn. Nevertheless, judging by the existence of the neologism *raihankkwŏk*, there must be many children in this situation. An official who is in charge of human rights at the UN office in Vietnam has said that some grandparents in Vietnam are so poor that they cannot afford to pay the fees to extend a visa, which costs around 60,000 wŏn to 70,000 wŏn (about $50 to $58). This sum is equivalent to one month's salary for an average Vietnamese worker.[45]

Despite such unfortunate incidents for *raihankkwŏk*, many Vietnamese women are eager to marry foreign men, for they see such a marriage as the best route out of poverty. In fact, some Vietnamese parents become economic beneficiaries by allowing their daughters to marry Korean men. According to a report filed by AP wire services, in Tan Loc Island, a Mekong Delta island, many residents there have replaced their thatch-roof shacks with brick homes with money from foreign sons-in-law, mostly from Taiwan and Korea. They have also opened small restaurants and shops, creating jobs in a place where people have traditionally earned pennies a day tending rice and other crops in the blistering sun. The luckier families received enough to build ponds for fish farming.[46] "At least 20 percent of the families on the island have been lifted out of poverty. . . . There has been a significant economic impact," according to Phan An, a university professor in Vietnam who has done extensive research in Tan Loc.[47]

Violations of Human Rights

Whatever the causes may be—dishonest matchmaking by international marriage brokers, spousal abuse, and cultural differences—the cases of human rights violations are one of the most talked-about subjects in the Korean mass media.

In 2006, a young Mongolian woman married a Korean man through an international marriage broker who failed to tell this bride-to-be that the Korean groom-to-be was deaf and sexually impotent. Soon after the marriage, the bride's parents-in-law insisted that she should be pregnant. As time went on, they began to complain about her sterility. After marriage, the Mongolian bride suffered mentally and emotionally from the tremendous stress caused by never-ending pressure from her parents-in-law. To make matters worse, her Korean in-laws refused to give her the 200,000 wŏn (about $166) per month as agreed to in the marriage contract, arguing that that she had failed to fulfill her end of the bargain by not bearing a child. This was money that her family in Mongolia had anticipated to be paid each and every month. She worked various odd jobs to earn that amount of money. Despite her effort, though, she was unable to earn enough to fulfill the commitment. Nor could she expect anything out of her husband because he was unable to function properly due to his physical handicap. Finally, the Mongolian bride gave up and went back home, arguing that the premarital conditions had not been honored by the groom's family.[48] This is not just an isolated case but a widely recognized problem, although there are no reliable statistical figures available.

In December 2006, with the help of an international marriage broker, a nineteen-year- old Vietnamese bride married a Korean man who was twenty-seven years older than she. They lived together for two years, and during this time the bride was frequently abused physically by her husband and suffered from long bouts of depression. One day she threatened to leave her husband and go home. In a drunken state the husband beat his Vietnamese wife and eventually killed her. As a result, the husband was tried and convicted. He received a twelve-year prison sentence from the Taejŏn Court of Appeals.[49] Also, in March 2007, a thirty-five-year-old Korean man married a twenty-one-year-old bride from Nepal, paying 18.5 million wŏn (about $15,416) to an international marriage broker, an amount that appears to be a bit higher than the average.[50] Each marriage broker charges a different rate, ranging from twelve million wŏn (about $10,000) to fifteen million wŏn (about $12,500). Most times, brides pay a token fee of 300,000 wŏn (about $250). In any event, after the bride from Nepal came to Korea, she claims she was literally "sold" to an old farmer who was physically handicapped.[51]

There have been some extreme cases in which cultural misunderstanding have led to disasters. Such tragedies remind Koreans that understanding and sensitivity to cultural differences are imperative in implementing multiculturalism in Korea. In January 2009, the Pusan District Court sentenced a forty-two-year-old Korean man to a thirty-month prison term with a three-year suspension after he was convicted of forcing his twenty-five-year-old wife from the Philippines to engage in nonconsensual sex. This was the first ever spousal rape conviction in Korea's judicial history.[52]

Perhaps this ruling signals a drastic change in a male-dominated conservative view on spousal rape, which was an almost unthinkable subject to be reported to the public. In the past in Korea, spousal rape has been regarded as a family matter and considered to be shameful, almost taboo to discuss publicly. The Filipina wife wrote a new chapter in Korean judicial history. Incidentally, according to a national survey conducted in 2008 by the then

Ministry of Gender Equality, prior to the landmark case 38.7 percent of respondents supported punishment for spousal rape. Twenty-six percent said that they supported it but that the time was not right for such a change in criminal justice. Finally, 35.2 percent were against it.[53]

The court ruling in the spousal rape case brought about an even greater tragedy. Five days after the court rendered its decision, the man convicted of spousal rape committed suicide by hanging himself in his apartment. Before this man committed suicide, he told a *Dong-A Ilbo* reporter that, although he forced his wife to have unwanted sex, he did not use violence. He complained to the reporter, saying that his wife was negligent in doing household chores and demanded money all the time to send to her parents in the Philippines. He told the reporter that he would appeal the case to the superior court. Nonetheless, instead of appealing the case, he committed suicide instead.[54] Despite this tragedy, the case reminds many Koreans that cross-cultural understanding is pivotal in dealing with married immigrants from other countries.

There are numerous incidents of domestic violence and human rights violations that stem mainly from two causes. The first is dishonest matchmaking on the part of marriage brokers—either by giving false information or by engaging in deliberate deception just to collect fees. The second is a failure on the part of a groom to honor a premarital commitment to assist the bride's parents back home.

International Marriage Brokers

Early on, the recruitment of foreign brides depended largely on international marriage brokers, often encouraged by the Korean government, mostly local and municipal. Later, however, the Korean government, as well as civic organizations, began to recognize that commercially minded brokers supplied inaccurate information about prospective grooms, even though paragraph two of the Management of Marriage Brokerage Act, promulgated on December 14, 2007, specifically prohibits the dispensing of false information regarding would-be brides and grooms.[55] Nevertheless, according to a report by the Ministry of Health, Welfare and Family Affairs in April 2009, a total of 316 (28 percent) out of 1,128 known matching brokerage firms have violated the existing laws and regulations.[56] Such unethical and illegal activities have been reported widely in various Korean newspapers.[57] In order to improve their tarnished image, brokers have initiated several measures of their own. At the same time, the Korean government has taken several steps to regulate the practices of international marriage brokers.

As a self-controlling measure, most brokers recently introduced the so-called guarantee of bride service—for six months or a year, the brides would not leave their husbands or file for divorce. The brokers also institutionalized counseling services for married brides to promote a harmonious marital life. If a divorce occurs in an international marriage due to the fault of the foreign bride, or if she leaves the family, the broker promises to introduce a new foreign woman to the Korean groom. The Korean man can go on another matchmaking trip, paying only for actual expenses incurred, such as airfare.[58] However, some foreign brides are skeptical about such counseling measures to sustain a fragile marriage. Kim Hyun Mee reports that "they [marriage brokers] tend to simply order the migrant women [foreign brides] to obey the demands of their Korean husbands and families, rather than making the service a venue for negotiations between husbands and wives. One Mongolian woman said to me that a broker once visited her household with an interpreter but spoke only to her husband without asking her anything."[59]

In order to regulate marriage brokers, on June 11, 2008, an executive order from the president of the Korean government took effect. It is called the Enforcement Rule of the Act on the Management of Marriage Brokerage. The order works in conjunction with a similar order passed by the minister of the Ministry of Health, Welfare and Family Affairs on June 13, 2008. Such measures require marriage brokerage firms to have a headquarters office with a street address. They must also deposit certain amounts of cash and carry insurance. All the firm's documents and contracts have to be translated into the native languages of persons who would be engaged in marriage, and mandatory training for marriage brokers is required. If any firm violates these rules overseas, the minister of the Ministry of Foreign Affairs and Trades should notify the minister of Health, Welfare and Family Affairs so that sanctions may be laid on the firm that violated the rules.

Despite such measures, as long as international marriage arrangements are regulated not by licensing but only registering, sanctions are ineffective. Furthermore, since most international marriage brokers do business in several countries, even if they violate the laws and rules of one country, they can easily move along to another country and continue business as usual. There is no accurate information on the number of international marriage brokers currently working, but their numbers are increasing steadily because one can go into the business simply by registering without being licensed. *Dong-A Ilbo* has reported that by the end of July 2010, there were 1,253 marriage brokers, an increase of 125 in one year.[60]

As late as July 8, 2010, a twenty-year-old Vietnamese bride living in Pusan, a southwestern port city, was beaten and stabbed to death by her forty-seven-year-old Korean husband. The husband turned himself in immediately after the incident. He told police, "I killed a person. I'm suffering from a mental disease. I killed her after hearing the voice of a ghost telling me to kill her while I was quarreling with my wife," he was quoted as saying in a police investigation.[61] He was arrested on murder charges the following day.

The death of this Vietnamese bride is tragic in two respects: First, she was murdered on only her eighth day living in Korea. She had no time to think about the "Korean dream." The fourth of five children in a poor family, she grew up in a small town in southern Vietnam, about a six-hour drive from Ho Chi Minh City. To earn a meager salary, she had worked as a housekeeper in Ho Chi Minh City to help her parents back home.[62] One of her older sisters married a Taiwanese man, and one of her nieces married a Korean man. Both of them live happily. Given this good track record, she decided to marry a Korean man; however, she did not know that he was a mental patient.

Second, a tragedy of this kind could have been prevented easily if international marriage brokers checked the medical records of brides and grooms and reported them honestly. In this particular case, police discovered that the Korean man had received treatment at a hospital for a mental disorder fifty-seven times, but the matchmaking company did not filter him from the list of Korean applicants.[63] The Pusan Metro Police Department is investigating whether the particular marriage broker falsified the record of the Korean man knowingly and intentionally.

Since this tragedy has been so widely reported throughout the country, there has been a public outcry condemning international brokers for their illegal and unethical handling of international matchmaking. The Vietnamese ambassador Tran Trong Toan, deeply saddened by the event, asked the Korean government to regulate international marriage brokers by laws as well as government policies.[64] Foreign brides held a rally in memory of the victim in front of the Human Rights Commission in Seoul.[65]

The Vietnamese bride's tragic death has drawn government attention. At a meeting with his newly appointed top aides, including Prime Minister Chung Un-chan [Un-ch'an Chŏng], President Lee Myung-bak ordered a full investigation of international marriage brokers.[66] Gender Equality Minister Paik Hee-young [Hyŭi-yŏng Paek] spoke out on the issue: "The Busan [Pusan] murder case of the Vietnamese bride shows that the rampant international marriage trend has fundamental problems which needed to be solved."[67] Accordingly, The National Police Agency launched a nationwide crackdown on all illegal acts of marriage brokering. The Pusan policy specifically looked into whether the broker was aware of the medical history of the husband who killed his wife and then withheld the information from the bride and her family.[68] The Korean government is reinforcing the regulations on marriage brokers to obligate them to offer accurate personal information on spouses.

Concurring with the crackdown on the illicit international marriage brokers, the Ministry of Justice announced, beginning in August 2010, that any Korean man who is interested in marrying a foreign bride, especially from China, Vietnam, the Philippines, Cambodia, Mongolia, and other Asian countries, is required to attend a four-hour "courtesy orientation session" (*soyang-kyoyuk*) regarding the proper procedure for international marriages, related laws, and cases of failed international marriages. This orientation session must be attended prior to engagement or marriage (*massŏn* or "mutual first").[69] The orientation is a prerequisite for obtaining a F-2 entry visa for a bride. Also, the Ministry of Justice announced a restriction on issuing visa requests made by Koreans registered as sex offenders, domestic abusers, ex-criminals, and mental patients.[70]

I am skeptical about how much a four-hour orientation session will improve the situation. With that said, though, anything is better than nothing. There is another cause for optimism. Given the widespread problems in international marriage brokering, the Korean government is seriously considering instituting a government-led nonprofit organization to handle legitimate international marriage arrangements, much like what Taiwan instituted in August 2009.[71] Perhaps the tragic death of the young Vietnamese bride will not have been in vain.

However, as long as there is high demand from both parties, brides and grooms, it will be difficult to enforce existing laws and regulations, no matter how tough the control measures are. Such is the case with drug enforcement. This analogy is apt for a situation where there is a high demand from users and a large pool of supply. The strong demand in some Southeast Asian countries for foreign husbands has been described vividly by the AP wire service:

> Nearly 70 young Vietnamese women swept past in groups of five, twirling and posing like fashion models, all competing for the hand of a Taiwanese man who had paid a matchmaking service about $6,000 for the privilege of marrying one of them. Sporting jeans and a black T-shirt, 20-year-old Le Thi Ngoc Quyen paraded in front of the stranger, hoping he would select her. "I felt very nervous," she recalled recently as she described the scene. "But he chose me, and I agreed to marry him right away."[72]

As for financial promises made before marriage and the frequent failure to honor them later, there is no easy solution so long as a great majority of brides (about 73 percent of them as aforementioned) marry for financial reasons. Even if grooms have good intentions to keep their premarital promise, many cannot deliver on their promise. That is because most of them (52.9 percent) have incomes below the poverty level. Foreign brides who wish to marry Korean men should be aware of this reality. If they did have a "Korean dream," it may not be realized as easily as they assumed it would.

HUMAN RIGHTS VIOLATIONS AGAINST CHILDREN OF "MIXED-BLOOD"

Korea's emphasis on ethnic homogeneity has been so prevalent that the United Nations Committee on the Elimination of Racial Discrimination (UN CERD) recommended that Korea stop using such expressions as *sunhyŏl* (pure-blood) and *honhyŏl* (mixed-blood). Despite the popular rhetoric on multiculturalism in contemporary Korea, many children born to cross-racial and cross-ethnic parents have been, and still are to a certain extent, discriminated against for their ethnic and racial origins.

According to the most recent report, the total number of children born to international marriages was around 121,935 in June 2010.[73] However, there were quite few children born to American military servicemen and Korean women before multiculturalism became popular in public discourse. For this reason, some academicians classify them into two groups: one group includes children born to American military servicemen and Korean women. These children are called "Ko-Americans" or "Amerasians." The other group has been labeled "Ko-asians" (children born to international marriages between Koreans and other Asians); these are children born to multicultural families beginning in the late 1990s and early 2000s.

The numbers of the first group were estimated to be ranging from 1,400 to 2,300 in the 1960s; this figure fell to 500 in 1990 as U.S. forces in Korea were drawn down.[74] These figures could be inaccurate. An official at the Korea National Statistical Office indicates that it is practically impossible to figure out the number of international marriages because birth certificates do not have any place to identify the nationality of the parents, the assumption being that all were Koreans.[75] The number of children who belong to the second group is rising rapidly—from 7,998 in 2006 to 13,445 in 2007; 58,007 in 2008 to 121,935 in June 2010. The estimate by 2020 is some 142,000.[76] All the figures vary from source to source since no official records are yet available.[77]

Regarding "Ko-Americans" or "Amerasians," Chŏn Kyŏng-su, a Korean anthropologist, and his colleagues have pointed out that until the growing number of Ko-asians forces public acknowledgement of this multicultural issue in contemporary Korea, the problems of Amerasians will continue to be overlooked and minimized in the minds of Koreans.[78] Prejudice and discrimination in the premulticultural era were directed against the children who had darker skin pigmentation, mostly children of cross-racial marriages between African American servicemen and Korean women. The nature and forms of discrimination varied—ranging from name-calling (with all sorts of epithets for darker-skinned people), humiliations of various kinds, obstacles to entering the labor market, and at times even beatings for no particular reason. The wrongs are too numerous to list.

A good many of those Amerasians immigrated to the United States, if they could identify their American father, and others have been adopted through various adoption agencies. Again, there are no statistics on adoption of children of cross-racial marriages. Adoption agencies such as Holt Children's Services, Inc., which has a fifty-four-year-history of arranging adoptions for ninety thousand children to overseas families, do not officially reveal the identities of the adoptive parents (mostly fathers). There is no way of knowing how many children from so-called *honhyŏl* marriages have been adopted. However, *Dong-A Ilbo* has reported that most of the adopted children were children of American servicemen and Korean women in the 1950s (the first adoption was in 1953 after the Korean War). From 1955 to 1959, almost 70 percent of 2,887 adoptions were children of interracial marriages. This percentage has dropped sharply to 10 percent in the 1970s.[79] Hines Ward, winner of the 2006 MVP award in American football's Super Bowl XL, was born in Korea to a Korean mother and an African American ex-GI. He is one of the many who went to the United States to avoid the discrimination prevalent in Korea. In September 2010, Ward was been named to the U.S. President's Advisory Commission on Asian Americans and Pacific Islanders.

Prejudice toward and discrimination against children born into multicultural families in the late 1990s and the 2000s has lessened remarkably as compared to that experienced by Amerasians. This lessening owes to the rhetoric of multiculturalism and the public campaign to reduce, or even eliminate, racial prejudice. Nevertheless, there are numerous incidents of continuing bigotry toward children of interracial marriages, particularly for children with dark skin. These abuses include *wangtta,* meaning teasing and bullying, which is equivalent to *ijime* in Japan.[80] Such ridicule makes the children of multicultural families feel stigmatized. Many children of multicultural families have experienced *wangtta*.[81] In fact, twenty-eight out of one hundred students have had such experiences,[82] and six out of ten are subjected to humiliation.[83] Because of such treatment, a seventeen-year-old girl from Mongolia said that she did not want to go to school because for her school was "hell."[84] Some parents petitioned school officials to remove a child whose mother is from Vietnam.[85] In an ethnographic report on two counties in south Chŏlla province, Chŏn kyŏng-su concurs with the reports made by journalists.[86]

According to a nationwide survey conducted from July to August in 2008 by the National Youth Policy Institute of the Korean government, out of 3,185 Korean youths, 56 percent of the respondents answered that they do not want to befriend children from multicultural families.[87] In the same survey, a great majority of respondents (85 percent) answered that they have never had any education on multiculturalism. Instead, 38 percent of the respondents are proud of the fact that Korea is a homogeneous and single ethnic nation. The percentage is higher among younger students (primary school, 49.1 percent; middle school, 37.8 percent) than with high school students (30.8 percent).[88] Such responses would not be surprising considering the fact that "Korean school textbooks still show what critics call 'an anachronistic misconception' that Korea is ethnically and racially homogeneous."[89] Such statements were explicitly written in school textbooks on Korean history and ethics, which were endorsed and approved by the Ministry of Education, Science and Technology. The rhetoric of multiculturalism has not yet found its way into school textbooks.

In early April 2006, the highly publicized visit of Hines Ward to Korea prompted many discussions about unfair discrimination against "mixed marriages" and the children born to those marriages. In response to a public outcry against unfair treatment in the past, all political party leaders promised to push for legislation to protect "mixed-blood" Koreans from discrimination in the workplace, schools, and other parts of Korean society. However, the outcry has since died down, and no significant reforms have been enacted.

The percentage of children from multicultural families who advance to high school after completing middle school is only 30 percent,[90] a figure that amounts to only a third of the 99.7 percent of Korean kids who do.[91] Among many factors, prejudice by mainstream Korean students toward children from multicultural families has been a major contributing factor for their loss of interest in schooling.

SOURCES OF PREJUDICE AND DISCRIMINATION

Ethnic Nationalism

In the previous chapter, I argued that the so-called ethnic nationalism that underlies the purity of Korean blood is not an integral part of Korean tradition. Nor is it true that Koreans lack a historical experience of living together with foreigners. As John Frankl,[92] Andre Schmid,[93] and Han Kyung-Koo have pointed out, "Traditional Korea had clear policy principles and practices concerning immigration and naturalization (*hyanghwa*). Moreover, traditional Korea did not consider itself to be an ethnically homogeneous state and did not discriminate against foreigners simply on the basis of their ethnic origins."[94] "To traditional Koreans," says John Frankl, "the nationality of Confucius and Mencius, or the fact that Jesus Christ was a Jew born in Bethlehem, is of no importance."[95] If this is the case, why do prejudice and discrimination against foreigners, particularly for married immigrants and their children, take place in contemporary Korea as described? Many NGO workers, scholars, intellectuals, and even government officials believe that ethnic nationalism is the major source of this bigotry. Nevertheless, in the context of Korea's long history, it is a relatively recent phenomenon.[96]

Some detailed accounts of Korean nationalism include works by Gi-Wook Shin and Andre Schmid. Like many scholars and laymen, Han Kyung-Koo characterizes Korea's version of nationalism as "an ethnic nationalism because Koreans not only say that they have a common language, history, and set of customs, but also that they are descendants of a common ancestor: Dangun [Tan'gun]."[97] The conception of ethnic nationalism, *minjok* (ethnic nation), began in response to the threat of Japanese domination of the Korean peninsula. In an editorial from January 12, 1900, in the *Hwangsŏng sinmun,* Sin Ch'aeho, a staunch advocate of the nationalistic concept, used a term with a meaning closer to "race" (or *injong* in Korean).[98] However, in a later editorial from June 1907, also in *Hwangsŏng sinmun,* "minjok-ism" [*minjokchuǔi*] lost any connotation of racial unity and began to denote only the people inhabiting the Korean peninsula.[99]

Thereafter many Korean intellectuals and laymen joined Sin's campaign and participated in the formation of Korean nationalism in their struggle for independence from Japan. Gi-Wook Shin points out that the idea of ethnic homogeneity was developed during the colonial period as a countermeasure against the Japanese propagandist notion of *naisen ittai* (a phrase meaning that Korea and Japan are one and the same). Japanese initiatives included several measures: use of the Japanese language; adoption of Japanese names by Koreans; and the assumption of Japanese customs and habits of daily life related to dress, food, housing, and more.[100] Ironically, though, Korean nationalism as led by Sin was obviously influenced by European thinkers, especially by Johann Gottlieb Fichte and advocates of German nationalism, thinkers who had also influenced the Japanese. Han Kyung-Koo states that "it would be correct to say that Korean ethnic nationalism was developed under the influence of Japanese as well as German nationalism."[101]

As Gi-Wook Shin suggests, perhaps "nationalism in itself is fairly harmless. Only when combined with other ideologies can its effect be felt."[102] Nevertheless, according to Gi-Wook Shin, "Ethnic nationalism has been combined with different forms of ideologies in modern Korea, the Left (communism) and Right (capitalism), modern (industrialization) and antimodern (agrarianism), authoritarianism and democratic politics, and local and transnational (globalization)."[103] Legend has it that Koreans are descendents of a common ancestor: Tan'gun, the legendary founder of Old Chosŏn in 2333 BC. He was believed to be the son of heaven, and his wife was purported to be a bear turned human. Tan'gun has become the symbol for promoting ethnic nationalism.

Nevertheless, *Samguk yusa* does not say anything about the Old Chosŏn people being a single ethnic group. Traditional Koreans during the Koryŏ and Chosŏn dynasties did not believe that they shared a common biological ancestor but considered Tan'gun to be the first king of Korea, not the progenitor of the Korean people. Indeed, not all Koreans are descendents of Tan'gun: perhaps some are, while others are descendents of naturalized immigrants from elsewhere.[104]

However, despite these facts, following Sin Ch'aeho, many scholars supported a nationalist historiography with the patriotic goal of writing "a new racial history of Korean independence." This new history was influenced by Korea's anticolonial resistance to the "Japanese imperialistic historical framework."[105] According to Han Kyung-Koo, "Even scholars fail to critically review this misconception and blame the Dangun [Tan'gun] myth as the source of ethnic nationalism in Korea. This misunderstanding is corroborated by so-called Korean familism, which emphasizes blood relatedness. Familism makes Korean ideology seem preoccupied with blood kinship, an archaic means of solidarity."[106] When Korea lost its sovereignty as a nation, its people dwelled on the importance of nationalism.[107] In such a social and academic milieu, Korean history books were largely silent on contributions made by foreigners. On this state of affairs, Hyung Il Pai elaborates,

> The elevation of Tan'gun to historical status is a direct challenge to Kija, a Shang aristocrat enfeoffed in Chosŏn at the time of the fall of the Shang dynasty (ca. 1000 BC). Kija was later followed by Wiman, a general from the state of Yan who arrived around 195–194 BC to set up Wiman Chosŏn and whose descendants later contested Han emperor Wu's invasion in 108 BC. Thus, the traditionally accepted dynastic state sequence of the Sam Chosŏn of Kochosŏn, Kija Chosŏn, and Wiman Chosŏn has been overturned in the revised Korean ancestral state lineage.[108]

Yi Chi-ran also does not fit in the theme of ethnic nationalism.[109]

Perhaps Sin's version of ethnic nationalism might be closer to "tribalism" than "nationalism," if we follow the definitions given by popular writer John Naisbitt, who offers these definitions:

Nationalism, which flourished from the 18th century until the end of World War II, is a belief that one's nation-state is more important than international principles or individual considerations. World War II put an end to the nationalism of Italy and Germany and greatly diluted the forces of nationalism in the West. *Tribalism* (emphasis mine) is the belief in fidelity to one's own kind, defined by ethnicity, language, culture, religion, or in this late 20th century, profession. And this belief is flourishing.[110]

If any Koreans still espouse ethnic nationalism as characterized by Sin and nationalistic historiographers, they may still be thinking in tribal rather than global terms.

Parenthetically, as Gi-Wook Shin has alluded, nationalism can lead to the compromise of rights. Han Kyung-Koo entertains some specific examples when he writes,

When nationalism was regarded as more important than any other universal values, democratic processes, freedom of speech, and human rights were subject to suspension for the sake of the nation. Park Chung-hee [ex-president who held power over some thirty years after the 1961 military coup] and Kim Il Sung [former North Korean premier and father of current ruler Kim Chung-il] were champions of nationalism in their own ways, as they both shrewdly manipulated nationalist symbols and values in their efforts to overcome supposed "national crises." Park competed not only with Kim over who was more nationalistic, but also with his political enemies, and student activists. With superpowers looking close by and national unification ahead, they found Japanese style German nationalism extremely convenient and attractive political tools.[111]

Gi-Wook Shin also concurs with Han Kyung-Koo's interpretation that "nationalism became a highly effective organizing and mobilizing force in both parts of Korea."[112] In spite of that, Shin points out that "Park's [Park Chung-hee's] nationalism did not necessarily lead to xenophobia."[113]

Saet'ŏmin or North Korean Refugees

It may be too hasty and premature to think that if Koreans could be free from ethnic nationalism and the myth of a pure-blooded nation, they would become more tolerant toward foreigners, immigrants, and any outsiders than ever before. In fact, ethnic or racial identity is not the sole factor leading to prejudice and discrimination. At times, social background appears to be an important factor, as evidenced by the more than 20,050 North Korean refugees who escaped the North after the Korean War and settled in the South.[114] North Korean refugees are the "brethren" of South Koreans, so to speak, if one uses criteria such as common ethnicity and homogeneity of culture. In fact, some of them had family members living in the South before and during the Korean War.[115] Despite the fact that both were a single nation for thousands and thousands of years, North Korean refugees are experiencing the same, if not worse, prejudice, discrimination, and stigmatization as foreign brides have experienced.[116] Various surveys indicate that North Korean refugees suffer the most from prejudice, a prejudice that considers them suspicious and culturally inferior.[117]

Indeed, the legal status of North Korean escapees is ambiguous. On the one hand, they are "political refugees" who escaped because they were not able to maintain a decent standard of living due to widespread poverty in North Korea. Whatever they did, they had no chance of improving their living conditions or of escaping omnipresent political oppression. On the other hand, they are "immigrants" because they left North Korea for South Korea voluntarily. In 2006, there was a systematic study of twenty-eight North Korean escapees ages twenty and older. Using in-depth interviews, researchers Cho Chŏng-a, Im Sun-hŭi, and Chŏng Chin-kyŏng found that the escapees experienced an initial cultural shock upon being transplanted from an underdeveloped, preindustrial society to a highly industrialized and technologically sophisticated society.[118]

Most escapees have faced difficulties adjusting to South Korea's ethos as a capitalistic society. They have suffered from having northern accents, lacking knowledge of English, and lacking basic computer skills. Most of all, they lack the kind of work ethic that comes from laboring under an incentive system that rewards quality work.[119] Escapees with children have struggled to pay for their children's education, which was free in North Korea. Also, paying additional fees for private tutorial lessons has presented another financial burden for them.[120] Most North Korean escapees, who were used to a strict patriarchal system in the North, can hardly understand the family practices of the South. This cultural difference has created a generational gap between parents who used to live in the North and their children who have grown up in the South. This gap has brought about conflicts and tensions between them.[121]

Whether or not the stereotypes are true, South Koreans tend to believe that North Koreans do not make for good workers and citizens. Once freed of coercive state control, they tend not to conform to social norms voluntarily. South Koreans believe escapees to have poor working habits as well as a tendency to seek easy jobs, complain a lot, and display a quick temper.[122] Because of such negative views of them by South Koreans, North Korean escapees, struggling to maintain their self-respect, often feel alienated from their southern "brethren."

Whatever their feelings might have been, other than some thick northern accents among North Korean refugees, there are no ways of making any distinction between North Korean refugees and South Koreans by appearance. Even when it comes to accents, some North Koreans have practiced enough to mimic the speech of the South. Nevertheless, the code numbers given to North Korean refugees in their national identification number (ID), roughly equivalent to social security numbers in the United States, are different from those given to South Koreans so that they can be easily identifiable.[123] Every Korean has to have this number; it is required in every activity for schooling and employment. Because the codes are used so widely, they can be misused and abused, which itself can be a violation of privacy. A good many North Koreans have been refused visas to travel to other countries, particularly China, a close ally of North Korea. And many of them have been banned outright from traveling to China.[124]

The children of North Korean refugees suffer from *wangtta* (bullying) much in the same way as children of multicultural families.[125] It is difficult for them to acquire jobs, and even when they are employed, their income tends to be about 57 percent of the average Korean's for doing the same job.[126] A recent report indicates that their wage is about one-third of the average Korean's wage.[127]

Yi U-yŏng, a senior researcher at the Korea Institute for National Unification, a government-owned research institute, writes that "Koreans tend to look down upon North Korean refugees much worse than general laborers from Third World countries. If some of them were hired as maids in Kangnam (south of the Han River, and known to be the most lavish residential area in Seoul) their wage will be lower than that of people from Third World countries. Their children in school are so bullied and stigmatized that a good many of them tend to withdraw from school."[128] In fact, the survey conducted by the National Youth Policy Institute of the Korean government, which was mentioned earlier, found that primary school students consider children of North Korean refugees least likely to belong to the category of "our group." Out of a possible high score of 5.0, North Koreas scored 2.74 points, much worse than whites (2.84 points), Korean Chinese (2.91 points), and children of multicultural families (3.12).[129] It would appear then that belonging to "our people" is not a matter decided only by one's ethnic or racial identity. Perhaps Han Geon-Soo is correct when he points out that "both nationality and social class function as vital factors in the matrix of the treatment of ethnic Koreans."[130]

The difficulties and hardships that North Korean escapees face in adjusting to life in South Korea remind me that we ought to rethink the traditional Korean perception of foreign immigrants. As John Frankl and Han Kyung-Koo maintain, discrimination against anyone in traditional Korea was not based on place of birth or ethnic and racial origin but on whether the person was *orangkae* (barbarian) or civilized.[131] Since barbarians can be civilized, one's intention to be "civilized (or assimilated)" would have been the determining factor in differentiating between "Koreans" and "non-Korean foreigners." In the Koryŏ and Chosŏn dynasties, Jurchens were classed as *organgkae,* but Yi Chi-ran, a Jurchen, was regarded as a Korean because he became a civilized person who discarded his old ways and adopted a Korean way of life. So did Kim Ch'ung-sŏn from Japan. Traditional Korean notions prior to the late nineteenth century about foreigners may still remain in the minds of contemporary Koreans.

In sum, despite all the recent rhetoric of multiculturalism, words and deeds do not always match. Korean citizens and the government strongly condemn ethnic nationalism as an outdated notion, yet "Korea's school textbooks still show what critics call 'an anachronistic misconception' that Korea is ethnically and racially homogeneous."[132] It is an irony that some Koreans are critical of incorrect information about Korea in the high school textbooks of other nations[133] while they do not acknowledge similar failings in their own textbooks. But if Koreans are serious about implementing multiculturalism, they should own up to the misinformation. Textbooks will be a major impetus for coming-of-age Koreans to broaden their perspectives. Young Koreans should not be indoctrinated by the century-old remnants of semitribalism—ethnic nationalism and nationalistic history. To that end, it has to begin with the fundamentals—education using up-to-date and accurate textbooks—not propagandistic nationalist rhetoric.

4

Tales of Foreign Brides Who Married via International Marriage Brokers

A Korean woman minister, Han Kuk-yŏm, who runs the Center for Human Rights for Foreign Brides (*Han'guk Ijuyŏsŏng Inkkwŏn Center*), once said that "it would be a lie if [Korean] parents were to say they would not mind if their children married foreigners."[1] She was frank and straightforward in reflecting the sentiments of elderly Korean parents and grandparents whose children and grandchildren would like to marry foreigners. I, for one, was hesitant to approve a request from one of my sons, who told me that he would like to marry a Caucasian woman who had been his high school sweetheart. My hesitation was based on possible cultural differences between the two families, not on her qualities and accomplishments or her family background. Her parents were my colleagues at the university where I taught. She had been a winner of the National Merit Scholarship and was educated at the top law school in the United States. Despite my reservations, they married anyway and have lived happily ever after with two fine sons.

Interestingly, my in-laws were typical white Southerners, who historically have had a reputation of being ethnocentric. Hence I thought that they would have been more averse to the marriage than I was. On the contrary, they were warm, receptive, and welcoming to my son as their son-in-law. Perhaps I had been narrow-minded,[2] while my in-laws had been open-minded. They had been so tolerant because they live in a multicultural society, while I had very limited experience living in a multicultural and multiracial society. Enculturation in a multicultural and multiethnic society from an early childhood seems to be a powerful, effective, and long-lasting influence when it comes to accepting the notion of "cultural relativism." My interest in Korean multiculturalism and foreign brides may be motivated in part by my family background of having a daughter-in-law whose ethnic background differs from my own.

This chapter describes from an ethnographic perspective the life stories of two Vietnamese women who married Korean men in the form of arranged marriages. While one bride failed to realize "the Korean dream" owing to a tragic incident, the other one is enjoying a happy married life. In order to understand the socioeconomic and cultural milieu of the two brides' home country, in November 2009, I made a field trip to Vietnam, which helped me fill in my knowledge gap of the society where many foreign brides come from.

ARRANGED MARRIAGE AS THE NORM
IN INTERNATIONAL MARRIAGES

While the primary goal of this chapter is to tell the life stories of two foreign brides, I want first to provide a little background on arranged marriages in Korea. Marriage by way of an international marriage broker is a form of arranged marriage, albeit one conducted by someone outside the family. Because Western readers may find such a cultural practice odd, it is worth discussing arranged marriages briefly in the context of Korea.

Among the estimated 181,671 multicultural couples in contemporary Korea, the manner of their marriage generally falls into one of two categories. The first and larger category is arranged marriage—arranged either by commercial marriage brokers, with the support of Korean local government, or by friends, acquaintances, and family members. Also, belonging to this category are people married by way of a religious organization such as the Unification Church (*T'ongilgyo*). The second category encompasses marriages of love where the bride and groom fall in love with each other. Some of these couples meet through work—in businesses, industries, and government agencies in Korea and elsewhere—while others meet while studying at school, training centers, and elsewhere.

Logic of the System of Arranged Marriage

When I taught a course on comparative family systems at a campus of the University of Tennessee, my students expressed curiosity about the system of arranged marriage.[3] Some of them asked how one could marry someone without first experiencing love or affection. I entertained my class with the following verse to illustrate the logic behind the system and its justification:

> I never knew what love was,
> I don't know what love is,
> I don't care what love is,

I don't intend to be told what love is,
Get Married?
Love does not lead to marriage but marriage leads to love,
If such a thing as "love" exists.[4]

Nevertheless, my verse was insufficient to convince American students of the logic of arranged marriage because most Americans have been so deeply enculturated in the system of free-choice marriage, in which love is supposed to lead to marriage, not the other way around. Indeed, as Francis L. K. Hsu has pointed out, "When two American lovers appear in public with their arms around one another, the rest of the world is excluded, if not ignored," yet "in China the term 'love,' as it is used by Americans, has never been respectable [in the past at least]."[5]

This does not mean that romantic love is a concept totally foreign to Koreans and other East Asians. In fact, the main theme of one of the most popular and beloved Korean novels, *Ch'unhyangjŏn,* tells the story of the son of a local magistrate who falls in love with the only daughter of a retired *gisaeng,* a female entertainer who serves as an escort at men's drinking parties.[6] As Stuart A. Queen and Robert W. Habenstein have reported, "In ancient feudal China, falling in love was not an unusual antecedent to marriage, although parental consent was necessary before the various ceremonies preparatory to marriage could go forward."[7] Even in the West, marriage resulting from romantic love has a relatively short history. Such marriage was not common before the end of the Middle Ages in Europe. In fact, "Marital selection in medieval England was a matter of clear bargaining and formal routines, in contrast to the romantic adventure it has become in modern England and America."[8]

Nevertheless, in modern times arranged marriages are minimal if not entirely absent in the West. Since Korea has experienced rapid industrialization, hyperurbanization, and increasing globalization, one may surmise that the traditional system of arranged marriage is gradually diminishing. Laurel Kendall, an anthropologist and expert on Korea, has observed that "today, as the workplace and the coeducational university provide unprecedented opportunities [for couples to meet], increasing numbers of women and men have a love marriage without a matchmaker's introduction."[9] It appears that a great majority of Koreans of marriageable age now favor love marriage over arranged marriage. Statistics regarding the number of people who practice arranged marriage as opposed to love marriage vary considerably, mainly because of varying definitions of *arranged marriage.*[10] For instance, if two people are introduced by a fellow worker or college classmate and later get married, this could perhaps be counted as an arranged marriage, even though the mutual friend presumably did not make the introduction with a future marriage in mind. Although the system of arranged marriage is on the decline, it has deep historical roots, and its current revival through international brokerage warrants a closer look at the system.

A BRIEF HISTORY OF ARRANGED
MARRIAGE IN KOREA

The system of arranged marriage in Korea was firmly established during the late period of the Koryŏ dynasty, when members of the dynasty were in close contact with the Yüan dynasty. In the later period of Koryŏ, while aristocrats practiced arranged marriage, commoners followed free-choice marriage. Koryŏ aristocrats used marriage strategically to expand the power of their families and increase their own access to power. "The more influential the family with which one formed marriage ties, the more quickly one might enhance the standing of one's own house and bring it into greater political prominence. There was a strong aspiration among ambitious young to marry with an aristocratic family member—particularly with the royal family clan."[11] The system of arranged marriage appears to have coincided with or paralleled the emergence of a social stratification system. Historically in Korea certain privileged classes have used arranged marriage as a major mechanism for maintaining or improving their own class status.

During the Chosŏn dynasty, arranged marriage came to be considered an ideal form and was firmly institutionalized. The *yangban* used arranged marriage to maintain their status quo. Consequently, during the Chosŏn dynasty, the system of arranged marriage contributed to class endogamy, in which most Koreans married within his or her own class. Nevertheless, among commoners free-choice marriage remained the norm.

The arranged marriage system began to decline when Korean society started to transform itself from a premodern into a modern society. Certain socioeconomic and demographic changes led to a transitional form of marriage. An individual might select several candidates and then ask his or her parents to choose from among them, or parents and kin would recommend several candidates and the individual would select from among them. One can surmise that today, while arranged marriages are still the means by which less educated, rural people acquire their spouses, highly educated and urban Koreans tend to choose their spouses themselves. Nevertheless, even today well-to-do Koreans often choose an arranged marriage in order to maintain their status or improve their socioeconomic standing.[12]

In traditional arranged marriages, matchmaking was done by relatives, most often female members, who would search for a spouse among their natal kinsmen and the relatives of their husband. The chosen man and woman would marry with the approval of the elders of both families. Most of the time, such approval was no more than a formality, because the male elders trusted that the female marriage arrangers, who belonged to both clans, would know the betrothed well.[13] The matchmakers would serve as bilateral sureties for both families since they were related to both. Also, because of such a selection process, the bride and groom tended to be of the same rank socially and economically.[14]

Because increasing urbanization eroded the tradition of arranged marriages, during the 1970s and 1980s a legion of unlicensed semiprofessional matchmakers (called Madam *Ttu,* or Madam Procure) emerged in urban areas. These matchmakers mostly arranged marriages between children of the newly rich and privileged. Madam *Ttu* matchmakers did not charge any fee for their work until the arrangement was finalized. Commissions would run about ten million wŏn (about $8,333).[15] However, at times, the commissions were so high that the practice was considered a real social problem.[16] Nowadays, this kind of matchmaking has diminished, although it has not disappeared altogether. It has been reported that some former Madam *Ttu* matchmakers have become consultants for commercial marriage consulting centers.[17]

Matchmaking as a Newly Emerging Business Enterprise

As the credibility and reputation of the Madam *Ttu* has declined, licensed and commercial marriage consulting centers (*Kyŏlhon chŏngbo hoesa*), which use computerized matchmaking and multimedia technologies, have become increasingly popular. Marriage consulting centers originated in Japan during the early 1980s, where such centers became popular and prosperous, with many branches opening throughout the country.

The first marriage consulting center in Korea was founded in 1986, and a few others followed soon thereafter. But in 1999, when the Family Ritual Code (*Kaejŏng ŭrye chunch'ik*) regulating marriage rituals was suspended, government licenses were no longer required to engage in commercial matchmaking. Since then, consulting centers have sprung up throughout the country, and their numbers have increased dramatically. Currently, there are over one thousand centers, ranging from small local ones with few members (applicants) to those with over forty thousand members. Some of the largest ones operate globally in the United States (Los Angeles and New York) and in New Zealand. Some centers also support home pages and videotaped narratives in English. In 1994, when I visited such a place in Seoul with my students during my tenure as a visiting professorship at Yonsei University, it looked like a small private counseling center. Now it has become a genuine business enterprise.

Anyone who wishes to register and seek a spouse has to be a member. Annual membership fees vary from center to center and by category of membership. An average membership fee runs from 880,000 wŏn (about $733) for a general membership to as high as 5.5 million wŏn (about $4,583) for a special membership, for those, say, with outstanding educational credentials or those with disabilities. One center that specializes in second marriage (or remarriage) offers three different categories of membership for women (though not for men, for some strange reason) and charges different membership fees: a general membership is 880,000 wŏn (about $733); a special membership costs 1.85 million wŏn (about $1,541); and a "noblesse" membership (for the well known or rich) costs three million wŏn (about $2,500). The total annual earnings of all Korean marriage consulting centers in 2006 were over seventy billion wŏn (about $5.84 million).[18]

By and large, it is known that a great majority of young Koreans prefer to have free choice in marriage. Many of them are affected by the rule of endogamy—a rule of marriage that requires persons to take a spouse from within their own social group as defined by class, kin, wealth, education, or some other form of social organization; for example, membership in the Unification Church. Arranged marriages in Korea—whether the result of relatives, a Madam *Ttu,* campus dates, or a marriage consulting center—tend to be endogamous. In traditional Korea, social class, particularly *yangban* status, was such a category of endogamy, but in recent times education has come to serve as the most important group boundary, as was demonstrated by a marriage center study.[19] The traditional Korean custom of arranged marriage helps to promote an acceptance of contemporary brokered marriages.

Any Korean man who lives in a rural village, has a limited education, and does not hold down a reputable job has only a remote chance of marrying a desirable woman. Consequently these men often turn to international marriage brokers, sometimes assisted by the local government, to acquire a bride. This is a "pull factor" in bringing foreign brides to Korea. At the same time, there is a "push factor"—namely, economic gain—that pushes foreign brides to marry Korean men. It is safe to say that a combination of these push and pull factors has fueled the growth of international marriages in contemporary Korea. Additionally, a latent factor behind the growth is a parallel tradition of arranged marriage in the foreign brides' home countries. Having laid out some background information on arranged marriages in Korea, I now turn to the stories of two Vietnamese brides.

THE INTERNATIONAL MARRIAGE OF A VIETNAMESE WOMAN WHOSE MARRIAGE ENDED IN TRAGEDY

Twenty-year-old Ttuet Huang (a pseudonym), originally from the southern Vietnam province of Dong Nai, was a victim of dishonest and commercially minded international marriage brokering. The broker or brokers who arranged Ttuet's marriage did not inform her that her prospective groom, forty-two-year-old Hong Kil-dong (a pseudonym), was mentally disturbed. I was unable to identify the broker and unable to find out whether the broker knew about Kil-dong's mental history. In either case, the broker should shoulder part of the responsibility for the horrific outcome that befell Ttuet.

Ttuet was born into a poor family, the second daughter of five children. Her family lives in Dong Nai province, which is east and northeast of Ho Chi Minh City, formerly Saigon, and northeast of the southern Mekong Delta region. The topography of Dong Nai province is flat with a few scattered mountains and a gradual declivity in the southward direction. The province is full of lakes, dams, and rivers. The economy of the entire region depends largely on farming, fishing, and forestry, such as rubber plantations. Plans for industrialization have yet to take effect. In 2009, per capita GNI for Dong Nai was about $1,367, which was less than one-half of the national average that year of $2,900.

Given the economic condition of Dong Nai, it is not surprising to see why quite a few brides from the area seek foreign husbands, mainly from Korea and Taiwan. The situation is similar to that on Tan Loc Island in the Mekong Delta. On Tan Loc Island, finding foreign husbands for young Vietnamese women is considered the best route out of poverty. By marrying foreigners from richer countries, daughters can potentially save their parents from destitution in old age, which many Vietnamese consider their great duty.

Ttuet's parents, a father and mother who were both fifty-six years old in 2009, have five children, including Ttuet. Ttuet has one older sister who is a full-time housewife; an older brother who works various jobs, including glass cutting; a younger brother who is studying at a vocational school to become an electrician; and a younger sister in high school. Ttuet's parents sell rice noodles, called *Pho*, on the street using a handcart, commonly called a "rear car" (*quan hang rong* in Vietnamese). But their business was not going well, so the family maintained only a marginal living. Despite the poor life of the family, Ttuet had managed to finish her middle school education. Ttuet's mother told me during my visit to her home in November 2009 that, although Ttuet wanted to pursue further study, in order to help out her brothers and sisters, she forwent further schooling to work on the farm. Her mother told me that Ttuet was a daughter of filial piety who was helpful to her siblings. While she was working on the farm, she learned that, were she to marry a Korean man, she could financially assist her parents.

By an arrangement made by a neighbor who knew an international marriage broker, Ttuet met her husband-to-be in Ho Chi Minh City and decided to marry him. In an international marriage, the groom usually pays all the expenses for the broker, but the bride has to pay some token fees for the matchmaking service. Each international marriage broker charges a different rate, ranging from twelve million wŏn (about $10,000) to fifteen million wŏn (about $12,500). Most brides pay a token fee of 300,000 wŏn (about $250). Ttuet paid 5.5 million Vietnamese dong (about $296). Tuet's parents borrowed the money from relatives and neighbors; the sum remained a family debt. Ttuet and her parents trusted that the debt would be paid off by the Korean groom, Kil-dong, as he promised to Ttuet before their marriage. Ttuet knew about the nearly twenty years that separated them in age, but she did not know that Kil-dong had a long history of mental illness. As long as Kil-dong took his medicine, he appeared to be normal. Ttuet anticipated that she would be happy with Kil-dong. Not only would she be able to pay off the family debt, but she would also be able to help her natal family financially. Eventually, she married and came to Korea in November 2007.

Kil-dong is the oldest child of five siblings, with one younger brother and three younger sisters, all of whom do fairly well as salaried workers in the city of Ch'ŏngju, the provincial capital of north Ch'ungch'ŏng province, not far away from their home. Kil-dong went to a regional college and got a job at a gas company in Seoul. In some ways, Kil-dong was an unusual person, peculiar for his clinical depression and occasional fits of epilepsy, but he was regarded as intelligent. As long as he took medicine regularly as the doctor prescribed, he could function normally. However, when he skipped his medicine, he became abnormal. Because he was smart, he finished college and passed the entrance examination to join a decent company, beating out a pool of highly competitive applicants. From there, he was promoted to a position as section chief of the company.

While he was working in Seoul, he fell in love with a woman who was a member of a new religious organization called Taesunjiligyo.[20] She told Kil-dong that if he would donate some seventy million wŏn (about $58,333) from his retirement allowance to the church, she would marry him. So he did. When he was ready to go to meet his fiancée's parents, she suddenly disappeared without leaving any note. He was despondent and did not know what to do. Finally he returned to his parents' home in Pukch'ŏn and told them all about it. His mother was so shocked about it that she got sick. Eventually, she died from the shocking event. After Kil-dong's return, his father sold 1,650 square meters of vineyard so that his son could marry a Vietnamese woman and settle in the city of Taejŏn. After Kil-dong married Ttuet, the couple lived with his father for a while, but his father insisted that his son should live in the city rather than remain on the farm. Kil-dong was able to acquire a decent job in Taejŏn, and the couple lived there happily for five months.

Because Kil-dong was so intelligent and also so skillful at acquiring a new job, he was able to find a new job easily. Even so, he was unable to hold on to any one job for long. In a deep depression because he skipped his prescribed medicine, he quit his job and returned to his father's home in Pukch'ŏn. His depression grew worse because he still refused to take his medicine, despite Ttuet's insistence that he should do so. While the couple was living in Pukch'ŏn, they thought they did not have much of a future. And, most painful for Ttuet, she would not be able to assist her family in Vietnam financially. Finally, Kil-dong instigated a dual suicide. They purchased the pesticide Sumithion, which is known to be so mildly toxic and so used widely in farming that anyone can purchase it without special permission. It is known to be safe unless one consumes an excessive amount at one time.

Before they attempted suicide, Kil-dong tried to kill his father. At three o'clock in the early morning on April 11, 2008, right before Kil-dong could stab his father, the father somehow awoke, and Kil-dong aborted his attempted murder. Afterward, Kil-dong's siblings realized that leaving their father at home with Kil-dong was too dangerous, so they promptly made arrangements to hospitalize Kil-dong in a mental institution. Miserable, Ttuet was left to take care of her father-in-law without her husband's help. Kil-dong's sister-in-law in Ch'ŏngju once asked Ttuet to come live with her, but she remained at her father-in-law's home. Deeply disappointed by all that had happened, Ttuet ultimately decided to commit suicide by taking an overdose of Sumithion. When she did, she fell into a comatose state. Despite her condition, Ttuet's father-in-law waited until the next day to take her to the hospital. People in the community commented that the delay was a sign of the man's below-average intelligence.

When Ttuet reached the hospital, she was nearly dead. The doctors at the hospital in Pukch'ŏn did whatever they could to save her life, including reviving her heart by electric shock. Ttuet was barely able to stay alive on life support. The doctors at the hospital commented that if she had been taken to the hospital sooner, she might have been spared the worst effects. For two months, Ttuet was unconscious and unable to recognize visitors. After three months in the intensive care unit, she was transferred to the general ward. Nonetheless, because her nerve system was badly damaged, she was immobile and her body shook all the time. She could not move her arms and legs, was unable to talk, and could not take meals. Since she could not take food through her mouth, doctors bypassed her damaged throat with a tube that delivered liquefied food directly to her stomach. All of her teeth were removed. Although her life was saved miraculously, the hospital bill was astronomical, and her family was unable to pay it. Worst of all, her husband was still confined to a mental institution.

The tragic story was relayed to the Korean public by a reporter at the *Yŏnhap* News Agency (*Yŏnhap T'ongsin*), and people began to send in charitable donations. Among the donors were individuals at the Pukch'ŏn county branch of public prosecutors and Kil-dong's family members. The total amount of donations reached some 8,600,000 wŏn (about $7,166). The hospital took over half the sum: 7.5 million wŏn (about $6,250). For continuing support, a minister of Pukch'ŏn, working with the Pukch'ŏn branch of the Center for Supporting Married Immigrants, a nationwide organization, led a campaign to raise some funds for Ttuet. After three months in the hospital having physical therapy, Ttuet's condition improved a little bit, and she was able to take a few steps with the help of therapists. However, her condition deteriorated when the outside temperature dropped with the coming of fall. Her muscles became stiffer as time went on; such stiffness is a typical symptom of Sumithion poisoning. Doctors informed the charitable association that the hospital could not offer any effective care for her. Because she was unable to talk, no one knew what she wanted. Doctors assumed that her spirits were as badly affected as her body, so they suggested that she go back to her family in Vietnam and seek out medical care in Ho Chi Minh City. The doctors thought she would be better off living at home than she would be staying at the Pukch'ŏn hospital. Ttuet was able to signal her approval of the plan with a big smile. She appeared to be very happy, and her morale went up. Finally, a minister who led the group who raised funds for her aftercare arranged for Ttuet to return to Vietnam.

Finally, on September 21, 2008, along with an interpreter, Ttuet returned to Vietnam with some money.[21] Those who raised the money thought Ttuet's family could use it to remodel their deteriorated house and upgrade the family business. They could also afford to take Ttuet to a hospital in Ho Chi Minh City, some 130 kilometers (about 82 miles) away. Ttuet's family later reported that her condition had improved since she had been undergoing therapy at a hospital in Ho Chi Minh City.

I decided to meet Ttuet and her family when I traveled to Vietnam to deliver a keynote speech at the International Conference on Korean Language

and Culture on November 16, 2009. The event was hosted by Vietnam National University at Hanoi. Before going to Hanoi, on November 13, 2009,
I flew to Tan Son Nhat Airport, in Ho Chi Minh City, to meet Ttuet and her
family in Dong Nai. At eight o'clock in the morning, November 14, 2009, I
traveled to Ttuet's home with an interpreter and a dean of the CUK, Jae Yoel
Lee, who was founder of the Korean Language Program at Hanoi National
University.

Life of Ttuet in Dong Nai

Seeing hundreds of taxicabs at the Tan Son Nhat Airport and countless cars
and motorcycles on the streets, not to mention the hustling, bustling business
activities at the lavish Renaissance Hotel and Resort in Ho Chi Minh City, I
wondered why so many young Vietnamese brides marry older Korean men
and go to live in remote farming and fishing villages in Korea. Looking
around Ho Chi Minh City, it did not seem possible that per capita income in
the county was only about $2,900. There were fine restaurants, shops, and
other signs of affluence. In short, the citizens of the former capital of South
Vietnam looked happy, dynamic, and energetic, and the city looked vibrant.

   However, as our van left the city limits, driving east and northeastwardly
toward Dong Nai, the paved road became so narrow and rough that two
cars could barely pass by each other. It looked exotic to see thousands and
thousands of rubber trees on plantations along the roadside. And, for the first
time, I had an opportunity to see river people who lived in shelters atop their
boats in a branch of the Dong Nai River. Their appearance was exotic to me,
an outsider, but it had to be difficult to live their way of life. There appeared
to be many of them. After we crossed the river, the road conditions became
worse, and individual dwellings looked rundown and wretched. After seeing
the living conditions in Dong Nai province, I was able to understand why a
good many young women in Dong Nai wanted to marry foreign men, especially from Korea and Taiwan.

   As we came to Ttuet's hometown, her father and brother were waiting
for us at a corner of the town. As they saw our van coming, Ttuet's father
suddenly disappeared, but her brother led us to the house through narrow
streets. Via the translator, we introduced one another and were led into the
house. Her mother, her brother, and her younger sister came into the room,
and finally Ttuet was led to the room. She sat on a chair quietly, but her body
shook badly. She was unable to talk at all, and I could not see a single tooth
in her mouth. Nevertheless, she smiled at me in a friendly way. Since Ttuet
could not talk, her mother and brother did all the talking. I asked all sorts of
questions about what had happened in her suicide attempt. Her mother gave

all the answers. I was curious how her mother was able to explain the circumstances of the event since Ttuet was unable to tell her about them. After
hearing lengthy explanations from her mother, I concluded that asking any
further questions would only lead to more unreliable answers. But Ttuet herself neither denied nor confirmed her mother's explanations with any gesture.

Nonetheless, according to Ttuet's mother, once she had returned to Dong
Nai and undergone treatment, including physical therapy in a hospital in
Ho Chi Minh City, her condition had improved remarkably. If her present
condition was indeed an improvement, I could not even imagine how bad
her condition had been previously. According to her mother, if she could be
treated continuously at the hospital, she could be cured. She admitted that
although the family receives some assistance from the Korean support group,
an amount of about $500 a year, the sum was insufficient to pay for her treat-
ment at the hospital. Ttuet's mother insisted that she needed more money so
that Ttuet could have the continuous treatment she needed. She asked me
whether there was any way I could raise further funds.

The amount of charity funding donated by people in the Pukch'ŏn region
varies from source to source. The Korean account does not match the account given by Ttuet's family. According to a report, the support group in
the Pukch'ŏn region raised a total amount of ten million wŏn (about $8,333),
which is not a small amount in terms of the Vietnamese dong, and gave it
to her when she returned to Vietnam.[22] The group wished, and assumed,
that charity funds would be used by Ttuet's parents to open a decent and
permanent *Pho* shop—a significant improvement over the handcart (*quan
hang rong*) operation on the street. This improved business arrangement
would then earn a steady income for the family. I myself thought that there
would be such a *Pho* shop. But Ttuet's father was out on the town and
avoided meeting us. One thing was obvious: their two-room dwelling was
renovated and looked clean and well kept. However, there was no evidence
of the *Pho* shop. My interpreter asked over and over again about the *Pho*
shop, but there was no answer. In the interpreter's view, there was no such
shop. The funds appeared to have been used in remodeling the house, and
any remainder had been used to cover living expenses. They did not say how
many times Ttuet visited the hospital in Ho Chi Minh City. Instead, Ttuet's
mother kept on insisting that the support group in Korea raise more funds
for Ttuet so that she could receive proper treatment.

According to the family, Ttuet's older brother held a job as a glass cutter,
but we did not ascertain any details about his work during the interview. Although Ttuet's father was not present at all during my visit with the family,
her older brother stayed with us the whole time. Our interpreter surmised that
he might not have a regular job. Instead, he showed me the original copy of

Ttuet's marriage certificate that indicated that Ttuet and Kil-dong are still married and not divorced. Her brother kept on insisting that, since they are still married, the Kil-dong family is responsible for supporting her financially. He did not fail to remind me that, as soon as she gets well, she will return to Korea. In my judgment, there is small hope that she will ever get well.

Before I left Ttuet's home, I posed a final question to her mother. I asked if she would allow Ttuet's younger sister to get married to a Korean man. She said that if there were a proper candidate, and if her daughter wanted to marry a Korean man, she would approve the matrimony without hesitation. Her daughter, who had been present throughout the interview, smiled to indicate her agreement. Ttuet also gave a big smile of approval. Even if she could not talk, she could understand what I had asked. Given this response, it would seem that Ttuet's suicide attempt and resulting grave illness did not make the family bitter toward Korea and Koreans.

As for Koreans, the tragedy of Ttuet aroused sympathy and regret over the treatment of foreign brides. Some expressed personal sympathy, and others donated charity funds. It is an isolated incident, yet most Koreans have expressed some sort of guilty feelings over the tragedy. Whenever such an unfortunate incident occurs, Korea as a nation tends to take responsibility for not preventing it.

On April 16, 2007, for instance, when a Korean student at Virginia Polytechnic Institute and State University in Virginia murdered thirty-two students and teachers in a random shooting, Korea as a nation was apologetic to Americans.[23] In response to such an unusual apology from Koreans at home and abroad, a friend of mine in the United States wrote me an email saying he could not understand why Korea had to be apologetic and carry deep feelings of guilt. If there was anyone other than Seung-Hui Cho to blame for the tragedy, Americans shared some responsibility for not taking proper care of immigrants. I was impressed by the comment, realizing that America was a genuine multiethnic and multicultural society. Most Americans think that Seung-Hui Cho was not a Korean citizen but a permanent resident of the United States who immigrated when he was eight years old. In middle school, he was diagnosed with and treated for severe anxiety disorder. In keeping with the interpretation of my American friend, Koreans are equally responsible for not treating Ttuet properly during the stage of her adjustment in Korea.

Ttuet's incident brought Koreans' attention to two matters: the first matter was the qualifications of international marriage brokers, along with their honesty and sense of responsibility. Korea's government, at both the national and local levels, has expressed a strong will to uphold the law that regulates international marriage brokers. The second matter of concern was the need for educational programs to assist foreign brides in learning the Korean language and culture. The CUK's Campaign is one of several such programs. The educational components include teaching the native language and culture of the foreign brides to their Korean families in order to promote cross-cultural understanding. From my visit to Vietnam I learned that, despite such an unfortunate incident as Ttuet's, Vietnamese women will continue to marry Korean men as long as an economic incentive exists. The recent steep rise in foreign brides in Korea attests to the reality of this trend.

Ttuet's story should not suggest that all brokered marriages are bound to fail. In fact, a great majority of such marriages are doing remarkably well. In order to correct the stereotype of doomed international marriages, I will discuss the case of a successful marriage between a Korean man and a Vietnamese woman.

HUANG'S REWARDING LIFE IN PUKCH'ŎN

I have chosen to describe the life of Huang (a pseudonym) because she came from Vietnam just as Ttuet did. Huang lives in the same Korean province—close to the place where Ttuet used to live—and her husband is below normal intelligence. Huang's life story can give us some clues as to why one international marriage might succeed where another might fail. Such a comparison might suggest key factors that determine the success or failure of international marriages. Also, this case can be representative of many other successful couples whose stories are not told in this book.

Huang was born in a farming town in the Bac Giang province of northern Vietnam, which is located east of Hanoi, the capital city of Vietnam. It takes about two hours by car from the capital to reach Huang's village. Since the province lies in the rural Red River Delta, the region is primarily dedicated to agriculture. Per capita income is about $1,000, which is lower than that of Dong Nai. Like Dong Nai, the province is striving for industrial development and working to attract foreign as well as domestic investment. Considering the relatively impoverished economic state of the region, it is not surprising that some brides in that region are seeking foreign grooms, preferably Korean and Taiwanese men.

Huang was born the fourth child of five. She has one older brother, two older sisters, and one younger brother. At the time I met Huang, her mother was fifty years old; her father died in July 2008 because of a heart attack. Huang's older brother, who works in a motorcycle repair shop, carries a heavy economic burden in supporting his family, which includes an elderly grandmother (seventy-five years old), his mother, and Huang's younger brother (twenty years old). Their living conditions are marginal, less than the average per capita income of the region.

A friend of Huang's family was once introduced to a Korean friend who makes frequent business trips from Korea to Vietnam. The friend recommended a Korean man named Sang-hun (a pseudonym) as a possible husband for Huang. Sang-hun was thirty-seven years old, fifteen years older than Huang, when they first met. At their first meeting in Hanoi, Sang-hun was enamored of Huang at once. He wanted to marry her badly. Huang's first impression was somewhat different. In an interview in January 2009 for the Korean independent documentary film *Theme Special,* Huang told a reporter that, while Sang-hun liked her very much, she found him odd-looking, with an unusually broad, large face. Despite divergent first impressions, the couple eventually married in Vietnam in the summer of 2006, and Sang-hun brought Huang to Korea.

Sang-hun was born in 1969 the youngest of three sons. His father was doing quite well as an engineer for a construction company and traveled widely throughout Korea. But he died when he was thirty-six years old. When Sang-hun was six years old, he began to fall into convulsions periodically; he still suffers attacks to this day. In appearance, there is nothing unusual about him except his unusually large face, as his wife Huang noted, and his heavyset body. His speech patterns are not as smooth as those of others, but his speech is sound, logical, and courteous. His expression of love toward his wife is straightforward and overt in front of others, which is not so common among his peers. Since he and his family knew that he would not fit into regular college life, instead of applying to a regular high school, he went to a vocational and technical school to specialize in electronics. Because he was classified as a handicapped person, he had a temporary menial job doing custodial work at a local rehabilitation center. His marriage turned his life around. He became one of the happiest persons around. He now smiles all the time and shows affection to his mother, brothers, and friends. He also shows deep care and concern for his in-laws in Vietnam.

The happiest moment came when Huang gave birth to a boy, Kyŏng-min, who, in 2009, was two years old. Everyone in the neighborhood loved Kyŏng-min because in that community there had been no child born for the last ten years. This situation illustrates well the effects of Korea's low birthrate, the lowest birthrate of any nation in the world for the past several years. Since then, three more children have been born, all to foreign wives. Multicultural families have helped to increase Korea's birthrate slightly.

Virtually every day, elderly women of the community came to Sang-hun's home to play with Kyŏng-min. Huang's house became the center for the elderly women in the community because they could gather together easily in the shop run by Huang and her mother-in-law. They call it a "super market," but in reality it is a small convenience shop that sells virtually everything. Nonetheless, the market is the major source of their family income since Sang-hun's salary is trifling. People in the neighborhood are fond of the two-year-old-boy and consider him a precious gift for the community. Kyŏng-min is a very cute boy and clever. Most of all, Huang is beautiful—her skin pigmentation is much lighter and whiter than most Korean women's. She is also kind, courteous, and humble in her manner. She treats elderly persons, especially friends of her mother-in-law and people in her neighborhood, with great respect. When I visited her in her house in December 2009, she treated me very well, providing various fruits and beverages. Although she appeared to be shy, she said what she wanted to say. Even Kyŏng-min behaved very well.

Among many other things, it does not take too long to understand why this particular international marriage works so well. I understood why as soon as I met Huang's mother-in-law (who was seventy years old at the time). She looked fierce in appearance at first—this had been Huang's first impression, too—but as soon as I started to talk with her, I discovered that she was a typical countrywoman full of humanity. She was kind and courteous in showing hospitality to a visitor. Although she has two older sons besides Sang-hun, she chose to live with Sang-hun to help Huang run the market and take care of Kyŏng-min. These activities are more a privilege for her than a duty.

It seemed that Huang's mother-in-law, and the other elderly women in the neighborhood, could not live without Kyŏng-min. They missed the child terribly when Huang, Sang-hun, and Kyŏng-min were away from home for two weeks to visit Huang's home in Vietnam.

The two-week visit in January 2009 was arranged by several Korean businesses that do business with Vietnam and the county office of Pukch'ŏn. They selected thirty members of model families, including Korean husbands and their children, and paid their expenses to visit Vietnam. It was a wonderful opportunity for Vietnamese women to visit their natal homes for the first time since they left for Korea. It was also a rare occasion for Korean husbands to meet their in-laws and relatives. For the children, it was the first time they had met family members, relatives, and friends of their mothers in Vietnam. To dramatize the occasion, the Korean ambassador in Vietnam attended a ceremony in the capital of Bac Giang in northern Vietnam. I was unable to attend the occasion, but it was narrated and videotaped by the crew of *Theme Special.* The scene was vivid, and the taping crew followed Huang and her family in Vietnam.

Before the trip, Huang arranged to visit the graveyard of her father-in-law along with her mother-in-law, husband, and Kyŏng-min. She paid her respects to her dead father-in-law, who had passed away quite some time ago. Such a deed and gesture touched many, including neighbors. In return, Huang's mother-in-law prepared all sorts of gifts for Huang's family members in Vietnam. Some items were in honor of Huang's father, who had died in July 2008. Sang-hun paid quite sincere and genuine respect to the grave of his dead father-in-law. It was genuine because Sang-hun dropped tears while he was observing the graveyard ceremony. Not only did Sang-hun have the opportunity to meet and know his in-laws, but he also realized how much concern they had for the welfare of his family. During his stay in his wife's home, he tried to install a television antenna, which is necessary since Huang's natal home is located in relatively remote farmland. Using his skill in electronics, he tried to be helpful. Huang's natal family was apologetic to their son-in-law for showing him a shabby home. They explained that the house was damaged by a bad storm a year ago. They had not been able to repair it because, according to custom, home repair had to wait until three years have passed since the death of a family member.

Throughout the trip, Sang-hun learned how hard going it is for someone who does not comprehend the language spoken around him. While Huang was busy renewing her relationships, Sang-hun was alone, wandering the town. He commented to the filming crew that his own experience in Vietnam made him realize how hard Huang's life in Korea must be since she does not command the Korean language. This was a useful lesson for Sang-hun to learn. Also, Huang's Korean mother-in-law has learned how important Huang and her precious grandson Kyŏng-min are to her. She told the filming crew during an interview, "I don't think I can live without Huang and Kyŏng-min." Neighbors informed me that Huang's mother-in-law started counting down the days until Huang's return. She often cried because she missed Huang and Kyŏng-min. The trip to Vietnam accomplished a lot, but the most important lesson learned was that Huang was indispensable to the family.

In sum, after learning about Huang and her life story, I propose that several factors have contributed to her happy life in Korea. Huang plays the typical roles of a loving housewife, a dutiful daughter-in-law, and a good mother. Huang fits an image of a traditional Korean woman and thereby satisfies the expectations of her husband, mother-in-law, relatives, and people of the community, especially friends of her mother-in-law. A growing women's liberation movement in Korea makes Huang look better and better to rural elderly people who retain yesterday's values. Furthermore, her courtesy, humble attitude, and nonthreatening manner have been praised by family members, relatives, and people from the community.

Also, Huang's marriage is based on the fact that—instead of relying on the help of outsiders, including local governments and volunteers who assist multicultural families—she studied diligently to learn the Korean language and

Korean customs by attending a language learning center in the community and watching educational television programs. She works hard until late in the evening to improve her command of the Korean language. Unfortunately, until I made contact with her, she was unaware of the CUK's Campaign. She told me, "I have to master the Korean language so that I can effectively help my son be a good student in school."

Huang's success is also based on the fact that Huang's Korean family is economically sound. The family gets a steady source of income from the store. Huang does not have to do extra menial work to generate additional income. Huang's husband did not owe any money to anyone for his marriage, and Huang does not have to send any money to help her natal family in Vietnam. Almost all family quarrels in international marriages are due to wives sending money to support their natal families back home. And most domestic discord owes to husbands failing to deliver on a promise to send money to their wife's family.

From my perspective as an anthropologist, the most important element for the success of her marriage is her mother-in-law's cross-cultural understanding, even though the family did not say so in so many words. During my visit to their home, her mother-in-law sang Huang's praises. I will close this chapter with her words: "How hard it would be to live in a society where customs are all different, and she cannot say what she wants to say. I am going to take care of her not like a daughter-in-law but just like my own daughter. She is polite, respectful to the elderly, and is not a spendthrift. Among other things, she gave birth to such a precious grandson. What else could I expect from her? She is our family treasure. I don't think we could find such a nice woman among native Korean women."

5

Stories of Foreign Brides Who Were Married by a Religious Organization

This chapter provides an ethnographic account of two foreign brides, both of whom married via an arrangement made by a religious organization, the Unification Church. The brides were bound in matrimony as part of a "mass wedding" (*haptong kyŏlhon*). The Unification Church was founded in 1940 by Moon Sun Myung [Sŏn-myŏng Mun]. It was formally established in Seoul as the Holy Spirit Association for the Unification of World Christianity, reflecting Moon's original vision of an ecumenical movement. The doctrine of the church is explained in the book *Divine Principle,* which draws from the Bible as well as from Asian traditions. The doctrine espouses a belief in a universal God.[1] According to Michael Breen, "Moon's view of God is quintessentially Korean, combining shamanist passion and Confucian family patterns in Christian form."[2] In the 1990s, Moon began to establish various peace organizations, including the Family Federation for World Peace and Unification. Members of the Unification Church are found in fifty countries. In Korea, members are estimated to be from 250,000 to three million.[3]

Among the practices of the Unification Church, the blessing ceremony is considered to be the most important ceremony in a person's spiritual life. The blessing ceremony removes the couple from the ranks of sinful humanity and makes them part of God's sinless lineage. Any children born to the blessed couple are free from original sin. Those who espouse the faith believe that matchmaking and marriage are the direct and perfect manifestation of a profound theology and worldview. The blessing ceremony was first held in Seoul in 1961 with thirty-six couples. Since then the scale and size of the blessing ceremony has become larger, as evidenced by a 2009 ceremony for forty thousand couples at Sun Moon University in Asan, Korea.[4]

According to church officials, from 1980 to July 2010, a total number of 145,742 foreign brides from various countries, including from Japan, the Philippines, Mongolia, Thailand, and other countries, married Koreans through the church.[5] The two Japanese brides whose stories are told in this chapter are among the 5,326 (2.9 percent of foreign brides in Korea) Japanese brides living in Korea.[6]

Most Koreans think that the phenomenon of multiculturalism in contemporary Korea began in the late 1990s and became more popular after 2000, as a large number of foreign brides, mostly from East and Southeastern Asian countries, married Korean men and came to Korea. However, international marriages conducted by the Unification Church began back in 1961. In my experience with the CUK's Campaign, I have found that most Japanese women who marry Korean men are married by way of the Unification Church. It is estimated that over 60 percent of international marriages between Japanese brides and Korean men are conducted by the Unification Church.

AN ETHNOGRAPHY OF A JAPANESE WOMAN WHO WAS MARRIED BY THE UNIFICATION CHURCH

This chapter begins with an ethnography of a couple who entered into an arranged marriage. The wife is a thirty-nine-year-old Tomoko Yuki (a pseudonym),[7] and the husband is forty-four-year-old Kim Ch'ŏl-su (a pseudonym). They married at a mass wedding back in 1999 when Tomoko was twenty-eight and Ch'ŏl-su was thirty-four. After the wedding, they lived in Yŏngwŏl (a fictitious name), in north Kyŏngsang province, where they managed a vineyard. They now have three children, two boys (eleven and five years old) and one daughter (ten years old).[8]

Administratively, Yŏngwŏl is classified as a city, but actually it is a farm-based rural community. Since there are no major industries located there, the population of Yŏngwŏl is decreasing by about 1.4 percent yearly. Currently, the total number of inhabitants—including the city and its immediate vicinity—are estimated to be around 120,000. Recently, the area has earned a reputation for producing fine quality grapes. Tomoko and Ch'ŏl-su own a vineyard, which generates a yearly income of some fifty million wŏn (about $41,666). Such an income is above average for farmers in the region.

I met Tomoko on January 24, 2008, in the city hall of Yŏngwŏl at a ceremony for those who completed the requirements for the Korean language proficiency certificate offered by the CUK's Campaign. At the ceremony, awards were given for a Korean writing contest, and Tomoko won first place. Her Korean proficiency was exceptional compared to the other contestants.

Tomoko's Background

Tomoko was born on March 20, 1971, in Wakayama, the capital city of the Wakayama prefecture in the Kansai region of Japan. She was the second of two daughters. When I visited Wakayama in March 2010, I was amazed by the rich history of this old city, with its numerous cultural and historical relics.[9] Tomoko has many memories of living in Wakayama. While some of them are good, others, she would like to forget. These bad memories include the loss of her beloved father, financial exigencies for her family, and her struggle to pursue an education and find a new world beyond Wakayama. She became nostalgic when she showed me the elementary school she once attended.

Tomoko's parents were originally from Kyushu, and most of her close relatives still live in Kyushu. Her sister was born in Kyushu as well. However, in 1965, before Tomoko was born and when her sister was eight months old, her parents moved to Wakayama because of Sumitomo Steel's expansion. Tomoko's father worked in the furnace area of the steel plant. He was promoted to the head of the smelting team. Because her husband had a solid job, Tomoko's mother remained a full-time housewife. Since the area where Tomoko's father worked required workers' constant attention, her father was a member of a three-shift team. The three-shift rotation meant that Tomoko's father did not spend a lot of time with the family. It seemed to Tomoko that her father worked all the time. She believes that her father might have suffered from job-related stress. He often worked a second job in a local supermarket to generate some extra income while her mother was occupied in making kimonos, the traditional Japanese dress for women.

Tomoko's father was active and athletic. He loved all sorts of sports and even participated in a local marathon. However, in order to cope with the pressures of work, he became a heavy smoker and drinker. These habits often brought about family squabbles between Tomoko's mother and father. However, Tomoko's family lived comfortably.

They lived in a house built by the steel company, so most of their neighbors worked for the same employer. It was like a company town. Tomoko remembers that her house was well furnished, with a refrigerator, a washing machine, and other appliances. Although most of the neighbors owned cars, Tomoko's family did not. Tomoko still remembers envying her car-owning neighbors, as she had to ride a bicycle most of the time. Nonetheless, the family was comfortable financially. Tomoko had a swing set and took piano lessons. She recalls having plenty of toys and dolls to play with. However, she does not have many memories of playing with her older sister, owing largely to the five-year age gap that separated them. Now, her sister manages a lavish restaurant and takes care of her mother, who lives with her.

Tomoko does not remember her primary school years aside from the thirty-minute walk it took her to get there, a walk she made even when it was raining. When she entered middle school, which had some one thousand students drawn from four elementary schools nearby, she rode a bicycle. She participated in various extracurricular activities, including basketball, swimming, and piano lessons. She also attended *juku* at least once or twice per week. *Juku* is a commercial tutoring service that offers supplementary education after school.[10] Such supplementary education helps some children enter elite high schools.

Only well-to-do parents can afford supplementary education for their children, and Tomoko's parents were able to do so. In fact, when she was in middle school, her parents built a new two-story house. She had high hopes of entering an elite high school. However, because her grades were not good enough to gain admission to an elite high school, she applied to the next best tier of high schools at the advice of her teacher.

Tomoko applied to a high school that was well known for its horseback riding program. However, when she entered the school, the school abolished the program. Instead of riding horses, she joined the school band and the *kendo* club. Ultimately she became team captain of the *kendo* club and earned a second-degree belt. *Kendo* is a Japanese sport of stylized swordplay using bamboo swords. Later, she joined the calligraphy club. Because of her practice at calligraphy, she writes Chinese characters very artistically. The Japanese use Chinese characters extensively, along with Japanese *kana,* which represent the syllabary portion of the Japanese writing system.[11] However, in her high school years Tomoko faced a series of misfortunes. Unexpectedly, her father lost his job at Sumitomo Steel. The steel company moved much of its steel-producing operations to China when Tomoko was in high school. The Wakayama steel mill of Sumitomo was downsized, and many workers at the Wakayama plant lost their jobs. Because of financial difficulties resulting from her father's unemployment, Tomoko's family faced bankruptcy. The newly built house was auctioned off. Her family was relocated three times, and family members had to adjust to very crowded quarters. She was commuting to school by train because it would take her more than forty minutes to get there on her bicycle. Her older sister was sent to live with Tomoko's maternal grandmother while attending junior college. Tomoko's parents had a very difficult time managing the family during their financial downturn. Tomoko herself was deeply saddened by her parents' troubles and had a tough time coping.

As Tomoko and I were looking at the scenery of Wakayama atop the Wakayama Castle, she pointed out the remnants of the Sumitomo Steel mill, a huge site. She recalled her father once saying that the "Japanese assisted

Koreans with steel and iron producing technology, but Korean steel plants outperform." Back then Tomoko was unaware of Korea as a nation and could not remember the name of P'ohang Iron and Steel Company (POSCO), but now she assumes that the country was Korea and the steel plant was POSCO. In fact, the initial installation of POSCO, founded by the Korean government, was based on Japanese technology. POSCO was first established in 1968, its operation starting in 1973.[12] Since Tomoko was born in 1971, her memory of her father's comment about POSCO might have been made when POSCO was in full production.[13]

Ironically, POSCO was the company that enabled the CUK to initiate the Campaign in 2007. Tomoko told me that whenever she goes to the Eastern Sea—passing by the main plant of POSCO—she is reminded of her father. In some sense she is still tied to the steel mill. After the closing of the Wakayama plant, according to Tomoko's mother, young people have been leaving the city. Citizens of Wakayama are suffering from a beleaguered economy. Tomoko's sister, who manages a restaurant, told me that her business is not doing well. She said, "You watch the street in the morning rush hour, and you hardly see any young salaried men going to work." I could tell that the city was suffering from a depressed economy.

Commitment to the Unification Church

As Tomoko suffered from her family's financial decline, her mother, who had earlier become a member of the Unification Church, persuaded her to go to church. She believed that the church might give Tomoko comfort, guidance, and direction in her life. Tomoko's experience with the Unification Church turned her life around. Eventually it led to her marriage to a Korean man.

While her mother was a Buddhist before becoming a convert to the Unification Church, Tomoko did not belong to any particular religion, as is the case with most East Asians: Chinese, Japanese, and Koreans. As Francis L. K. Hsu has said, "Ask any number of Chinese what their religion is and the answer of the majority will be that they have no particular religion, or that, since all religions benefit man in one way or another, they are all equally good."[14] Most Japanese and Koreans would respond similarly, so Tomoko's conversion to the Unification Church was not as exclusive as most Westerners might think.[15] In fact, Harumi Befu, a Japanese anthropologist who has worked in both Japan and America, has observed syncretism in Japan: "The same person may worship deities of different religions without any feeling of conflict. For example, a Japanese [person] might pray at the Buddhist altar at home in the morning and go to a neighborhood Shinto shrine in the afternoon. . . . Moreover, there are religious edifices which enshrine deities of different religions. For instance, there may be a Buddhist temple on the premises of a Shinto shrine, or vice versa."[16]

Koreans are also nonexclusive in their religious observance. A Korean anthropologist, Cho Hŭng-yun, has written, "On a given weekend within a family, the mother-in-law goes to a shaman to attend a *gut* (a shaman ritual), one daughter-in-law attends a Christian church, another has joined a new religious group, and yet another visits a Buddhist temple. Meanwhile, the father and head of the household participates in a discussion among Confucians while mountain climbing."[17] Given the religious practices of most of East Asians, the Japanese in particular, Tomoko's commitment to the Unification Church is not as binding as Westerners might expect. I do not mean to belittle Tomoko's commitment to the church, but it appeared to me that she turned to the church primarily for moral and spiritual support during the time of her family's economic hardship. Her mother may have introduced her to the church, but once a member, Tomoko looked to her peers for emotional support and fellowship.

The Unification Church claims to have 460,000 followers in Japan. However, Hiroshi Yamaguchi, who heads a group of three hundred lawyers who have brought lawsuits against the church, claims the number is much lower, about ten thousand active members. Yoshifu Arita, a journalist who has monitored the church for ten years, estimated membership at about thirty thousand in 1996.[18] Although there is a branch of the Unification Church in Wakayama, Tomoko attended a church in Osaka, which is located some forty minutes' driving distance from Wakayama by express bus or train. I asked Tomoko why she attended church in Osaka instead of Wakayama. She replied, "Because I was always adventurous and interested in big cities." Indeed, Osaka is Japan's second largest city, home to nearly twenty million people. It is the commercial capital of Japan. While spending time in Osaka and associating with friends who attended prestigious high schools there, Tomoko discovered that her school in Wakayama was not as prestigious as those that her Osaka peers attended. Because of this she felt so inferior to her peers.

Tomoko attended a *juku,* which was run by the church in Osaka. She had hoped to study the arts at an art college, but owing to the financial state of her family, she instead took the advice of her *juku* instructors to specialize in tourism at a vocational and technical junior college. Once she started attending the church and associating with her friends in church, she began to learn the Korean language. The Korean language is important because the founder and leader of the Unification Church is a Korean and members of the church are Koreans. The book *Divine Principle,* which contains the teachings of the church, holds that a man born in Korea in the early twentieth century received from Jesus the mission to become the second coming of Christ. Members of the Unification Church believe this messiah is Moon Sun Myung.

Life in the Church

Before she attended junior college, Tomoko moved into the church dormitory in Osaka. Later, when she started going to college, she commuted from school to the church dorm. When she started attending school, she envied her college classmates who came from well-to-do backgrounds. At times, she felt looked down upon by students whose family backgrounds were more affluent than hers. Despite this, she had no option other than staying in the church-run dorm and going to school. Members of the church had been so kind to her. Whenever she was unable to attend school due to sickness, her fellow churchgoers expressed concern for her welfare. She was grateful for their concern, even if they were not family members. She also played piano for the church choir.

During her college years Tomoko did not concern herself with dating, as most young women her age would. The church has rather rigid restrictions on dating and courtship among church members and those outside the church. The church advocates sexual abstinence until marriage. Tomoko recalls more of the church's rigid rules. She had to wake up at four o'clock in the morning to attend a prayer meeting. After class, before she returned to the church dorm, she had to report her whereabouts to the church office. Most times after school she had to work various part-time jobs, including odd jobs at the local bank and tutoring middle school students in English. Since the Japanese economy was strong in the late 1980s, Tomoko remembers there being plenty of part-time jobs available. During a break from school she was once paid 1,300 yen (about $13) per hour at a garment manufacturing company. Whatever she was paid, though, Tomoko had to give her earnings over to the church. In return she received an allowance.

In spite of all the difficulties, in 1989, when she was in her final year of junior college, Tomoko had an opportunity to travel to Korea by ship. She was interested in Korea because it was Moon's home country. While there she visited various places, including Sun Moon University, founded by Moon Sun Myung, and other universities.[19] After visiting the universities, Tomoko hoped to have the opportunity to study at one.

She graduated from a junior college in 1989, but she was not excited about her graduation because her future prospects were not promising. However, since she had specialized in tourism, Tomoko secured a job as a clerk for a travel agency. Because she had knowledge of computers, she was assigned to the accounting department. She started to learn accounting and bookkeeping; eventually she earned a license as a certified accountant. Because the company had a nationwide network in Japan, with branches all over Japan, Tomoko's daily workload was heavy and very demanding. While she was working for the company, she became interested in her job. She also visited her family home in Wakayama whenever she could. Because of her involvement in various church activities, such as choir, she practiced at piano and became very good at it.

At twenty years old, for the first time in her life, Tomoko began dating a man who was the section chief of the company she worked for. Yet she was deeply conflicted about her relationship because of the church's practice of arranged marriage consecrated by the blessing ceremony. She told me that she felt guilty dating someone against the will of the church. She did not know what to do about it. On the one hand, were she to follow church rules, she would lose her boyfriend. On the other hand, if she chose her boyfriend instead, she would defy church doctrine. Tomoko was in deep distress over her dilemma. At times, when going to work, she fainted in the subway. Finally, she was diagnosed as having panic disorder. Because she was not functioning properly, she wanted to quit to work, but her company did not accept her resignation. In spite of the panic disorder, she continued to work for a while. This was in 1992, and Tomoko recalled that a good many Japanese women married Korean men and went to live in Korea.

While she was suffering from panic disorder, her father was fighting against cancer. Knowing that there was a good doctor in Tokyo, her father was taken to a large hospital in Tokyo. Finally, she was allowed to resign from her job in Osaka to nurse her father in Tokyo. By arrangement of the Tokyo branch of her company, Tomoko was able to rent a room in Tokyo. While she was going to the hospital frequently to tend to her father, Tomoko became acquainted with a head nurse at the hospital. Some time thereafter the hospital offered Tomoko a job as a nurse's aide. It was a new beginning for her. While she worked at the hospital, she thought about a new career in nursing, but she wanted to continue to play piano as well. At the same time, she started to learn the Korean language intensively by hiring a private tutor who was a college graduate and native Korean woman. This instruction added to the knowledge of Korean she already had.

Marrying a Korean Man

While she was working at the hospital, she worried about the condition of her father. At the same time, when she was just about ready to marry a Korean man through the blessing ceremony arranged by the church, she could not forget about her boyfriend in Osaka. With all the pressure she became panicky. She had been hospitalized a few times before when her panic disorder had become severe. Despite the problems with her mental health, in 1995, a twenty-eight-year-old Tomoko agreed to marry a thirty-four-year-old Korean man named Ch'ŏl-su, who graduated from high school and managed a vineyard in Yŏngwŏl in north Kyŏngsang province.

Even if they agreed to marry through the church, Tomoko was not sure she should marry a Korean man. Her father strongly opposed the marriage. Perhaps her father did not have as strong a commitment to church doctrine as her mother did. Tomoko pondered her marriage while postponing the actual wedding. While Tomoko was hesitant, and even reluctant to marry, Ch'ŏl-su fell in love with her because she was so charming and attractive. Ch'ŏl-su called her virtually every day and went to Japan to see her several times. Ch'ŏl-su's love and affection for Tomoko was more intense than any ordinary "love marriage." In a sense, Ch'ŏl-su thought that it was the best thing that had ever happened in his life. He was persistent in his desire to marry Tomoko. In 1998, while she pondered matrimony with Ch'ŏl-su, Tomoko's father died. It was one year before she decided to get married. The marriage finally occurred in 1999. Tomoko and Ch'ŏl-su ended up having three wedding ceremonies: one in Japan for Tomoko's family, one in Yŏngwŏl with Ch'ŏl-su's family, and one in Seoul as part of a mass wedding of the church.

Ch'ŏl-su, who was thirty-four years old and had attained only a high school education, was the last son of six children. Chŏl-su's father had died years prior, but his seventy-three-year-old mother lived with Ch'ŏl-su, even though he was the youngest of her three sons. Ch'ŏl-su owns about nine hundred square meters of vineyard. Before Tomoko came to live in the house, the old house of some sixty square meters must have been small, old, and dilapidated. But I did not see their old house. When I visited them in 2009, the old house had been torn down and a new one stood in its place. (I was able to see the old house in a film made by Japanese television.)

When Tomoko first came to the old house, she was washing clothes by hand and doing most of the household chores manually. The new house, however, was built in a Western style. It was clean, attractive, and appointed with modern amenities: hot and cold running water, a refrigerator, washing machine, television, computer, a landline telephone and mobile phones, and built-in air conditioning. It appears that Ch'ŏl-su has made every effort to please Tomoko, working harder than ever before in his vineyard to generate more family income. Tomoko also worked as much as she could in the vineyard, but she said that she was not really cut out to be a farmer or farmer's wife. Because she is allergic to certain weeds in the vineyard, she has to stay away from it a lot. During my visit to their house, her husband and mother-in-law were working in the vineyard because it was harvest time. When we went for lunch, her husband hauled a pickup load of harvested grapes to an agricultural co-op to sell.

Their annual income put Tomoko and her husband in the top 2 percent of multicultural families according to a 2009 survey conducted by the Ministry for Health, Welfare and Family Affairs. Economically, Tomoko's family is doing fairly well by Yŏngwŏl standards. She also enjoys having the conveniences of a modern home. However, from the very beginning she has had difficulty adjusting to rural farm life in Yŏngwŏl. Although Tomoko's hometown was only a regional city, it was industrial and prosperous until the Sumitomo plant shut down its operation. The city had a twenty-story modern hotel, many lavish restaurants, and very decent shopping malls. If one needed more, one could easily travel to Osaka. As I compared Wakayama with Yŏngwŏl, I wondered how she could cope with life in Yŏngwŏl.

Problems Adjusting to an Alien Town

Tomoko seemed to find it hard adjusting to rural life in Yŏngwŏl. There was nothing else for her to do except work in the vineyard, spend time with family members, and watch soap operas in the evening with her mother-in-law. There are virtually no cultural activities to speak of in Yŏngwŏl. More than the locale and lack of cultural activities, Tomoko seemed to have trouble relating with the people around her. The people of Yŏngwŏl and her family members, her mother-in-law in particular, struck her as very abrupt, blunt, and curt. Among Koreans, the brusque manner of the people of Kyŏngsang province, particularly north Kyŏngsang province, is well known. But people from that region usually defend them. They say that despite their curtness— enhanced by their regional dialect—they are actually kind and friendly. I came from that region, so I know the situation firsthand. For a polite Japanese woman such as Tomoko, it is difficult to discern friendliness behind a brusque manner. Tomoko admits that she was hurt a lot emotionally before she came to understand Korean culture, especially the behavior of Korean mothers-in-law toward their daughters-in-laws.

Tomoko told me that she had made extra effort to be a good wife and daughter-in-law. At times, she has been totally exhausted physically as well as mentally. Tomoko said that she could have won the "Most Filial Daughter-in-law Award" if the city of Yŏngwŏl had such an award, like most other Korean cities and counties. In fact, in Korean cities and counties that do have such an award, a good many Japanese women who married Korean men have won it. Tomoko's statement suggests that she has worked hard to accommodate the needs of her husband's family and to overcome cultural differences.

In so doing, she has been recognized by her family, relatives, and even the entire community.

In 2001, two years after her marriage, Tomoko gave birth to a boy named T'ae-ho. In 2002, she gave birth to a daughter, T'ae-hŭi, and in 2004 she gave birth to a son, T'ae-yŏng. While all the children have typical Korean names, Tomoko also gave them Japanese names. She said she came up with the names herself. She insisted that, since they are half Korean and half Japanese, they should have Japanese names in addition to Korean names. I sense that although she is married to a Korean man, currently lives in Korea, and is capable of passing the Korean language examination required for naturalization, Tomoko retains her Japanese identity. Her legal status in Korea is that of a "permanent resident." Not hiding her inner feelings, she told me, "Someday I might go back to Japan, as you went back [to Korea] after thirty-six years living in the United States."

Tomoko has persevered remarkably well through all the hardships and difficulties she has confronted in her years of living in Korea. She has suffered culture shock, loneliness, and dejection after giving birth to and rearing three children. Tomoko has been broken down both physically and emotionally. She has been plagued by melancholy and a mild form of hypochondria. She sought professional help. But since Yŏngwŏl is a small city, she could not find an expert who could converse with her in Japanese. Tomoko is fluent in Korean, but she figured that she could not adequately describe her inner feelings and delicate state of mind in the Korean language. Eventually she found a physician in Seoul who is fluent in Japanese. She visited the physician and found his advice very helpful in overcoming her emotional crisis.

I asked Tomoko, "Even if you had hard times, in the midst of the struggles, you have been depicted as one of the happiest women in the whole world according to Japanese TV. Were you not?" She replied, "I just acted in accordance with the direction of the producer. I think most people would act the same as I did in a feature film." She told me, "If I met you for the first time, and you asked me so many sensitive questions, I would have answered the same way I did for the television film. Since we have met several times, and you even visited my mother and sister in my hometown of Wakayama, I feel like I can tell you anything. Most of all, I should tell you the truth." Apparently she had more faith in an anthropologist's work.

Since overcoming her struggles, she has devoted her time to introducing Japanese language and culture into the local kindergartens and elementary schools where her children attend. She is very active as a key member of the Committee for Cultural Exchange between Korea and Japan (*Han'il Munhwa Kyoryu Hoeŭi*) in the Yŏngwŏl region. She feels she is playing the role of cultural broker between Japanese and Koreans. She is very proud of that. And, in her free time, she competes with other foreign brides in various Korean language contests. She almost always wins them, including one sponsored by the CUK. Now she is regarded as a celebrity in the city where she resides.

Is She a Celebrity or an Integrated Member of the Community?

For anybody who does not know about her Japanese identity, and as long as she does not speak the Korean language, it is impossible to tell that Tomoko is Japanese. Even though she speaks Korean fluently, she still has a noticeable Japanese accent. Despite this, Tomoko does not think she has been discriminated against for being a foreigner. Whenever she is invited to talk about Japan and Japanese culture at civic organization gatherings, such as when she teaches the Japanese language at local schools, she usually dresses up in a kimono and brings along some Japanese artifacts. She never hides the fact that she is Japanese; on the contrary, she is proud of her Japanese identity.

Tomoko has not been discriminated against on the basis of her morphological characteristics such as skin color, hair texture, and others. Foreign brides from other countries do not enjoy this advantage; this includes brides from Southeast Asian countries such as the Philippines, Vietnam, and Cambodia; and Caucasian brides from Uzbekistan, Russia, and other countries. However, Korean animosity toward the Japanese does flare up whenever the two countries have a political confrontation over sensitive issues, such as the issue of the "comfort women" (*Chŏngsindae*). Korean women, some of them pregnant, were drafted and some others were kidnapped by the Japanese authorities and kept in brothels for Japanese soldiers in the war zone during World War II.[20] Since Japan has not officially acknowledged doing this, a handful of survivors who went through the inhumane ordeal and their sympathizers demonstrate periodically in front of the Japanese embassy.

Tomoko became uncomfortable when there were furious disputes between Japan and Korea over territorial claims to Dokdo [Tokto],[21] which is an islet of about 187,453 square meters. Korea claims it as Korean territory based on records that date back to the sixth century. Korea also points to a Chosŏn Empire ordinance of 1900 officially incorporating the islet into modern Ullŭng county in north Kyŏngsang province. Japan claims the islet based on records of its own. Japan classifies the islet as part of Okinoshima in the Oki district of the Shimane prefecture. The Japanese call the islet Takeshima. There have been several rounds of dispute over the islet since 1952. The dispute escalated further when Japan's Shimane prefecture assembly designated February 22, 2005, to be "Takeshima Day," a declaration meant to reinforce Japan's claim to the islet. Since then, there have been furious demonstrations and protests against Japan's claim.[22]

Since Yŏngwŏl is part of north Kyŏngsang province, of which Dokdo is an integral part, its citizens became angry about Japan's territorial claim. In response to the move made by the Shimane prefecture of Japan, citizens of Yŏngwŏl organized a mass protest against Japan in March 2005. Tomoko recalls the mayor of the city calling her husband, Ch'ŏl-su, before the protest gathering. The mayor asked him to serve as the head of the anti-Japanese rally. Tomoko believes this request was strategic and symbolic. If the protest was led by a man who was married to a Japanese woman, the symbolic effect would maximize the impact of the protest. Ch'ŏl-su could hardly refuse his role as chair of the demonstration because of his wife's Japanese identity. It was on short notice, but Tomoko's entire family attended the gathering. Tomoko came dressed in traditional Japanese garb as she usually does when attending a city event. On this occasion, she did not think through this decision very carefully.

The crowd carried anti-Japanese placards. They shouted and chanted anti-Japanese slogans. They burned Japanese flags. As the protest became more intense, Tomoko felt pressured to trample on the Japanese flag. She did not know what to do. She tried to understand Koreans' anti-Japanese sentiment. Nonetheless, as a Japanese national, she could not tread on the flag of her native country. Sensing her difficult position, Tomoko's mother-in-law helped Tomoko to slip through the crowd and escape. Tomoko was grateful to her mother-in-law for her smart thinking. When it was over and the mob mentality broke its hold over the gathering, she spoke to several people in the community who had attended the protest. They told Tomoko, "We did not mean for you to do that, and we all understand you. We believe that you are one of us." Such comments are one reason why Tomoko does not feel she has been discriminated against for being Japanese.

Later, Tomoko heard that in some other towns, some churches had asked all brides from Japan married to Korean men to dress up in traditional Korean clothes (*hanbok*) and bow to members of the congregation as a gesture of public apology. Knowing this had taken place, some women at Tomoko's church told her not to do that, even if the church were to adopt the same practice. In fact, it never happened in her church and in the city as a whole. She regrets that Japanese who have nothing to do with the territorial disputes between Japan and Korea are sometimes trapped and put in an uncomfortable position.

Tomoko believes that her children have not been discriminated against in school by their peers for coming from a multicultural family. In fact, Tomoko has enjoyed her status as a foreign guest, even if she is not a fully integrated member of the community. I concur with her perception and compare it to my own time spent living in a foreign country. When I used to live in a small town in the American South, I was always addressed as "doctor" and was seldom if ever addressed on a first-name basis, as was the case with others around me. In that way I stood out and was not a fully integrated member of the community.

Her Career Ambition and Her Obsession with Her Children's Education

Tomoko is a committed member of her chosen religious faith, and she does not regret that her marriage was arranged by the church. Instead, she is determined to make the most of her situation in the future. When she was younger—during high school and junior college years—she was a multitalented person. She created art, played piano, and studied nursing, etc. Now, she emphasizes her experience living in Korea and speaking the language competently. She also emphasizes her tie with the Japanese language and culture. She seems to be doing what she can to be the best housewife, daughter-in-law, and mother of three children. At the same time, Tomoko would like to cultivate her own career as a professional. She has set three goals: First, she would like to attain a four-year college degree; second, she would like to play an active role in promoting cultural exchange between Japan and Korea; third, she would like to provide the best educational opportunities she can for her three children.

First of all, Tomoko has committed herself to pursuing a professional career. To do that, she realized that she has to have a four-year college degree (a bachelor's degree). She told me, "I am good enough to teach the Korean language to Japanese who would like to learn the Korean language, and, also, I can teach Japanese to Koreans who would like to learn the Japanese language. Actually, I have been teaching some informally. But I cannot be certified officially because I have only a junior college degree (an associate's degree). So, even if I passed the Korean language competency examination with fourth degree (4 *kŭp*) certification, I would remain a private tutor. For a certified position, I have to have a four-year college degree."

When I visited her home in 2009, she was in the process of inquiring into the application procedure at a college in Taegu, the provincial capital of north Kyŏngsang province and the third largest city in Korea, where there are several colleges and universities. However, it would be difficult for her to take courses at any university in Taegu because it is about twenty-eight miles away. To travel there takes about an hour and a half either by car or by train. In order to overcome the problem of travel, she chose an online university, where students can take classes via the Internet. When she applied to a cyber university, she was accepted with a full scholarship. Since she already has an associate's degree, she received transfer credit for junior college courses. She is at the level of a sophomore. She is thinking ahead toward graduate school. If she finishes her bachelor's degree successfully, she could certainly go on to graduate school to become a professional.

Second, she is determined to dedicate her time and effort to playing the role of cultural broker between the languages and cultures of Japan and Korea. She teaches Japanese language and culture classes at local and regional schools. The schools have benefited immensely from the instruction, as it broadens students' parochial perspectives. She said, "It is regrettable to see that foreign brides are not trying to mingle with other parents of Korean students in local schools where their children attend. Perhaps it is because of their incompetence in the Korean language, I guess." Not only does she teach at school, she also actively participates and even chairs the Committee for Cultural Exchange between Korea and Japan (*Han'il Munhwa Kyoryu Hoeŭi*) in the region. Since she has an intimate relationship with other foreign brides in general and Japanese brides in particular, she has been a valuable leader for the committee. She maintains a good reputation in the community, and leaders in the community appreciate her contributions.

Third, she shows a keen interest in her children's education. Like other Korean parents, Tomoko wants to provide the best education possible for her children. Indeed, most Korean parents are obsessed with their children's education. The great emphasis on education in Korea has brought about a highly competitive entrance examination system described as "examination hell." Many Korean parents are determined to sacrifice everything so that their children can obtain good scores on the College Scholastic Ability Test (CSAT). Most Koreans seem to think that receiving degrees from top-tier universities is almost the same as passing the high civil service examination (*kwagŏ*) during dynastic times. Graduates of the nation's top universities have a better chance of obtaining employment in government and leading businesses, and even have a better chance of attracting desirable marriage partners.

In order to enter a first-tier university, a student's preparation has to start in kindergarten. What school one can attend is determined by residency within the districts, and preference for certain school districts affects where people choose to live. Seoulites tend to move from poor school districts to better ones within Seoul. A school district located south of the Han River called Kangnam (literally meaning south of the Han River) is known to be the best. Kangnam's many private tutoring institutes, called *hakwŏn* (equivalent to Japan's *juku*), are crowded with students. Competition on entrance examinations in Japan, as Tomoko had experienced in her school years, might be as severe, or even worse, than it is in Korea.[23] In order to take advantage of these resources, parents who can afford it purchase houses or apartments in the district, while others rent a room or apartment in order to meet the residency requirement. Because of the demand, real estate prices in that district are outrageously high.

Parenthetically, Korean mothers obsessed with their children's education are aptly called "Kangnam mothers." The Kangnam mother phenomenon is also prevalent in Japan. Tomoko herself went to a *juku* when she was young, so she is familiar with the competitiveness. Tomoko's zeal for her children's education is no less than that of the Kangnam mothers. Perhaps it may even be greater.

Tomoko does more than the most devoted Kangnam mothers. While most Korean mothers only emphasize the Korean language in their children's education, Tomoko gives her children bilingual instruction. She teaches Japanese to her children at home using Japanese school textbooks she brought from Japan. Assuming that young children can learn two or more languages simultaneously without difficulty—as demonstrated by most European children—she started teaching them the two languages side by side. According to a survey conducted by the Ministry for Health, Welfare and Family Affairs from May to November 2009, the problem of speech impediment is widespread among children in multicultural families. Of 121,935 children of multicultural families throughout the country, almost 40 percent were found to suffer from improper language development and some form of speech impediment.[24] Tomoko's children, however, do not have a noticeable accent when speaking Korean, and they excel in school. Perhaps it is because Tomoko is fluent in Korean.

As practice in the Japanese language, Tomoko's children talk to their Japanese grandmother over the phone. I went to Wakayama, Japan, in March 2010 with Tomoko and her eleven-year-old son T'ae-ho. Tomoko was visiting her mother, who was recovering from a minor surgery. She wanted T'ae-ho to attend a Japanese school for two weeks to acquire some experience in a Japanese school. When we arrived in Japan, I wondered whether T'ae-ho could speak any Japanese because he did not speak it at all on the first day of the visit. He clammed up, so to speak. On the second day, however, when we visited the Wakayama Castle with several others, he started to talk to his mother in Japanese and converse fluently with his cousin, Tomoko's sister's son, who lives with his maternal grandmother. If Tomoko continues her bilingual instruction, her children will benefit from growing up in a multicultural family. In fact, in November 2010, T'ae-ho was nominated by the county to participate in a national bilingual contest for children of multicultural families.

Looking to the future, Tomoko was not sure whether she would remain in Yŏngwŏl for the rest of her life, relying on the limited income generated by the vineyard, even if her family income is higher than that of most multicultural families. She seems not to like living in a rural town after having grown up in an urban milieu in Wakayama and Osaka. She knows that there are very limited career opportunities available in a rural town. More important, she knows that the quality of education her children would receive in a rural town could not compare to that available in a large city such as Seoul, especially the Kangnam district. She casually told me during our conversation that her husband told her, "I don't mind going to Japan, if I can get a decent job there." She might go back to Japan and become a certified Korean language teacher. She could continue to play a pivotal role as a culture broker between Japanese and Korean cultures. Even if she were naturalized as a Korean citizen, she would still retain her Japanese nationality. It may be that not only is her ethnic identity and nationality strong, but she also likes to have options: career options, choices of places to reside, and many others.

An Incompatibility between Tomoko's Aspirations and the Role as Being a Dutiful Housewife

The more that Tomoko receives recognition from leaders of her community, the more her husband and mother-in-law worry about her. While at first they supported her involvement in community activities, they now express worries over whether she can remain the wife of a farmer in a rural community, far from cultural and educational activities. Their concern grew only larger when Tomoko enrolled in a four-year college.

Most Korean men who marry foreign brides and have attained only a limited education do not want their wives to become professional persons. They are even reluctant for their wives to make contact with outsiders. They worry that their wives might eventually leave them. It is an irony that most Korean husbands wish their wives to be upwardly mobile while remaining homemakers, good mothers, and dutiful daughters-in-law. For these reasons, the CUK's scholarship program, partially funded by Goldman Sachs, may not be as vital as I hoped it would be, if Korean husbands do not support their wives in pursuing college scholarships. Tomoko has to be careful in her pursuit of professional advancement so that she does not risk alienating her Korean family. No doubt, though, Tomoko has the potential to go far.

WINNER OF THE 2008 "MOST FILIAL DAUGHTER-IN-LAW" AWARD

The second story I want to relate in this chapter is the story of forty-two-year-old Takako Miyamoto (a pseudonym), a Japanese bride who married forty-seven-year-old Han-bin Lee (pseudonym), a Korean man, through the Unification Church in 1999 in Seoul. When they married, Takako was thirty-one years old and Han-bin was thirty-six years old. After the wedding, they went to live on the outskirts of the city of Mulp'o (a pseudonym), a small rural city in south Kyŏngsang province.

Takako was born in the rural town of Miyaki, Japan. She was the second of three children, having one older brother and one younger sister. Her parents were high school graduates engaged in farming and raising livestock. One might say that Takako was a farm-oriented person. After graduating from high school, she helped her parents raise livestock before getting married.

Although Takako and Tomoko have similarities—both are Japanese nationals, members of the Unification Church, and the wives of Korean men—they differ in other respects. While Tomoko graduated from junior college, Takako has only a high school education. Tomoko is urbane in her values, active in the community, oriented toward her professional goal, and highly involved in her children's education. Because of her background in rural Japan, Takako adapted well to rural life. She is fond of home life and conforms to the existing rules. Unlike Tomoko, Takako is at home on a farm, so she adjusted better to life in Mulp'o than Tomoko adjusted at first to living in Yŏngwŏl.

On September 15, 2009, when I visited Takako's home in Mulp'o, her husband was working at the co-op office, where he inspects and sorts fruit that farmers bring there to sell. His title is "fruit appraiser." According to personnel who work for the office of the Multicultural Family Assisting Center at Mulp'o, Han-bin does not make much money at his seasonal job as a fruit appraiser. It is not known how the couple manages to make a decent living. When I saw Takako's second-story room, it looked very humble. However, I did see a laptop computer, and Takako was very good at using it. She was able to take courses on the Korean language and culture via the CUK's Campaign.

Despite their low income, Takako carries herself well and is polite and humble when receiving a guest. She was one of the most hospitable persons I have ever encountered. She prepared fruit and tea for us. She has two children, a nine-year-old daughter and an eight-year old son. Her daughter was almost a copy of her mother: polite, clever, and beautiful. Her son was good-looking and healthy, but he was restless and hyper. He was so disruptive that it was hard to carry on a conversation in his presence. His older sister tried to take care of him by taking him outside to play with her. Even though she was only one year older than her brother, she behaved so maturely, showing care and love.

The Burden of Japanese Guilt and Filial Piety

At dinner with her family at a local restaurant, Takako's eighty-one-year-old father-in-law, Tong-ho, joined us. He told me about his previous occupation as the branch manager of the delivery department of a leading Korean newspaper. He told me about Takako's untiring care for his eighty-year-old wife when she was sick. Right after the marriage, as soon as she arrived in Mulp'o, Takako started to take care of her mother-in-law, who was sick, physically handicapped (classified as a second-grade disabled person), and immobile without assistance. Takako's mother-in-law was unable to control her bladder and bowels. Takako had to change soiled bed sheets, and at times she had to carry her to the hospital on her back since they have no automobile.

For such dutiful care, everybody in the community talked about her, and finally the city recognized her by awarding her the "Most Filial Daughter-in-Law Award" (*Hyobu-sang*) in 2008. In fact, feature stories about her were reported widely throughout the nation, and Sun Myung Moon's book published in 2009 also carries a feature article about her filial piety.[25] When I asked how she could care for her mother-in-law with so much dedication, compassion, and filial piety, she answered by simply saying, "I just did it in the same way as my mother did for my grandmother." Most people in the community commented that "not many Korean daughters-in-law could do as Takako has done for her mother-in-law." At the time I visited Takako's home, her mother-in-law had been placed in an institution where she could be cared for.

Takako's father-in-law dominated our conversation. He told me about his most difficult years in the Iwatae Coal Mine as a conscript worker mobilized by the Japanese authority during World War II. In fact, during the war, as fighting intensified, Japan carried out a total national mobilization policy and put into effect a variety of extraordinary measures, including the mobilization of Korean manpower. A great many Korean laborers were involuntarily brought to Japan and various war zones to make up for deficient manpower. The comfort women were part of the forced mobilization. Mobilized Koreans were made to work in munitions plants and coal mines, or they were made to perform other kinds of physical labor. Some were sent to war zones. Some 71,941 were sent to Japan, Sakhalin, and Southeast Asia.[26]

Tong-ho's work in the coal mine was so hard that he stayed hungry all the time. At one point Tong-ho escaped from the mine, braving the guards. He walked all the way to Simonoseki, a journey of several days on foot.[27] Finally, he was able to catch a ship going to Pusan, a southern harbor city. He barely made it back to Korea before the war came to an end. Tong-ho told me that he could never forget the ordeal he had to endure in the coal mine and his dramatic escape from it. He said, "How could I not condemn the brutal, inhumane, and atrocious Japanese colonial policy. After conscription, I became viciously anti-Japanese and was a Japan hater."

Tong-ho found it unacceptable when his son mentioned his intent to marry a Japanese woman by arrangement through the church. Tong-ho told me frankly, "I told my son, 'hell no.'" His anger against the Japanese exploded, and his resentment became so strong that he told his son, "If you marry a Japanese woman, I will take your name out of our genealogy, and I will not think of you as my son and a member of our family." Despite his father's vehement opposition to the marriage, on February 7, 1999, Han-bin and Takako were married in Seoul. Then the couple went home to Mulp'o. According to Takako, her parents-in-law, especially her father-in-law, did not even open the door for the newlyweds.

Later, Tong-ho and his wife ended up living with their Japanese daughter-in-law. It was Tong-ho, instead of Takako, who told me about domestic relations between them. He treated his daughter-in-law harshly, at times abusing her verbally. Tong-ho told her, "My treatment of you is nothing compared to what the Japanese did to me when I was a conscripted worker in a Japanese mine." Whenever he abused her, Tong-ho said, "She politely told me, 'On behalf of the Japanese who mistreated you and other Koreans during colonization, I apologize to you.'" Tong-ho said that she never showed any discontent at his verbal abuse. Nor did she grumble over his moaning about what the Japanese had done to Koreans. At times, Tong-ho made anti-Japanese statements at clan meetings in the presence of Takako, but she took it well. Every clan member has praised her for her humble attitude and polite manners. Most of all, Tong-ho was impressed by her filial piety in taking care of her sick mother-in-law. Tong-ho told me, "Through Tomoko I learned that, even if I could not forget what I went through during my time as a conscripted worker, I should not direct my anti-Japanese feelings at individual Japanese." Tong-ho said, "Takako taught me the difference between the Japanese colonial policy and innocent Japanese." In fact, some Japanese have been and still are sympathetic to Koreans who had to endure the colonial experience. Takako must be one of those.

Takako, who said nothing while her father-in-law spoke, commented quietly, "I can understand my father-in-law's sentiment against Japan and the Japanese. If I were him, I might have done the same. If I could have any wish come true, I hope that he would forgive what the Japanese did to Korea and Koreans, and especially to him." Tong-ho replied, "I did. As you know, I don't do that anymore." Even if Japan as a country might be reluctant to admit its guilt for past wrongs, Takako, as an individual, has done her share of atonement. Takako can play the same role as Tomoko is playing—that of a cultural broker promoting fellowship and friendship between Japan and Korea. All in all, I had a pleasant dinner with Takako and her Korean family. In all honesty, when Tong-ho accompanied his daughter-in-law to our interview, I thought that his presence might inhibit Takako from talking freely, but it turned to be better having Tong-ho present, as he told me his feelings openly.

More Committed to Her Religion Than to Her Career

Any attempt to compare Tomoko and Takako might not be fair. Takako is slightly older and less educated than Tomoko. While Tomoko is urbane, Takako is at home on a rural farm. Tomoko is more career-oriented and less committed to her religious beliefs. Takako is more home-oriented and is deeply committed to her faith. Takako believes that her marriage is a God-given fate. She said, "To take care of an old and sick mother-in-law and to marry a foreigner are duties passed to one by the hand of God." She expresses no regret nor complains about her present situation. While Tomoko's sphere of interaction is communitywide and she is involved in various nonchurch activities, Takako limits her activities to the church. She sometimes attends church-organized special activities such as yacht sailing, swimming, and camping. She does not actively participate in the school activities of her children.

Tomoko's and Takako's involvement in and attitude toward their children's education are different. While Tomoko likes to teach both languages, Korean and Japanese, to her children, Takako said that she does not want to teach her children Japanese. She wants her children to learn only Korean at this early stage because she believes that "if I teach them Japanese, their native Korean accents and pronunciations might not be the same as native Korean children." She wants her children to be able to speak the Korean language the same way as native Korean children do. Since her children are doing well in school, especially with the Korean language, she does not believe that her children have any speech impediment. They are just as normal as any other native Korean children. Regarding the scholastic performance of her children, she said, "Unless someone tries really hard to discern my children's identity, no one can tell they have a Japanese mother. They look the same as other Korean children, and they talk just like the others do. Thus, they have never been discriminated against for anything."

When I asked about her future, I learned that she still retains her Japanese citizenship and stays in Korea as a permanent resident. For the time being, she is satisfied where she is and what she is doing. She said, "If any change would come, it must be God's will, and I will take it as it comes." Indeed, she is not pursuing any professional career or has any plans to go back home after her children have grown up. While Tomoko has visited her mother and sister in Japan several times and calls her Japanese relatives frequently, Takako has never been back to Japan since she left in 1999. She said that she did not have any time at all while taking care of her mother-in-law. Only recently has that changed since her mother-in-law's placement in an institution. She is indeed a devoted wife, daughter-in-law, and full-time mother.

A Full-time College Student

In my observation of her, Takako appeared to be very clever and very skillful in using a PC to access the Internet. She has been polishing her IT skills ever since she began taking courses as part of the CUK's Campaign. She was willing to take advantage of a special admission program created for foreign brides who are married to Korean men and living in Korea. She applied for a scholarship and was admitted to the CUK with a scholarship. Just before enrolling as a freshman in January 2010, the university lost contact with her. The university admission office was wondering what had happened to her. Later, someone reported to the school that her husband was killed in an automobile accident. I was reluctant to call her or visit her. I have been told that she overcame the tragedy and is now enrolled. She is also working in the afternoon. Since it is an online university, her daytime job does not interfere with her studies. The tragedy that befell her husband might cause Takako to change her mind about a career. Perhaps her sister, who also married a Korean man and lives in the vicinity of Seoul, might give her some comfort. At present, it is uncertain what Takako will do in a long run after the death of her husband.

In summing up, life histories differ from person to person, even for two women married through the same ecclesiastical arrangement. The life stories of two Japanese women can in no way speak definitively for the 5,326 Japanese women married to Korean men. Nor do their stories epitomize all international marriages arranged by a religious organization. Quite the contrary, in fact. As I have tried to demonstrate in this chapter, each life story of a foreign bride differs from others in significant ways. In full knowledge of this, I have made an effort to tell personal life histories as a way of understanding the human condition of foreign brides who live in Korea. As seasoned anthropologists have recognized, and as I quoted earlier, life histories are "useful for examining the patterns of general values, foci of cultural interests, and perceptions of social and natural relationships."[28]

It appears that as long as foreign brides play their roles as good mothers, loving husbands, and dutiful daughters-in-law (as traditional Korean family norms require) they will be received well. Nonetheless, it would be a pity were they not to use their talents for their families and Korean society. There are many talented foreign brides who could pursue professional careers and make positive contributions to their adoptive society.

6

Foreign Brides Who Fell in Love with Korean Men

The previous chapters discussed the life stories of foreign brides who married Korean men either by arrangement with a professional international marriage broker or with a religious organization. This chapter tells the life stories of foreign brides who married Korean men because they fell in love. Owing to the overwhelming number of arranged marriages through international marriage brokers (and the criticisms surrounding such marriages), stories of couples that married out of love have been mostly overlooked or ignored. In order to present a balanced view, this chapter describes marriages of romantic love and tells stories of these foreign brides adjusting to life in Korea.

A WOMAN FROM HUNCHUN (HUNQUN), CHINA

It was on June 16, 2007, when I first met a thirty-three-year-old Chinese woman named Wang Qun (a pseudonym) in the conference room of the CUK. On that day I announced the winner of the autobiography contest for foreign brides sponsored by my university, the CUK. The contest is part of the CUK's Campaign. Qun's entry, the winning autobiography, began like this:

> Having lived eight years in Korea, I am now seeing my loneliness and sad feelings, which I had when I first came to Korea, change gradually toward overflowing joy and happiness. I came to Korea in October 1999. In 1995, when I was a senior in college, I met a Korean missionary in Russia (Vladivostok); we fell in love with each other and promised to marry. Upon graduation, I was offered a good job with the Chinese government and was assigned to Vladivostok to assist Chinese businessmen in Russia. It was a well-paying job, but I had to

give it up because I promised the Korean missionary, my would-be husband, that I would marry him. I promised him that I would go with him wherever he went as a missionary to share the joy and sadness together. It was not an easy choice for me to make. . . . [She concluded her description, writing,] By and large, most Koreans are polite, well-mannered, and warm. I hope that someday when I visit my native country [she used the expression "my mother's country"], I can brag about Korea—my adopted country—as a respected nation in the world community.

Qun has been naturalized and has attained Korean citizenship.

Qun was the most beautiful, elegant, and graceful Chinese women I have ever encountered. She had a total command of the Korean language—accurate pronunciation, a proper choice of words, and syntactically sound sentences in her writing. She spoke the Korean language better than I did, except for an occasional North Korean accent on some words. Her forty-four-year-old husband, Lee Chong-o (a pseudonym), who accompanied her, was handsome and cheerful. He brought along their cute eight-year-old son to the award ceremony. It looked as though they were an ideal couple.

At the time she won the award, Qun was working as a translator of Russian and Chinese on the islets of Ch'ŏn-do (a pseudonym) in the south Chŏlla province. Chong-o was minister of the Full Gospel Church in the city of Ch'ŏn-do.[1] Ch'ŏn-do is the third largest island (430 square kilometers) of Korea, and its population was 34,119 in 2009. However, the island is experiencing a steady population decline of some six hundred to seven hundred persons annually.

Qun as a Native of China's Gateway to Eastern Russia and North Korea

Qun was the second child of a college-educated father and a mother with a high school education. Her father was an ex–civil servant in the local government, and her mother has been a full-time housewife throughout her married life. Qun's family was not rich but comfortable enough financially to provide a college education for the children. They even provided Qun with an opportunity to study abroad in Vladivostok, Russia.

Qun's extraordinary proficiency in the Korean language and her marriage to a Korean may have some direct and/or indirect connection to her birthplace in Hunchun. Hunchun, a county-level city, is located in the Yanbian Korean Autonomous prefecture in the Jilin province of northeast China. It borders North Korea (north Hamgyŏng province) and Russia (Primorsky Krai), has over 250,000 inhabitants, and stretches for 5,145 square kilometers. Yanbian is south of Heilongjiang, east of Jilin's Baishan City, north of North Korea's north Hamgyŏng province, and west of Russia. Yanbian is designated an autonomous prefecture due to the large number of ethnic Koreans (estimated to be some 867,048 in 2007) living in the region.[2]

Korean migration into this region began at the tail end of the nineteenth century. Those who came were for the most part escaping economic hardship under Japanese economic exploitation.[3] Because there were so many Korean-speaking ethnic Koreans around her, it may have been natural for Qun to learn the Korean language from peers and friends. Since Hunchun is adjacent to three countries, she also could have learned Russian in the same way. Since she lived with so many ethnic Koreans, Qun might not have felt that Koreans were aliens or strangers.

After finishing high school, Qun entered Yanbian University and majored in the Russian language. The university was founded in 1949. It is a provincial public university of the People's Republic of China, located at Yanji, in the Yanbian Korean Autonomous Prefecture in the Jilin province. Yanbian University's aim is to educate the Korean minority in northeast China; it is the only university in China that has both Korean and Chinese as official languages. The student population is over sixteen thousand. Looking ahead to a career that would capitalize on her Russian language skills, Qun wanted to study at a university in Russia. She preferred to study at a university in Vladivostok on account of its geographical proximity. At the time, many Chinese traders and businessmen were travelling to Russia, Vladivostok in particular. Vladivostok is Russia's largest port city on the Pacific Ocean and the administrative center of Primorsky Krai. It is situated at the head of Golden Horn Bay, not far from Russia's border with China and North Korea. It is the home port of the Russian Pacific fleet.[4]

Before she graduated from Yanbian University, Qun transferred to Far Eastern National University in Vladivostok to study the Russian language. Established in 1899 as an institution of higher education, Far Eastern National University was closed in the late 1930s under Joseph Stalin and later reopened in 1956. Currently, the university is top rated, with over four thousand faculty members and over forty thousand students; it is the oldest and largest university in eastern Russia.

Encountering a Korean Missionary in the Romantic City of Vladivostok

In 1995, when she was a college senior preparing for graduation, Qun went to Lenin Square in the city of Vladivostok, along with several of her friends, to take a walk and chat.[5] She encountered a Korean missionary, Chong-o she later learned, who was sent there by the Full Gospel Church (*Sunbogŭm Kyohoe*). He was preaching to the Russian audience in Korean, and an ethnic Korean Russian was translating his sermon. The translator was a *Koryŏ-in*, meaning literally a Korean descendent whose ancestors immigrated to Russia from the Koryŏ dynasty (918–1392). Koreans immigrated to Russia, especially to the Maritime Province, including Vladivostok, during the imperial Chinese dynasty of Qing (1644–1911), which is equivalent to the later part of the Chŏson dynasty (1392–1910). A further wave of immigration took place after the Japanese annexation of Korea in 1910. Although they were no longer living under the Koryŏ dynasty in the Korean peninsula, they were familiarly referred to as the Koryŏ people (*Koryŏ-in*). A good many Koreans, including Korean independence fighters, immigrated to Russia following the nineteenth-century Japanese invasion of the Korean peninsula.

The translator for Chong-o's preaching was a Korean Russian physician whose grandfather had immigrated to the Maritime Province after Japan occupied Korea in the early 1900s. Since Qun was able to speak Korean fluently and was curious about Chong-o's preaching, she talked to him. He was delighted to meet her and was excited to learn that she could speak both Russian and Korean fluently and was very familiar with Vladivostok. During my interview with Chong-o in February 2010, he told me that "it was so exciting to meet Qun that I almost felt like hugging her." It just so happened that Chong-o's Korean Russian translator was just about ready to leave Vladivostok for another part of Russia. In fact, it was his last time translating for Chong-o. If Chong-o could not find another bilingual translator soon, he would not be able to continue his missionary work in Russia. Thus meeting Qun by accident was almost a miracle for him. Destiny seemed to have had a hand in bringing them together.

Because Chong-o could not wait any longer before recruiting a new translator, he asked Qun whether she would be available to interpret for his next sermon. Qun was hesitant about saying yes. Before coming to Russia, she went through a series of orientation sessions for Chinese students planning to study abroad. Qun was instructed to keep a distance from strangers, foreigners in particular. (Even though China has begun to open itself up economically to the outside world more than ever, it is still a communist country in its political system.) Despite such a hindrance, Chong-o was persistent and persuasive in his effort to recruit Qun.

Chong-o made frequent contact with Qun, trying to persuade her to be his interpreter. However, Qun did not want to meet Chong-o alone because she was afraid that a rumor could spread, a rumor that she was dating a stranger—a foreigner no less. At this point in time, Qun preferred that Chong-o visit her at her residence, one she shared with an elderly Russian woman. The woman could serve as a guarantor that their meetings were about business, not romantic. Chong-o visited Qun so often that the Russian woman might have suspected their relationship. However, at that time neither Qun nor Chong-o had any feelings of love for each other. (I suspect, though, that as Qun is so beautiful, Chong-o had to have been attracted to her.) Chong-o was so persistent that Qun finally agreed to interpret his sermons.

On the first occasion, Qun had some difficulty translating the sermon. Although she was proficient in the Korean language, she lacked any knowledge of Christianity in general and the Bible in particular. Unable to understand the meaning of the examples Chong-o cited in his sermon, Qun could not translate them properly. Qun told me during my interview with her that it was the most embarrassing and humiliating experience she has ever had. From that moment on, Qun began to study the Bible intensively. The more she read the Bible, the more she became interested in it. Whether or not she was aware of the fact, she found herself becoming immersed in Christianity. At the same time, since they were so frequently in contact, Qun and Chong-o began to like each other's company very much. However, they denied falling in love at that time. They told me that their feelings of love did not begin until they were separated from each other upon Chong-o's return to Korea.

In 1996, while this was going on, Qun graduated from Far Eastern University and had to go back to China. Chong-o was told by his church to return to Korea. They both had to leave Vladivostok and would be separated from each other. Upon returning to Hunchun, Qun had a lucrative job under the Ministry of Foreign Affairs assisting Chinese businessmen in Vladivostok with their business dealings. She had the opportunity to meet many Chinese businessmen. When she returned to Vladivostok, Qun attended a Korean Presbyterian church in Vladivostok and became a committed Christian. After his return to Korea, Chong-o called Qun virtually every day. At that time, the rate for international phone calls was outrageously high. They both told me that their phone calls were so expensive that they were spending most of their money paying phone bills. It was during this time that they realized they were in love.

During my interview with Qun I asked her what aspects of Chong-o were the most attractive to her and led her to marry him. Qun told me, "Of course he is a good-looking man [he is indeed], but more than his physical looks, I admired him for his indomitable courage." According to Qun, at the time Chong-o lived in Vladivostok, law and order were lacking. The situation was almost chaotic. Gangsters or *mafiosi* dominated the city. Lurking in the entrances of apartment buildings, muggers waited to steal money from incoming people. Such crimes occurred even more frequently in inexpensive apartments. The primary target was foreigners, especially Asians, Koreans in particular. Even though it was dangerous to live in such a building, Chong-o, with his meager missionary means, could only afford to live in an apartment with lax security. One day, at the stairway of his apartment building, several gangsters suddenly attacked him with knives. He was badly wounded and lost a lot of blood. His face was torn up, and he had to get several stitches at the hospital. Qun told me that even though Chong-o carried out exhausting missionary work in the face of apathetic audiences, he seemed never to have been too discouraged to continue. Nor for that matter did he speak ill of the mobsters. Even in his hospital bed, Chong-o did not express bitter feelings against his assailants.

The other aspect Qun admired most about Chong-o was his high standard of morality. Qun said that Chong-o might be a wretchedly poor missionary financially, but he was the richest man morally and spiritually that she had ever met. Chong-o looked especially virtuous next to some of the Chinese businessmen Qun had translated for in Vladivostok. She witnessed risqué private lives. Among businessmen and government officials, rampant rumors and reports of sexual indiscretion were not unusual. At least one time during her college years and even after she had a governmental job, she envied the elite occupations of business executives and high-ranking civil servants. But, after seeing some sleazy behaviors from those elite people, Qun began to envy the lives of clerics who maintain high moral and ethical standards. The more she learned about the world of business and politics, the more she began to like Chong-o. Qun told me that she chose to become the wife of a clergyman, and she is committed to living the life of a clergyman's spouse.

In 1998 Chong-o had to return to Korea following a change of leadership in his church. He got caught up in power struggles within the church. After his return, he decided to go to Australia for his overseas study. He was trying to redirect his career. But his life in Australia was not easy. The language barrier was a major stumbling block; he also struggled to support himself financially. Nonetheless, he told me that despite his hardships he did not stop calling Qun, even if he had to skip meals. He said that his bill for overseas phone calls reached unbelievable amounts. He admitted that he was unable to concentrate on his studies, the reason for his being there. Finally, after less than a year, Chong-o came back to Korea.

Fortunately, the year when he returned to Korea, Chong-o was reinstated in his ministry and assigned to a small pioneering church (*kaech'ŏk kyohoe*) on a remote island called Ch'ŏn-do on the extreme southern tip of the Korean peninsula. There were very few members of the congregation on the island, so the offering box was empty at most times. Moreover, Chong-o could not expect any donations from wealthy donors. Most who attended services were not regular members, and they were economically and socially deprived. Some who attended were foreign brides who had married Korean men.

Despite these difficulties, Chong-o was never tardy when calling to convey his love to Qun. Finally, via phone calls, Qun and Chong-o agreed to get married as soon as possible. By separating for a year or so, they had tested their love and realized they wanted to make a life together. Only two steps were left: One was getting parental approval, even if less than a blessing, from both families; and the other was getting permission from two governments. This was an essential requirement for Qun. She needed an exit visa from the Chinese government to leave China, and she needed an entry visa from the Korean government to enter into Korea.

Obstacles Are Everywhere

When Qun asked her parents for their approval of her plan to marry, they were adamantly opposed to it. Her father opposed the match much more so than her mother did. He went on and on about many potential problems that could arise in an international marriage as a result of cultural differences. Furthermore, her father did not particularly care for Chong-o's career as a clergyman of meager financial means. If Qun were to marry him, she would shoulder a heavy financial burden. The influence of long years spent living in a communist country did not predispose Qun's father to think well of Chong-o. He did not say so out loudly, but after seeing most Chinese Koreans in his own province living with the secondary status of an ethnic minority, his impression of Koreans was not particularly positive. He told Qun, "I did not provide a good education for you to marry a foreigner." He never forgot to remind her that he even supported her overseas study at a fine Russian university. Her mother was not necessarily supportive of Qun's marriage, but she was more sympathetic to the idea than her father was. Qun realized that at least there was a chance she could persuade her mother to be on her side, so she persistently urged her mother to support her marriage.

The situation with Chong-o's parents was no different; their opposition to an international marriage was just about as strong. Their opposition, however, had some additional dimensions: the negative public image of foreign brides who marry Korean men. There were, and still are to some degree, stereotypes of foreign brides as troublemakers who cause family squabbles that lead to verbal and physical abuse, and even divorce. Most of all, they had a reputation for constantly nagging their husbands about money. In fact, a significant number of foreign brides do marry Korean men to assist their natal parents back home with living expenses. I have witnessed so many family squabbles and even seen divorces take place because Korean men did not keep their promise to support their bride's natal families. Some men make such a commitment before marriage but then find themselves unable to honor it. Chong-o's parents did not want their daughter-in-law to be classed with foreign brides whose reasons for marrying are primarily financial. They said, "We could not explain to everybody, saying 'my son and daughter-in-law are not the same as others. They married because they loved each other.'" It was not easy for Chong-o to persuade his parents and get their blessing.

Qun thought that if Chong-o could meet her parents and appeal personally to them, they might give permission, even if they would not welcome him with open arms and an open heart. Qun was confident that her parents would like Chong-o because he is good-looking and has a cheerful personality. Qun found such an opportunity at her second brother's wedding in 1998. Chong-o attended the wedding in Hunchun, met Qun's parents, and asked their permission. Their attitude was "how dare he attend a family wedding without their approval in advance." In their opinion, Chong-o's worst mistake was presenting a document issued by the Korean government stating that Chong-o could marry Qun. The plan backfired for Qun and Chong-o, as Qun's parents were furious over the document and were adamantly opposed to the marriage.

An additional temptation to thwart their marriage came from Qun's employer at Vladivostok. Knowing that Qun might resign from her job to marry, her employer offered to raise her salary threefold. It was an unprecedented and surprising offer. Not many people could turn down such an exceptional offer. Qun's father could not believe how his daughter could turn down such a lucrative offer to marry a foreign man.

Almost all parents think that their children are superior to others; hence no potential partner could ever be good enough for their children. Also, in the process of making concessions, most mothers tend to be more sympathetic to their children's choice of a prospective mate than most fathers. When there is disagreement between fathers and mothers, mothers almost always win over fathers. Fathers may yell a lot in the process, but quiet wives tend to win over husbands in the end. It was no exception in the case of Chong-o and Qun. Qun's mother persuaded her husband not to oppose his daughter's marriage so vehemently. While Qun's father pretended not to give permission, her mother told her that she would go with her to Beijing for an exit visa application.

Obtaining an exit visa in China was not any easier than winning parental approval. It required elaborate documents and papers, including a certificate certifying that Qun is single and was never married before. The document also had to certify her and her fiancée's intention to marry, along with detailed plans for the marriage itself. If Qun could not meet these requirements, she could not apply for an exit visa. Without an exit visa, she could not apply for an entry visa from the office of the Korean Consulate General. Since Qun went to Beijing, she could apply for the entry visa from the Korean Consulate General's office in Beijing.

When Qun and her mother went to Beijing, they learned that processing all the documents in Beijing would be notoriously slow and complicated. Sometimes it can take several months. Since the process takes so long, most applicants cannot afford to stay in hotels or motels. Instead, most rent rooms in private houses or cottages, similar to bed and breakfast inns in the United States. However, such facilities in Beijing do not compare favorably with their American counterparts. While inexpensive, they are also filthy and crowded, with several people sharing one room.

Qun's application was rejected the first round as soon as she filed it. While Qun and her mother were staying in Beijing, they learned that there were many people waiting for the same approval. Some wound up drinking, smoking, and engaging in immoral behaviors out of frustration and disappointment. Qun and her mother had begun to worry about how long they would have to wait in Beijing and what might happen to them while they were there. Upon a second round of applying, Qun got lucky. Her application materials were approved. Qun and her mother were very surprised that they were rejected only once and approved so quickly. Everyone awaiting approval of their papers envied their good fortune. They were free from a trying, uncomfortable situation.

They later learned that Chong-o used all the contacts he had in Korea and mobilized them to assist Qun's application. Now, Qun was ready to apply for an entry visa at the Korean Consulate General's office. Again, Chong-o pulled all the strings he had. It was a long and complicated procedure, but finally Qun was set to leave her homeland of China and start a new life in her adopted country of Korea.

A Wedding and a New Life in Korea

Qun landed at Inch'on Airport, in the vicinity of Seoul, on September 28, 1999. From the airport, she had to take a long trip to Mokp'o in south Chŏlla province, where her wedding was scheduled to take place the next day. At first, she wondered why her wedding was scheduled to take place in Mokp'o instead of where her groom was doing ministerial work in Ch'ŏn-do. It was a small church wedding, but there were plenty of blessings from family members and church people.

Mokp'o is a port city on the southwestern tip of the Korean peninsula. The city has turned out so many excellent artists, musicians, and writers it is known as the "city of art." At first, Qun thought she would be living in Mokp'o. Their wedding took place there because it is the largest and closest city to Ch'ŏn-do, where the newlyweds were supposed to take up residence. When the couple left Mokp'o after the wedding, it was already dark, so Qun did not know where she was going. By automobile it normally takes about fifty minutes to an hour to travel from Mokp'o to Ch'ŏn-do. However, the trip requires crossing a long bridge. Before a bridge was built that connected Ch'ŏn-do to the mainland, one had to cross by ferry boat. Qun told me, jokingly, during our interview that on that night she wondered where Chong-o was taking her: "I thought he was going to sell me to someone." She was really disappointed to see poverty-stricken scenes of small houses in farming and fishing hamlets. It was incomparable to the city of Mokp'o.

Qun was shocked even further when she arrived at Chong-o's cottage. It was not decent enough for the newlyweds to live in on the night after the wedding. Qun thought that since he was a minister of a church, Chong-o should have housing provided by the church. But since his was a pioneering church, there was no such perk given to the minister. In the single room, there was a single bed, which squeaked noisily as she tried to sit on it. Besides the bed, there was no chair or couch in the room where one could sit. Actually the room was so tiny that there was no room for a chair, couch, or tea table. The bathroom was small, shabby, and in need of repair. Qun could see rats running all over. Before marriage, Qun had been determined to endure the humble life of a clergyman's wife. She thought she was prepared for the mental and emotional challenges it would bring, but she did not expect to live in such awful conditions.

Nevertheless, she could not walk away from the situation, knowing how hard she had struggled to get married. She decided that poverty should not be an obstacle in their marriage. While adjusting to living in poverty and carrying out stressful daily work, she made a long-range plan. First, in order to be the wife of a minister in a Christian church, she thought that she should learn more about Christianity. Qun thought that her self-taught knowledge about Christianity was not enough. To attain a formal education in Christian theology, she signed up for correspondence courses offered by a local theology school. At the same time, she convinced Chong-o to take graduate courses in social work because most of his missionary work relates to the field of social work directly or indirectly. Sometime later, he earned his master's degree in social work.

In the meantime, Qun was thinking about a way of earning extra income so that she could help out her husband. She began to assess her own qualifications and thought about how she might apply her skills in her immediate surroundings. The islets of Ch'ŏn-do consist of 230 small islands; of them, over 185 islets are uninhabited. Only forty-five are inhabited by people.

Ch'ŏn-do is well known for three things. One, it is a historical site where Admiral Yi Sun-sin, naval commander of Left Chŏlla province, destroyed the Japanese fleet. During the second attack of Japan, led by Toyotomi

Hideyoshi in 1597, Admiral Yi Sun-sin took advantage of the unusual current of Uldolmok. With metal "turtle ships" (*kŏbuksŏn*), he managed to destroy the Japanese fleet, preventing them from moving north and affecting a link with Japanese land armies. Ch'ŏn-do is separated from the mainland by Myŏngyang Strait, and so this naval event is known as the sweeping victory of Myŏngnyang. Ch'ŏn-do is now spanned by the 484-meter-long Ch'ŏn-do bridge. Apparently the Japanese were unaware of the unusually fast current of Uldolmok, which is under the Ch'ŏn-do bridge. Admiral Yi Sun-sin is regarded as the most respected admiral in Korean history. Bronze statues at the entrance to the bridge commemorate his victory. There is also a statue honoring him in the square of Kwanghwamun, the heart of downtown Seoul.

Also, Ch'ŏn-do is known to be a site where the "Miracle of Moses" takes place annually in the middle of March, according to the lunar calendar.[6] The expression, "Miracle of Moses," was coined in 1971 by the former French ambassador to Korea, Pierre Randy (1971–1975), after he witnessed the scene. Later, Japanese television, NHK, telecast the scene. The miracle is this: In the middle of March a land bridge forms about 2.8 kilometers (1.75 miles) long and 40 meters (0.25 miles) wide. The land bridge forms between Moto-ri and Hoedong-ri, presumably due to the ebb and flow of the tide. It takes about ten to twenty minutes, depending on the sea wind, to form a land bridge. It lasts for one to two hours.

During that time, people can walk along the land bridge and pick up shell-fish, small octopuses, and sea cucumbers. It has been so widely publicized since 1975 that many tourists come just to witness the "miracle." In order to attract tourists, Ch'ŏn-do celebrates an annual festival during the formation of the land bridge. The festival draws tourists from around the country and the world, particularly from China and Japan. One may be surprised to learn that Ch'ŏn-do draws over one million tourists yearly. The number of tourists increases year after year. Qun thought that she might have a role to play in the tourism industry as an interpreter and guide, especially for Chinese and Russian tourists.

Furthermore, since there is a shipyard of Hyundai Heavy Industry near Ch'ŏn-do, which employs over 3,300 (plus 6,639 workers who work as various subcontractors), there are many foreign businesspersons who visit the town. I have been told that among the foreign businesspersons and engineers there are quite a few Russians. When I spent a night in February 2010 at the Hyundai-owned hotel after meeting Qun on my way back home, I encountered several Russian businessmen and engineers in a coffee shop and lounge of the hotel. Were it not for the shipyard, it would be hard to imagine there would be so many foreigners in such a small town. Qun saw an opportunity to play a role using her linguistic skills in Korean, Chinese, and Russian.

Qun decided that her proficiency in Chinese, Korean, and Russian was an ideal combination for the community, but she had to make opportunities happen on her own since few people in the community knew about her knowledge of languages. In order to make her longtime dream a reality, she contacted a local primary school. She inquired about teaching Chinese, but she did not get a definitive answer from the school. In the meantime, as word got around that Qun was willing to teach Chinese to anybody interested in learning it, she began to tutor several people in town. Suddenly, she got an offer from a school on a tiny islet that was not nearby. It was great for Qun to know that some schools were interested in her linguistic knowledge. However, the job came with a meager salary, and to reach the tiny island she had to get up early to catch a ferry boat. Despite this, the job was a good start.

As it became known that she was teaching in a school on another island, people in the town where Qun lives took notice. Eventually the town's school invited her to teach a class. This opportunity was nice because people in the town recognized her credentials. For her, the job was convenient (as she did not leave home early to catch a ferry), and it came with better pay. During this time, the county's tourist bureau realized that her foreign language proficiency was valuable. Although it was a temporary job, she became a full-time translator and guide for the county. Because of this, she gained more self-respect. Around the time when she won the essay contest held by the CUK, she was serving in that capacity for the county.

Despite her stressful financial situation, Qun was able to sustain a normal family life. She knew well that she had to help her husband bring in more income. In spite of this, Qun did not complain to her husband about her situation. She told me, "I might have been very poor, even now, but I never believed that I myself was a poor person. In fact, I am very rich spiritually." While she was struggling to increase the family income, she gave birth to her first child, a son, the year after their marriage in 1999. She had a second child, a daughter, in 2006. While taking care of her two children, she was still able to carry out her social activities.

Perhaps the worst deprivation for Qun, with her two children, her chores, and the work she did as the wife of a clergyman, was the lack of an automobile. Anyone who is familiar with life in farming and fishing villages in rural Korea would understand how hard it is to live without an automobile. There is no public transit available such as one would find in a major metropolitan area. Therefore, those who live in these villages have to walk most of the time.

Since Chong-o was able to devote his time and energy to establishing his pioneering church, he finally built his own church on a hilltop at the edge of downtown Ch'ŏn-do in 2009. It was a small church building, but it could accommodate some one hundred attendees. Chong-o proudly showed me the church and told me, "After I acquired this lot, Qun and I actually built this church." It is made of bright orange adobe and looks exotic, elegant, and charming. It is visible from a distance. The interior is not well furnished, but it has most of the essentials, including benches, tables, a dais, and a lighting system. However, for financial reasons, a heating system was not installed. When I toured the church, I felt quite chilly, even in late February. There were several portable electric heaters sitting around to heat the church.

Qun and Chong-o told me that since it is a pioneering church, most members of the congregation are underprivileged people—economically, socially, and in other ways. Many members are part of multicultural families from various countries. Since Chong-o and Qun knew that I was campaigning on behalf of multicultural families, they were very supportive of my effort. We had a mutual understanding. Most of the congregants are in need of help from the church, so they can offer the church no more than moral support. When I looked at the collection box, it looked empty. When I dropped an envelope into the box, I heard a hollow sound. It must have been empty for quite some time. Nonetheless, Qun and Chong-o were very proud of the church they had built.

When we later went out to a local restaurant for dinner, I noticed that Chong-o was driving a new van. During dinner Chong-o explained to me how he got the van. When Qun and Chong-o went to Mokp'o, where they had their wedding ceremony, they went to a car dealer to rent a car. Unexpectedly they met a former Korean businessman who was doing business in Vladivostok. They knew him well. And he turned out to be the automobile dealer. As they were catching up, the dealer asked Chong-o to drive a van that might be suitable for his missionary work for the church. Chong-o and Qun told me that they met so many people willing to help them. They firmly believe that "God helps those who help themselves."

After obtaining her Korean citizenship, Qun now works for the county as a civil servant dealing with foreign visitors: tourists and foreign investors. In the little spare time she has, she assists multicultural families, especially foreign brides. At times, some of the local people have become so jealous of her work that they have made false accusations about her. Since issues of multiculturalism have become popular, some individuals and organizations, even some local governments, often compete with one another to win grant money to assist multicultural families. Qun and Chong-o were falsely accused of abusing an office space of the county government-owned building by a retired local journalist. Qun and Chong-o were using the office space to assist foreign brides who live in the county for meetings and counseling services, but the journalist brought about litigation because he was competing with Qun and Chong-o for a funding project regarding assistance program for foreign brides. Before the case went to court, however, it was resolved.

A Successful Foreign Bride and the First Naturalized Chinese Korean in Ch'ŏn-do

Now that the church is built, Qun likes to devote more of her time to church activities than to other work. She told me that she was seriously considering quitting her civil servant job to make more time for the church. However, since the county has been well served by her dedicated service, it seems highly unlikely that the county would let her go without protest. Not only is she is well liked by the citizens of the county and its environs, but she is also almost a celebrity. When I dined with the president of the local historical and cultural society, Qun was spoken of favorably. The president asked Chong-o, "How in the world did you end up marrying such a beautiful and charming lady?" Chong-o smiled proudly.

Even if Qun does end up quitting her county job, she is determined to live in Ch'ŏn-do as the first Chinese Korean ever to do so. She wants to serve the church and its congregants. Because of her linguistic talent, she could hold a lucrative job in a bigger city, but she has no longing to move. For this reason, she may be unique as a foreign bride. She does not long to live in a city, acquire wealth, earn fame, or anything like that. She appears to be happy "spiritually"—to use her own word—and has done the best she could have.

Qun's success in adjusting to the Korean way of life can be explained in the following way: First, Qun did not marry Chong-o for financial gain. Qun and Chong-o married based on unconditional love. Also, Qun's natal family is well off, enough so to send her overseas to study in Russia. Her father was an ex-civil servant and has maintained a respectable social status.

Second, Qun's success owes to her not having any unrealistic expectations about Chong-o's future prospects. While some foreign brides might have a wild dream about their future husband winning the lottery or having some similar stroke of luck, Qun knew from the outset that Chong-o was a clergyman with a small income. Qun chose a husband of solid moral character. Since marrying Chong-o, she has become a Christian who loves to help others. She has become as Christian as her husband is.

Third, Qun and Chong-o have maintained a loving, harmonious family life. They have an adorable son and a charming daughter. Their two children are vivacious, cordial, and cheerful. There is an old saying, "If one can cultivate his morals, then one can manage a family [or household]; further, if one can manage his family or household, then he can govern a nation." It would seem that Qun has proven the truth of this old saying. Regardless of income or financial state, Qun and Chong-o have maintained a harmonious family life.

Fourth, as a college graduate, she is educated enough to apply herself in her social and cultural milieu. She has tried to match her talent and knowledge to her circumstances. In so doing, she has earned respect from the community. She feels that she has made a positive contribution to the community. Ultimately, she has become a professional and has earned celebrity status in her community.

Fifth, Qun's self-motivation may have been the most important factor of all. She has been motivated on her own—not by her husband or by outside aid organizations or by local and national government. Qun developed her own adaptive strategies. During the late 1960s, I worked as part of a team evaluating an antipoverty program in Atlanta, Georgia. I observed that many recipients of government aid were not self-motivated. In such a situation, the government cannot motivate people. People must help themselves. Similarly, there are all sorts of aid programs to assist foreign brides as they adjust to Korean society, yet these programs are not effective when foreign brides are not self-motivated. Qun's story shows how important self-motivation is for foreign brides. Regarding this, a growing number of self-motivated foreign brides are critical of the approaches made by Korean government, NGOs, and various volunteer organizations, which have a tendency to provide blanket assistant programs. Instead they are asking for specific programs whereby foreign brides can apply their specific skills and abilities.

On a final note, crucial elements are the nature, personality, and educational background of a foreign bride's Korean spouse. Qun's success is owed in part to her husband, Chong-o, who should receive some credit for the happy outcome. As an old Korean saying has it, "If we are going to unfold a large sheet of a paper, it takes at least two persons to make it straight." Perhaps a better translation would be "One hand clapping never makes a distinct sound."

The characteristics of Qun's life story could not be applied to foreign brides in general. One might say that Qun was able to adjust to life in Korea because of her college education and professional knowledge. Not to be overlooked as well is her Korean language proficiency and knowledge of Korean culture. She did, after all, grow up in an ethnic Korean autonomous district and studied at Yanbian University, a bilingual school. One should also note that Qun married for love rather than economic gain. While these factors may be significant, they are not "sufficient conditions" for foreign brides' successful adjustment to life in Korea.

In counterpoint to Qun's story, there are two other stories to briefly relate: One is the story of a woman from Mongolia; the other is the story of a Korean Chinese woman, *Chosŏnjok*. Both of these women married for love.

A MONGOLIAN PHYSICIAN

This life story shows that a college degree with professional training and a marriage based on love does not necessarily make for a happy married life. During my fieldwork, I encountered a forty-three-year-old Mongolian woman, Tsedengor (a pseudonym, Tsend hereafter), who graduated in 1989 from Mongolian Medical University in Ulan Bator (the capital city of Mongolia) and became a licensed physician in Mongolia.

In 2008, Tsend came to Korea as a student to study at a university in Korea. Soon thereafter she met a forty-six-year-old Korean man who had graduated from high school and was working as an executive in a small private firm in a regional city. Tsend fell in love with him. She married him the same year she came to Korea. The couple now has a two-year-old son, and they live in Pakch'ŏn (a pseudonym) in north Ch'ungch'ŏng province. Since her husband has a steady job and a fairly good salary by rural standards, she did not have any problem adjusting to her living conditions. However, she was troubled by her eighty-year-old mother-in-law who has no formal education. The trouble arose from cultural differences and a language barrier.

Her trouble started with her misuse of Korean terms of address. The Korean language has two sets of terms of address: one for a junior who is younger than the speaker, and another for a senior who is older than the speaker. These terms differ from titles in English such as Mr., Mrs., and Ms. When a Korean child or a junior addresses a senior, such as a mother-in-law, that person has to use one set of expressions, and conversely, when a senior addresses a junior, that person uses another set of expressions. For instance, to a child or junior, one can say, "*Pab mŏkŏ!*" (Eat the meal!); but when addressing seniors such as a mother-in-law, one would say, "*Chinji chapsuseyo!*" (Please eat the meal!). Without knowing the difference Tsend used the informal expression indiscriminately, telling her elderly mother-in-law, "*Pab mŏkŏ!*" as though she were a little child. Her mother-in-law took for granted that Tsend would know the subtleties of the Korean language. Having no experience with foreigners, she thought that Tsend used the junior expression because Tsend looked down on her for being so elderly and uneducated. Tsend, however, could not help it because she did not learn Korean before coming to the country. Tsend did not have any friends or have contact with outsiders. She simply picked up Korean by listening to her mother-in-law and husband speak to younger people.

When it reached an extreme stage, the mother-in-law beat Tsend with her cane. The beating continued and worsened. Finally, Tsend decided to file for divorce. I wondered where her husband was during this time of conflict. After all, they married out of love. It seemed that Tsend's husband did not intervene in the conflict.

Knowing the seriousness of her situation, the Pakch'ŏn branch of the Center for Supporting Multicultural Families (*Tamunhwakajŏng Chiwŏn Center*), a national organization, has begun to intervene for arbitration. Due to the zealous effort made by the Pakch'ŏn director over a year, their marriage has been saved for the time being. The director of the center has made every effort to explain cultural differences to Tsend's mother-in-law. The director also instructed Tsend in the proper use of Korean. The trouble started because Tsend had not had any contact with people outside the house. This happens to many foreign brides because relatives worry that they might speak ill of the family or leave their husband for the promise of a job. Since Tsend was unable to learn proper Korean, the center advised her on what to do. She signed up for the CUK's Campaign. As soon as Tsend started using honorific expressions properly, her mother-in-law became happy.

Nevertheless, Tsend's problems were not completely resolved. Not only was her problem the physical abuse perpetrated by her mother-in-law, but she also agonized over not being able to practice medicine. Even though she is licensed as a physician in Mongolia, she cannot practice medicine in Korea. The Korean government does not recognize the credentials of foreign medical schools. Furthermore, because she lacks proficiency in the Korean language, she cannot get another type of job in health care. For the past three years, her frustration has grown. Her decision to file for divorce might have had something to do with her frustration over her thwarted career.

Her limited proficiency in the Korean language prevents her from seeking work other than that of a full-time housewife. Even the birth of her son did not make her empty feeling go away. As long as her Korean language skills do not improve, she may not be able to pass the state-given examination required to become a Korean citizen. She is still a Mongolian national. She was so preoccupied by her limited knowledge of Korean that I asked her, "Would you recommend that any Mongolian woman marry a Korean man?" Immediately she answered no. She told me that Koreans are very kind to Mongolians and live better than Mongolians economically. Also, since Koreans look like Mongolians morphologically, she has never experienced any discrimination. Nevertheless, she asserted that she would not recommend to any Mongolian woman that she marry a Korean man because of the "language handicap," unless there would be a way for the new bride to learn Korean before coming to the country.

Tsend's struggle with the language contrasts with the linguistic proficiency of a Mongolian assistant I came to know during the CUK's Campaign. She was a graduate student at a Korean university who assisted the Campaign in helping Mongolian brides. She was as fluent in Korean as any native speaker. She did not even have a foreign accent. In fact, since she was speaking both Mongolian and Korean so well, I thought she was a native Korean who learned the Mongolian language. I asked her, "How and from where have you learned the Mongolian language so well?" She thought I was joking. Nevertheless, I vaguely remember that when I was studying anthropological linguistics, my instructor told me that Korean and Mongolian both belong to the Ural-Altaic language family. Therefore, a Korean would find it much easier to learn Mongolian than Chinese or other languages. An analogy would be the kinship of German and English. Perhaps Tsend's difficulty in learning Korean may be her own individual difficulty.

After speaking with the director of the Pakch'ŏn branch of the Center for Supporting Multicultural Families, I made an arrangement for Tsend to start another career in Korea outside the field of medicine. With the urging and encouragement of the director, she applied for admission and was accepted to study in the Department of Continuing Education at the CUK beginning the spring semester of 2010. I have heard secondhand that she has experienced some difficulties in keeping up with schoolwork given her lack of Korean language competency. Faculty and staff at the university are not yet ready to evaluate her progress, so her future prospects are unknown. Through the Campaign, I have tried to help foreign brides adjust successfully to life in Korea. If Tsend withdraws from school, I fear that her life in Korea may not improve. From Tsend's story I have learned that successful international marriages do not depend solely on the mode of marriage—either a brokered marriage or a marriage of romantic love. The reader may remember the story of Huang, who came from the Bac Giang province of Vietnam. She married by a brokered arrangement, yet she is making a smooth adjustment to her new country. Since Qun was so successful in adjusting to life in Ch'ŏn-do, people may surmise that attainment of higher education is a determinant of successful adaptation. However, the story of Tsend suggests otherwise. Even a licensed physician like Tsend could not find her niche in Korea. Also, remitting money to a foreign brides' family is often a negative factor in international marriages. Such a generalization does not work in Tsend's case, though. She does not ask for money and her husband did not promise any; still, her marriage does not seem especially happy.

A *CHOSŎNJOK* BRIDE

Thirty-year-old Lee Arim (a pseudonym, Li Yalin in Chinese pronunciation) is a *Chosŏnjok*, meaning a Korean Chinese whose nationality is Chinese. China does not recognize dual or multiple nationalities. Currently, Arim lives in Hakch'on (a pseudonym) in north Kyŏngsang province, near P'ohang, where POSCO's main iron and steel plant is currently located. Arim's great grandparents are from P'ohang. They immigrated to Manchuria in the early 1900s to seek a new livelihood when the Korean peninsula was annexed by Japan. To Arim, coming to Korea is a sort of homecoming.

Arim was born in 1980 in a small farming town, Ch'ŏlyŏng, about two hours' driving distance from Shenyang, which is a subprovincial city and the capital of the Liaoning province in northeast China. Shenyang is an important industrial center in China. It is the transportation and commercial center of China's northeastern region. Arim was used to living in a small farming town, and she was unaware of much of the outside world. Although there were some ethnic Koreans where she grew up, there were not as many as in the Jilin province. Arim grew up Chinese instead of maintaining a strong Korean ethnic identity. Since she is a third-generation Korean Chinese, anyone who talks to Arim will likely take her to be Chinese, not Korean or of Korean ancestry. Her accent is characterized by a glottal pronunciation of certain Korean words. This is typical of native Chinese speaking Korean. During our conversation she often referred to China as "our country" rather than Korea. It reminded me of when I taught at the University of Tennessee. In my East Asian course, whenever I said "in our society," some students were confused by what country I meant—Korea or the United States.

I have chosen to tell Arim's story as an example of a foreign bride who married out of love. Her story offers evidence counter to some common assumptions, namely that most Koreans believe that all overseas Koreans have strong Korean ethnic identities; are familiar with Korean culture, including the Korean language; and would like to live in Korea. Through my lengthy interview and intensive contact with Arim, I learned that the above assumptions are not always true.

In 2006, Arim married Kim Ki-su (a pseudonym), who was thirty-five years old at the time. In 2004, Ki-su's great aunt, who lives in P'ohang, Korea, also had relatives in Ch'ŏlyŏng near Shenyang, China. When she visited Ch'ŏlyŏng, she met Arim and thought that she would be a good bride for Ki-su, even though Ki-su was ten years older than Arim. Upon her return to Korea, she passed on this recommendation to Ki-su's family. With a proper arrangement, Ki-su went to China and met Arim. Arim's friends in Hakch'on, particularly foreign brides, said that as soon as Ki-su met Arim, he "fell in love at first sight." When I asked Arim to corroborate this, she smiled and avoided a direct answer. However, Arim told me that Ki-su strove for a year to win her love. Also, there was no reason Arim's parents would oppose such a marriage. Although Ki-su was a bit older than the average age of grooms, he was good-looking and the oldest son of a family who owned a large expanse of farmland and a sizable apple orchard. Arim told me that her and her parents' only reservation was that Ki-su appeared physically weak. Even now he cannot engage in hard physical work without tiring easily.

Via international phone calls, their love took hold. It seemed, however, that Ki-su was more enthusiastic about marriage than Arim. Finally, in December 2005, Arim came to Hakch'on. The wedding occurred on March 26, 2006. Now they have a four-year-old son. Since they can afford it, Arim has her own automobile. She is able to go wherever she wants. She is one of a very few foreign brides who can afford to do whatever she wants. She is well dressed and has expensive accessories. She does not look like a country woman by any means; rather, she looks like a well-to-do Seoulite.

However, despite these favorable conditions, she is not free of difficulties. Her first difficulty is with the Korean language. She told me that since she is *Chosŏnjok*, everybody expects her to be fluent in Korean. This assumption is well founded. According to a survey conducted by the Korean government in 2010,[7] a great majority of *Chosŏnjok* (96.6 percent) were able to speak Korean fluently. Arim belongs to a tiny minority (3.4 percent) who have difficulty communicating in Korean. She told me about her case apologetically, "When I grew up in Ch'ŏlyŏng, all my friends were Chinese, and I went to school where everyone spoke Chinese." As a third-generation Korean, she did not have much exposure to the Korean language and Korean culture. She is gradually learning the basics of Korean, but since she started a junior college near Hakch'on, she has had difficulty following lectures. She has had even more problems with reading and writing. She told me that she spends most of her evenings studying the Korean language.

The fundamental problem lies in cultural differences. Most Koreans, including her family members and relatives, think that she should have no problems understanding Korean culture, and they expect her to behave in accordance with Korean customs. She said, "If I were from Vietnam or the Philippines, they would not expect as much as from me. But since I am of Korean ancestry, they expect more from me. But, you see, I am Chinese and just happen to be of Korean ancestry." She continued, "Let me tell you the most difficult part in terms of culture. I, as the wife of the eldest son, have to prepare food for *chesa* rituals (ancestor worship rituals), but I have not seen such a thing in my family back home in China. Chinese do not observe ancestor worship as Koreans do. In China we just prepare some Chinese bread and serve a humble meal on a special occasion during the year. It is not like ancestor worship on annual death days of the ancestors. I just do not know which food can be placed where on the table for the worship rituals. Most native Koreans, including members of our family, do not understand that I am a foreigner just like those from countries other than China." Perhaps most Koreans think of *Chosŏnjok* like Arim's family members do. Among foreign brides, *Chosŏnjok* constituted the single largest group in 2007: 36,051 (30 percent of all foreign brides) out of 120,146 foreign brides.[8]

Arim is gradually learning the Korean language and Korean culture. However, she still does not understand the role of being the wife of the eldest son in a family with one older sister-in-law and one younger brother-in-law. She admits, "I have learned that in Korea, the wife of the oldest son acts as if she is mother of the family. I am not familiar with such a role." However, she thinks that her priority is to learn the Korean language and worry about customs later. In fact, she enrolled in the CUK's Campaign and finished the entire curriculum at the basic and intermediate levels. She received a certificate for her completion of the courses. She is learning advanced Korean while she attends a local junior college. She said, "The best way to learn advanced Korean is to take courses in college. In so doing, I have opportunities to talk to classmates and professors, and they correct my writing when I submit my papers."

She is very open, active, and likes to make friends and acquaintances. She also participates in community activities. She can do so because she is better off than most foreign brides economically. She admits,

> "I know that I should make more frequent contact with native Koreans, including family members and relatives of my husband, but I am more comfortable associating with fellow foreign brides. In fact, my best friend is Japanese, and she lives near where I live. Since she is eight years older than I am, I call her *ŏnni* (older sister), and she acts as if she is my older sister. The major reasons why I am associating more closely with other foreign brides than with native Koreans are these: First, we share common experiences, good or bad; we are empathetic and sympathetic with each other; and most of all, we can improve our Korean since that is the only common language we can communicate with. You know, it is hard to understand, but it is true. When I started talking Korean with my strange accent and stumbling over certain words, most people did not want to carry on a lengthy conversation with me because it would be hard for them to follow my talking."

I can appreciate her honest admission. It reminded me of an experience I had at Emory University in Atlanta, Georgia. I asked to have an American student as my roommate, assuming that by sharing a room with an American student I would have a chance to improve my English. However, my roommate grew tired of carrying on conversations with me because of my rudimentary English. We ended up speaking only two words to each other when we woke up—"good morning"—and when we went to bed—"good night." I did not have much chance to learn English from my roommate. The next semester, I shared a room with a student from China. Since neither of us could speak the other's native language, we had to communicate in English. I ended up practicing English more with a Chinese student than with an American student. It seems that Arim has had a similar experience.

Arim told me about her way of overcoming cultural differences by talking directly about them. "At first, I just took all the blame resulting from cultural differences. I learned that by doing that, they thought I was making those mistakes knowingly. Now, after having a child, and having lived long enough, I have begun to tell them I am making such mistakes because I do not understand Korean culture. Having Korean ancestral roots does not necessarily mean that I have mastery of Korean customs, including etiquette." Perhaps most Koreans might think in such a way, but Arim is different from other *Chosŏnjok*. According to the counseling corner of the bulletin board of the Missionary Board for the *Chosŏnjok,* most *Chosŏnjok* are very reluctant to tell their personal stories to others, including the counselor, due to their cultural orientations.

Arim is a beautiful woman, so one can see why Ki-su could fall in love with her at first sight. She comes across as a quiet, sweet person. She speaks in a soft voice with great sincerity. But she is very determined to accomplish her goals. She has taken Korean lessons on-line and other college courses. She studies very diligently every night after her son goes to bed. She was fortunate enough to be able to invite her parents, her father (sixty-one years old) and mother (sixty years old), to Hakch'on. They live in the same town as Arim. She is determined to make Hakch'on her and her parents' permanent home.

The three brides described in this chapter share a commonality: they married out of love. Foreign brides who marry Korean men out of love appear to have a better chance for a successful marriage than those who marry by arrangement of an international marriage broker. However, as was shown in the case of Tsend, a marriage of love does not result in success automatically. On the basis of these cases, it seems to me that successful marriages result from a combination of two factors. One, foreign brides have to make every effort to succeed on the basis of their own initiative and motivation. No one can do it for them. Two, their husbands and their Korean family members have to be accommodating—careful not to make assumptions about a foreign wife's language proficiency or cultural knowledge. Sometimes, though, as was seen in the cases of Tsend and Arim, in-laws need to have their false assumptions pointed out to them. Outside assistance or aid could possibly hinder or weaken foreign wives' ability to be self-reliant. The Korean government and volunteer organizations have to nurture their abilities by helping them help themselves.

The Characteristics of Korean Multiculturalism and Its Outlook for the Future

Multiculturalism in Korea is still mainly at the level of rhetoric and it is largely focused on foreign brides in "multicultural families." This chapter discusses the characteristics of Korean multiculturalism and its future prospective.

FOREIGNERS WHO CHANGED CURRENT KOREAN DEMOGRAPHICS

Contemporary Korean demographics began to alter in the late 1990s as new waves of over 1.13 million foreigners from 180 countries came to Korea: These immigrants include 557,000 foreign workers from 180 countries, both legal and illegal; 181,671 spouses of Koreans from 67 countries; 82,000 foreign students from 175 countries; 18,000 North Korean escapees;[1] and 121,935 children born into multicultural families.[2] Korea's policies toward them and treatment of each group vary.

Foreign Workers

Once a "labor-exporting" country, Korea suddenly became a "labor-importing" country after hosting the 1988 Summer Olympics in Seoul. Korea was unprepared to deal with an increasing number of foreign workers, so from 1987 to 1991, there was no policy for foreign workers; from 1991 to 2003, the government implemented a system for guest workers; from 2003 to 2006, the government implemented both an employment permission system and a guest workers system; and since 2006, the government has combined those systems and consolidated its policies under the Employment of Foreign Workers Act.[3] The act specifies that foreign workers are allowed to enter Korea legally but cannot stay longer than three consecutive years for the purpose of work. There is an exception, though: qualified workers who meet certain conditions specified in the act (article 18) can extend their visas for two additional years but no more than five years in total. After five years, foreign workers have to return home and can apply for reentry after six months.

The five-year term limit is to prevent workers from applying to become permanent residents. Also, foreign workers cannot bring their spouses and children along when they enter the country. These stipulations serve as de facto prohibition against foreign workers becoming Korean citizens. Some foreigners marry while in Korea and have children; still, they cannot stay in Korea beyond a maximum of five years. At times, this limitation brings about serious violations of human rights.[4] Because of the restrictions, the number of foreigners who come to Korea decreased by ten thousand from 2005 to 2010.[5]

Knowing that a five-year term limit is unfair, some activists are critical of the policy and demand that every foreign worker, either legal or illegal, be entitled to human rights.[6] However, some Korean sociologists, Yoon In-jin for one, assert that at present it is unwise to open up the domestic job market to foreigners by allowing persons to enter or leave Korea without any restrictions.[7] There is a widespread belief among Korean workers that immigrants take jobs away from citizens and remit their earnings to their native countries. On May 13, 2010, the Korea Development Institute released a report stating that some 690,000 foreign workers out of 1,168,000 foreign residents in Korea are "encroaching" (*chamsik*) on the Korean job market.[8] *Chamsik,* meaning "eating into," suggests possible bias or bigotry against immigrants. However, despite the presence of foreign workers in Korea, there remains a critical shortage of labor in the so-called three-D jobs—dirty, dangerous, and difficult. When it comes to immigrants and the job market, there are contradictions between public sentiment and demographic data.[9] And the labor shortage will only grow worse if declining birthrate projections prove to be correct.[10]

Illegal Foreign Workers

When it comes to the estimated 174,049 illegal workers in Korea, Korean sentiment is strongly against their remaining in the country. Illegal workers do not have any legal protection from possible prejudice and discrimination. Any effort to treat them the same as legal workers would not get any real support from the Korean public.

Exclusion of illegal immigrant workers from the benefits of multicultural policies is not limited to Korea. According to Will Kymlicka, most countries of northern Europe contain large numbers of illegal immigrants, asylum seekers, or guest workers, but they are not the subject of multiculturalism or multicultural policies.[11]

Double Standard

While Korean policies on the employment of foreign workers are rather strict, Korean policies toward overseas ethnic Koreans are liberal as long as those living abroad can prove they are of Korean descent. In dealing with overseas Koreans, according to the Immigration and Legal Status of Overseas Koreans Act, the Korean government should treat foreign nationals and permanent residents who come to Korea the same as Korean citizens, except in terms of political rights, enfranchisement, and suffrage. However, in terms of eligibility, the original act (passed on September 2, 1999) applied to overseas Koreans who had retained their Korean citizenship (and to their immediate relatives and descendents) and who had left the country after 1948, the year when the Republic of Korea was established. Most Koreans who live in the United States and Western European countries were eligible since many Koreans immigrated to those countries after 1948. However, most ethnic Koreans living in China, Russia, and Central Asia did not meet the criteria until the law was amended in 2003.[12]

Because of preferential treatment of overseas Korean descendents, under the category of "visiting employment" (*pangmun ch'widŏp*, visa category H-2), some 297,756 persons without Korean citizenship are working in Korea with no three-year term limit. (However, people in this category must apply to renew their visa every three years.) Here are figures for these foreign nationals by nationality: 290,710 from China, 4,419 from Uzbekistan, 2,069 from Russia, 418 from Kazakhstan, and 140 from other countries.[13]

The Korean Nationality Act was amended in April 2010, and effective beginning January 1, 2011, certain foreign nationals are allowed to apply for "plural citizenship."[14] This amendment is part of an effort to recruit highly qualified workers to meet the country's labor needs. Essentially, the amended act allows highly qualified, talented, and resourceful foreigners to obtain Korean citizenship without renunciation of their original nationality. The law thus allows for a system of plural nationality.[15] Despite such an accommodating policy, it remains to be seen how many qualified foreign nationals will take advantage of it. So far, many unskilled workers have come to Korea, but few highly qualified and resourceful foreigners have done the same. Currently, of 557,000 foreigners working in Korea, only 19,917 (3.5 percent), excluding English tutors, are professionals—a category that includes professors, artists, musicians, and others.[16] The amended Korean Nationality Act is a manifestation of Korea's "utilitarian" point of view.[17]

Korea is not alone among countries that offer dual citizenship and give preferential treatment to particular kinds of immigrants. Peter Kraus and Karen Schönwälder, both of whom are political scientists, have reported on the case of Germany: "Dual citizenship is officially still unwanted, and the current citizenship law includes strict measures against its expansion. Nevertheless, as exceptions were granted, for example, to ethnic Germans who were allowed to retain their Polish citizenship, to Iranians who were not released from their former citizenship, as well as, for a time, a significant number of Turks, estimates put the number of Germans also holding another citizenship at several hundred thousand."[18] Also, Jürgen Habermas, a German philosopher, states that "foreigners who are willing to renounce their previous citizenship can be naturalized only after they have been living in Germany for at least fifteen years. In contrast, the so-called *Volksdeutsche* or ethnic Germans—primarily Poles and Russians who can prove their German ancestry—have a constitutional right to naturalization."[19] Moreover, children born to foreign immigrants who cannot prove German ancestry do not automatically receive the rights of citizenship.[20]

Looking back in Korean history, we find periods where foreign immigrants were actively recruited. In the early period of the Koryŏ dynasty, Koryŏ made every effort to recruit talented immigrants in order to establish an ambitious new dynasty modeled on China. Talented immigrants included men of letters, scholars, bureaucrats, writers, translators, and artisans. Even ordinary people were recruited and placed in strategically important places for defending the northern frontiers. Also, when Mongols relocated almost 10 percent of the total Koryŏ population (206,800 out of 2.1 million people) to Mongolia, Koryŏ had to recruit foreign immigrants to fill the vacuum created by the exodus.[21] The situation is similar today, as demographics and economics force contemporary Korea to open up its immigration policy.

In the process of recruiting foreign immigrants, Koreans have maintained a contradictory and double standard: they are open, hospitable, and even eager to recruit talented immigrants, but they show much less hospitality to unskilled and illegal laborers. Throughout Korea's history, Han Chinese have received much better treatment than immigrants from elsewhere, especially northern nomadic tribes. This is because most Han immigrants were upper-class men of letters, scholars, bureaucrats, and other skilled men. According to Han Geon Soo, it is true that "both nationality and social class function as vital factors in the matrix of the treatment of ethnic Koreans. In the end, Korea's multicultural landscape is composed of multiple layers made up of the varied social classes and different genders of the participants. The multicultural space and circumstances formed in each layer are different."[22] In my interviews most foreign brides from China and Japan told me that their children are less likely to experience prejudice and discrimination than are children of other ethnic groups and North Korean refugees.

Foreign Students and North Korean Escapees

Another group helping to make Korea a multiethnic and multicultural society is foreign students. Currently, there are some 82,000 foreign students from 175 countries studying in Korea: Chinese students are the largest in number with 63,161, followed by 3,965 Mongolians, 2,909 Vietnamese, 1,825 Japanese, and others. The number of foreign students has increased eight times from 2003 to 2010. They are pursuing various degrees: bachelor degrees (forty-one thousand students), master's degrees (eleven thousand students), and doctoral degrees (three thousand students).[23]

North Korean escapees (*talbukcha* or *saet'ŏmin*) are another group diversifying South Korean society. North Koreans are in a unique position among immigrants. They are the same as other political asylum seekers, yet, in a sense, they are in their own country when they escape to South Korea. While the UN recognizes the two Koreas as independent, sovereign nations, the Korean Constitution delineates Korea's territory as encompassing the entire peninsula, both North and South. Because of the Constitution, North Korean escapees do not have to apply for citizenship to live in South Korea. Their legal status is indeed ambivalent. The complexities and contradictions of South Korea's treatment of immigrants are well illustrated by the nation's treatment of North Korean escapees.

FOREIGN BRIDES

Some 161,991 Korean men who married foreign women have formed what are commonly referred to as "multicultural families." When foreign women marry Korean men, they are considered to be one of "us" or "ours" (*sijib-onda*). By contrast, when Korean women marry foreign men, they tend to think of themselves as outsiders or "theirs" (*sijib-ganda*), meaning "going away from home for other families or foreign countries."

Traditionally, Koreans tend to emphasize oneness or "Koreanness," particularly toward family members and members of kin groups. If necessary, Koreans are flexible enough to expand the scope of their oneness to include nonkin members such as those who came from the same region or those who attended the same school. These are known as "fictional" kin.[24] While foreign brides who marry Korean men are included within the cultural boundaries of "Koreanness" or "ours," as kin or at least fictional kin, other foreigners—foreign workers, foreign students, and even North Korean escapees—do not belong to the culturally defined category of "oneness" and thus become subject to distrust and differential treatment.

Korea's Multicultural Program for Foreign Brides

While traditional immigrant countries such as Australia, Canada, and New Zealand have an official multicultural policy under the central government, Britain and the United States do not have nationwide multiculturalism policies at the federal level.[25] In Korea, there are no explicit multicultural policies at the national level. However, in May 2005, the Korean president issued a statement pointing out that "moving toward a multiracial and multicultural society is a general trend that we cannot go against!"[26] Additionally, the Multicultural Families Support Act was promulgated on March 19, 2010, to assist multicultural families in maintaining a stable family life, in improving their quality of life, and in promoting social unity and harmony. Also, on December 14, 2007, the Management of Marriage Brokerage Act was passed to regulate international marriage brokers and thereby prohibit the dispensing of false information. Furthermore, on June 11, 2008, an executive order came down from the president for regulating marriage brokers.

Because most legislative acts, executive orders, and aid programs concern foreign brides, Korean intellectuals characterize Korean multiculturalism as a movement catering to foreign brides.[27] For foreign brides, requirements for naturalization are relaxed, and they receive aid from the government.[28] Since there are virtually no multicultural policies in place for other immigrants, multicultural polices in Korea are effectively limited to foreign brides. Some Korean scholars characterize the multicultural policies for foreign brides in Korea as government-led ones.[29] However, Yoon In-Jin asserts that Korean policy is not entirely either "state-led" or "citizen-led" but is more or less an outgrowth of "policy networks" among the government and NGOs.[30] Still others such as Han Geon-Soo dismiss multiculturalism in Korea altogether by stating bluntly that it is a "rhetorical concept" or "political slogan."[31]

Even if Korean multiculturalism is government-led, government policies are very loose. Tellingly, the Korean government did not even keep accurate statistics on foreign brides until June 2010. Prior to that time, each branch of the government kept its own statistics; the result was incommensurable information. At first the affairs of foreign brides were assigned to the Ministry of Gender Equality. Later, when the central government was reorganized, the affairs of foreign brides were reassigned to the Ministry for Health, Welfare and Family Affairs. Even though the affairs were assigned to a specific department, they came under the purview of many ministries, including the Ministry of Education, Science and Technology; the Ministry of Culture, Sports and Tourism; the Ministry of Food, Agriculture, Forestry and Fisheries; the Ministry of Justice; and the Ministry of Public Administration and Security. Because the affairs were spread across many governmental departments, the central government thought about consolidating them into the Office of the Prime Ministry. For some reason, though, the affairs were reassigned to the Ministry of Gender Equality and Family after the unit of "family affairs" was taken from the Ministry for Health, Welfare and Family Affairs and given back to the Ministry of Gender Equality and Family.[32]

During the CUK's Campaign, whenever the team visited the offices of local governments—provinces (*to*), cities (*si*), counties (*kun*), and townships (*myŏn*)—seeking administrative assistance, we were usually assigned to the office in charge of gender equality (women's affairs: *yŏsŏngbu* or *yŏsŏnggwa*). And most of the time, social workers from the office accompanied our team. Sometimes our team received a cool reception from accompanying officials, although some officials were extremely kind and helpful. On occasions when they were unwelcoming, they usually complained that "this is our job and our domain. Why does a university have to bother with our job! We also teach the Korean language, and Korean language teachers make home visits for one-on-one instruction." One officer from a provincial headquarters followed our team around, questioning our instructional methods: "How can foreign brides learn language over the Internet? It won't work." We knew, though, that traditional in-person instruction has its own difficulties. There are not many teachers available to make home visits, and instructional time is limited to eighty hours per bride. Such instruction does not sufficiently prepare foreign wives for the examination that is required for naturalization.

Many agency personnel have something of a "turf" mentality when it comes to the social services they provide. To illustrate this mentality, I will relate the story of a rejected donation. Although most Korean homes have one or more PCs, some do not have a computer. Members of these families have to use public computers available in the locality where they live. I made an arrangement with POSCO, the sponsor of the CUK's Campaign, to send their used computers to some foreign brides living in rural regions. POSCO repaired the computers and even delivered them to two provincial offices (*toch'ŏng*) for no charge. However, one provincial office refused to accept the computers, citing two main reasons: First, the CUK is not an agency authorized to provide social welfare services; second, the CUK's address is not in the province.[33] While one provincial office was willing to redistribute the refurbished computers without mentioning the role of the CUK, the other province refused the computers outright. This is a classic example of a bureaucratic organization invoking technicalities to preserve its domain.

A major arm of the government assisting foreign brides is the Center for Supporting Multicultural Families (*Tamunhwagajok Chiwŏncenter*), which is not under the auspices of the government per se but is a sort of consignor delegated by the Ministry of Gender Equality and Family to implement governmental programs and policies. It was founded on the legal basis of the Multicultural Families Support Act promulgated in March 2010. The Center for Supporting Multicultural Families (hereafter Center) implements various programs to assist foreign brides. There are now some 159 Centers in provinces, metropolitan areas, and counties throughout the country. The tasks of the Center are numerous and various in kind: training personnel, publishing magazines on multicultural family issues and news, keeping up public relations, and coordinating communication among related agencies. Centers at local levels—cities and counties—offer Korean language lessons, lectures on the nature of multicultural society, self-help meetings, counseling, and vocational education.

Besides the various governmental programs sponsored by the Center, some twenty NGO groups are actively assisting foreign brides. Most of the programs offered by NGO groups overlap with those of the Center, such as counseling and Korean language lessons. Some of the groups compete for funding to operate their projects. One official of a NGO group supported by a religious group was almost antagonistic to the CUK's Campaign, asking us not to bother promoting such a service on his "turf."

The Contents and Characteristics of Multicultural Policies for Foreign Brides

Throughout my fieldwork during the CUK's Campaign, I did not encounter any case of international marriage between a Korean woman and a foreign man; such marriages are considered peripheral in dealing with multicultural families.[34] Most programs are designed to turn foreign brides into properly assimilated Korean women[35]—meek and polite homemakers who are good cooks. This profile of a proper Korean wife is based on paternalistic, patriarchal, and chauvinistic notions.[36] Those who design multicultural policies assume that foreign brides are subject to "cultural amalgamation," as Oh Kyŏng-sŏk and others have witnessed.[37] In addition to teaching the Korean language, most programs emphasize cultural assimilation rather than respect for and recognition of wives' various native cultures. The programs teach wives how to perform the rites of tea ceremonies, how to wear traditional Korean women's clothes (*hanbok*), and how to emulate traditional mannerisms.[38]

The assimilationist approach of these programs can be illustrated by an example. On December 10, 2010, the Presidential Council on National Branding, the government-owned public relations organization, presented cookbooks written by foreign brides to the Ministry of Justice. The cookbooks, featuring recipes for traditional Korean food, were published under the auspices of Daewoo Security in seven different languages and were meant to be distributed to foreign brides.[39] The council thought that the book would be a valuable kitchen reference for foreign wives. However, one of my foreign wife informants commented to me that such books are not critically important for advancing genuine multiculturalism. This informant thought that such an effort promotes a public image of foreign wives as homemakers for rural Korean families. The informant commented further that multicultural polices ought to aim at reducing the heavy burden placed on foreign wives for their being ethnic and racial minorities and for their being women in rural Korean society.

Policies to alleviate the burden, however, are lacking. Discrimination and prejudice are especially felt by wives with darker complexions who come from poor countries. These wives are often identified as service line workers or domestic workers.[40] I hope that such a stereotypically negative image will not fully and permanently take hold in Korea as it has in other places.

During my time promoting the Campaign, I observed some patterns among the husbands of foreign wives: most do not have steady jobs; most are low-income earners; most are notably older than their wives; many have sick or elderly parents; some have physical and mental handicaps; and some have children from previous marriages.[41] As for their wives, I observed the following patterns: a good many are younger than their husbands; a good many have junior college and bachelor degrees with specific skills. (This is especially so for some Filipinas who teach English in local schools where a native English teacher is critically needed.) Any uniform policy for foreign brides should be reevaluated because each foreign bride's needs are not the same. The CUK's Campaign assists able and qualified foreign brides to enroll in college, trusting that foreign brides who have a high level of educational attainment have a better chance of excelling than their Korean husbands.

As it happens, a great many foreign brides live in Korea's most traditional and conservative regions: rural farming and fishing villages. While these areas are home to various ethnic and racial groups, they retain values and norms tending toward the traditional, parochial, and paternalistic. Foreign wives are pressed into playing traditional Korean women's roles while young Korean women have left these rural areas for cities and industrial zones where such roles are not so strongly enforced. Foreign brides suffer more from the burden attached to traditional gender roles than they do for being racial or ethnic minorities.

Dilemma of the NGOs

Currently in Korea, more than twenty NGO groups are interested in multiculturalism. They are active, vocal, and eager to implement multiculturalism in Korea, focusing on foreign brides. However, despite their high hopes and expectations, almost of all of them are poorly financed, if financed at all. To launch their programs, they have to apply for grants from the government. The government allocated some $50 million in 2010. (This allocation has increased 5.5 times since 2007.[42]) The number of foreign brides has increased from 126,000 in 2007 (with a budget of $9 million) to 181,671 in 2010 (with a budget of $50 million).

In order to receive some governmental funding, NGO groups must compete for the limited amount allocated. Since there are virtually no governmental budgets allocated for other immigrants, NGOs are interested in multicultural families with foreign wives.[43] Another financial hindrance for NGOs comes with long-term projects. Because NGOs must apply for grants yearly, a failure to win a grant anew could halt a long-term project underway. Consequently, most of the grants are one-time offers and can hardly be used to fund a long-term project.[44] Moreover, when government is the funding agent, it would not be easy to eliminate the government's temptation to monitor the funded projects.[45]

Some native Korean scholarship is critical about the direction of NGO's multicultural initiatives, saying that their programs are focusing on assimilationist efforts, which counterpose the liberal Western model of multiculturalism.[46] Another problem is the sheer youth of the multiculturalist movement. Since the movement has been around for only a decade at most, there are not many qualified personnel with experience in cross-cultural studies to handle sensitive issues. According to Yoon In-Jin, many of those involved in the affairs of multicultural families are insensitive to cultural differences. Therefore, their programs are based on their own frame of reference, which may be colored by traditional Korean values: paternalism, patriarchy, and ethnic homogeneity. Hardly anyone addresses the issue of gender equality for foreign wives.[47]

Most programs sponsored by the government (central as well as local government), NGOs, and various other volunteer groups compete with one other to support foreign brides without knowing their essential needs. Anthropologists call this misinformation an *etic* assumption—an outsider's view—rather than an *emic* viewpoint—an insider's perception.[48]

FOREIGN BRIDES

While conducting my fieldwork, I encountered, interviewed, and conversed at length with many foreign brides. On December 21, 2009, when I was visiting a local branch of the Center for Supporting Multicultural Families, the director gave me an essay written by a Chinese bride.[49] She introduced herself as coming from Harbin, a subprovincial city and the capital of Heilongjiang province in northeast China. She came to Korea in 1998 and has worked for another local Center since 2008. No date for the essay was given, but I assume it was written in late 2009. The Chinese bride who wrote it expressed a strong opinion. Since she articulates her point of view so well, I quote her at length:

> The Korean government, central as well as local, and various volunteer organizations, tend to believe that foreign brides need financial assistance out of "pity." Consequently, a lot of money has been spent to help them, which is good. However, since money has been spent in such a way, the public has formed the negative view that the government and organizations "ladle out" taxpayers' money unreservedly. This creates a negative image of foreign brides. There is a program called "home visiting educational program" in which an agency person visits an individual foreign bride's home and gives all sorts of advice, including advice on child-rearing practices. It may be helpful, but it is a classic example of wasting public funds. If the outside agency is going to run multicultural family affairs, foreign brides may become so used to receiving aid from society that they might lose their ability to be independent. It would not help foreign brides in the long run. Most of all, we foreign brides are not pitiable people, even if some of us are struggling financially. Foreign brides are not destined to depend on aid from governmental welfare funds. We are confident that we can live independently.

In her writing she is highly critical of some existing government programs that assist foreign brides. Questioning current policy, she thinks the Korean government does not make a deliberate effort to figure out what foreign brides think and want.

According to her, most existing policies are far from what foreign brides want. Some of them are unrealistic, and others are not particularly useful. Most of them are "nice things to do" but are not "urgently needed programs." Specifically, she writes that "there are programs for appointing 'mentors'" who assume "fictional mother- or sisterhood roles as though they are the mothers or sisters of the foreign brides. These programs are rather silly." She asks, "Who said we needed fictional adoptive mothers or adoptive sisters?" Indeed, as it stands, brides may have enough troubles already with their real mothers-in-law and sisters-in-law.[50]

She goes on to say that "government and society should teach the Korean public to respect foreign brides as human beings, not as 'human-machines' [to bear many children to make up for the shortage of labor resulting from Korea's low birthrate]. Also, Korean government and society should not force foreign brides to learn the Korean language and Korean culture unilaterally for the purpose of assimilation. Instead, they have to urge the country to learn about other cultures so that, with some cross-cultural understanding, Koreans can create a genuine multicultural society." She concludes by writing, "We are not asking a lot. We just ask to be treated as respectable human beings, not as alien species from exotic cultures. Reducing if not altogether eliminating prejudice, discrimination, and special treatment in every aspect of Korean society will permit foreign brides to adjust." In her writing this bride appears to be a genuine anthropologist.

Regarding government aid for foreign brides, thirty-three-year-old Maria Lee (a pseudonym)[51] from the Philippines told a reporter that she once received a twenty kilogram bag of rice from the office of *tong* (a local administrative unit that is often called *ri,* or village, in rural regions) free of charge. Officials assumed that all foreign brides would need such aid. In the Philippines, Maria Lee was the daughter of a rich department store owner. She was a medical school student at Ateneo de Davao University, lead vocalist of the school band club, and third runner-up in the Davao regional beauty contest for Miss Philippines in 1994. In 1994, when she was nineteen years old, Maria met a Korean man, Tong-ho Lee (a pseudonym), at her father's department store when he came in as a customer. Tong-ho was the second mate (*hanghaesa*) on a Korean merchant ship anchored at the port of Davao City, located on the island of Mindanao in the southern Philippines. Tong-ho was so attracted to the beauty of Maria that he resigned from his sailor's job and went to the Philippines to win her love. Finally, because of his persistent efforts to win her heart, Maria dropped out of medical school and married him in 1995. In 1998, three years after she came to Korea, Maria became a naturalized Korean citizen. Now she has two children, a boy and a girl.

Recently, she has appeared in movies and television programs. She also participated in a project called "a migrant wife as 2010 local council member" led by the Center for Korean Women and Politics and supported by the Ministry of Gender Equality. In the June 2 nationwide local elections, her name was mentioned as a possible candidate in the Seoul metropolitan council election by the ruling Grand National Party. Although she did not make the final list, she is interested in politics. She would like to be at the forefront of making "a better society for children of multicultural families, who may otherwise continue to face prejudice in the future."[52]

She is particularly dissatisfied with the term *multicultural family* (*tamunhwa kajŏng*) because the term creates so many distinctions between ordinary Korean families and families of international marriages. The term carries a sense of being underprivileged, low class, and in need of government assistance.[53] She has often been assumed to be a maid or cleaning lady as soon as people identify her as a foreign bride. She related this story: "My family and I once participated in a program for multicultural families to promote 'social unity and harmony.' When the participants were moving to another place by bus, a staff member of the program announced loudly to the participants, 'multicultural families ride this bus, and Korean families take the other bus!'"[54] According to Maria, despite all the good intentions behind the program, a simple announcement nullified everything. To Maria, the term *multicultural families* is counterproductive when it comes to fostering social unity and harmony.

CURRENT STATUS OF KOREAN MULTICULTURALISM

Despite all the rhetoric on multiculturalism in Korea, there are some gaps between words and deeds. Agencies involved in multicultural affairs are typical bureaucratic organizations, and some of the personnel maintain a strongly bureaucratic attitude. Every agency involved in the multicultural effort is competitive, and programs overlap. Programs for foreign wives are designed to assimilate them rather than recognize and respect their cultural differences. Blanket aid programs for multicultural families are inefficient and ineffective. Most of all, there is a lack of cultural awareness programs for Korean members of multicultural families. Korea needs well-qualified personnel with some cross-cultural experience to run the multicultural programs effectively.

Korea's Ranking in Terms of Multicultural Policies

Keith Banting, a professor of public policy at Queen's University, and his associates published an interesting report rating twenty-one select countries in terms of their multicultural policies (MCPs).[55] The researchers rated the countries according to eight criteria: "(1) Constitutional, legislative or parliamentary affirmation of multiculturalism, at the central and/or regional and municipal levels; (2) the adoption of multiculturalism in the school curriculum; (3) the inclusion of ethnic representation/sensitivity in the mandate of public media or media licensing; (4) exemptions from dress codes, Sunday closing legislation, etc. (either by statute or by court case); (5) allowing dual citizenship; (6) the funding of ethnic group organizations to support cultural activities; (7) the funding of bilingual education or mother-tongue instruction; (8) affirmative action for disadvantaged immigrant groups."[56] Each country's rating was calculated on a scale of zero to eight possible points. The countries included in the study were rated as follows: Australia 7.0, Austria 0.5, Belgium 3.5, Canada 7.5, Denmark 0.0, Finland 1.0, France 2.0, Germany 0.5, Greece 0.5, Ireland 1.5, Italy 1.5, Japan 0.0, the Netherlands 4.5, New Zealand 5.0, Norway 0.0, Portugal 0.0, Spain 1.0, Sweden 3.0, Switzerland 1.0, the United Kingdom 5.0, the United States 3.0.[57]

Korea was not included this analysis, but how might Korea have fared? Korea does not have a national level of policy for all immigrants (item 1) other than an executive order from the president, but we should give some credit to Korea for enacting the Multicultural Family Support Act, even though it pertains only to married immigrants. Also, regarding item 5, Korea allows a multiple citizenship (not dual citizenship) for qualified foreigners beginning January 2011. Also, there are some assistance programs for foreign brides through the Center for Supporting Multicultural Families. Although an exact score for Korea may be impossible to figure, Korea would likely receive some points, enough to rate it higher than countries that scored no points at all. Korean multicultural policies look better than those of some other countries, even if Korea still has a long way to go.

Characteristics of Korea's Multiculturalism

By and large, there are two large factors that hinder implementing multicultural policies from catching up with rhetoric: one is the century-old myth of a pure-blooded nation. This belief is particularly common among older Koreans who were indoctrinated into the myth from a young age. Some Koreans, including some policy makers, urge foreign brides to assimilate into Korean culture based on the idea of a single-ethnic origin. Younger Koreans who are free from the old myth are more likely to support a multiculturalist agenda.

A second hindrance is Confucianism. Pointing a finger at Korea's deep-seated Confucianism, Han Geon-Soo characterizes current multicultural policies as "paternalistic."[58] There is a strong hierarchical social order in Confucianism rooted in five relations: ruler–subject, father–son, husband–wife, older brother–younger brother, and friend–friend. These hierarchical pairings inform some of the ideas surrounding foreign immigrants: "Within a Confucian culture, with its emphasis on family, minorities are seen as younger brothers, as occasionally disobedient ones. Confucian obedience involves minority groups conforming to Confucian norms, maintaining unity and correct relations."[59] Chinese minority policies have been influenced by the Confucian order: while Han Chinese are the rulers, barbarians and outsiders are subject to their rule. According to Baogang He's report, Marxists did not get away from such a hierarchical order and instead replicated aspects of traditional hierarchy.[60]

Confucianism originated in China (551–479 BC) and was introduced to Korea during the Three Kingdoms period (37 BC–AD 935). In their devotion to the Confucian creed, Koreans seem more Confucian than the Chinese, particularly when it comes to Neo-Confucianism.[61] Wei-ming Tu, a renowned authority on Confucianism at Harvard, has written, "Confucianism, for instance, featured prominently in Korea, especially in the Yi [Chosŏn] dynasty. Indeed, from roughly the end of the 14th century to as recently as the 20th century, Korean culture has been greatly shaped by Confucian thought."[62]

Owing to Confucianism's influence in Korea, reports Han Geon-Soo, "International marriages are sometimes used as a pretext for turning the marriage and the relationship between the mother-in-law and daughter-in-law into one of master and servant. Some Korean husbands and parents-in-laws justify this hierarchical relationship by arguing that they have spent big money to 'buy the bride.' Such attitudes reduce the issues faced by marriage-based migrant women to raw domestic violence and human rights abuses."[63] From my observations, foreign brides are most likely among foreign immigrants to settle permanently in Korea, and they are subject to the strongest and harshest demands for assimilation into Korean culture. Han Geon-Soo reports on this aspect: "According to various surveys, they [foreign brides] have no opportunities to enjoy their native countries in their everyday lives in their host country. One mother-in-law even went as far as to throw a foreign dish prepared by her immigrant daughter-in-law out of the kitchen."[64]

In my estimation, Korean multiculturalism is moving away from the tradition of ethnic nationalism and the policies of assimilation and moving toward a genuine liberal multiculturalism modeled on the West. Koreans have come to understand that multiculturalism respects cultural diversity, but many have not yet reached a state of understanding where endorsing multiculturalism also entails respecting the right of minorities not to be assimilated into Korean culture at the expense of their native culture.[65] For this reason, Korean multiculturalism is in a period of transition. I am reminded of Korea when I read Peter Kraus and Karen Schönwälder's description of incipient multiculturalism in Germany: "[M]ulticulturalism in Germany has so far mainly existed at the level of discourse and not as a consistent political programme. No present or past federal or regional government has subscribed to an explicitly multicultural agenda. And, yet, elements of multiculturalism policies do exist."[66]

Korea is not an immigrant country, and the term *multiculturalism* is a recent introduction into public discourse. However, Korea has its own tradition and history of peaceful coexistence among immigrants from a variety of places. On the basis of this history and the current trend of globalization, Korea is striving toward a liberal model of Western multiculturalism. There are several positive indications that this societal shift will come to pass.

A FUTURE PERSPECTIVE ON A WESTERN LIBERAL MODEL OF MULTICULTURALISM IN KOREA

Today, many Koreans—especially scholars, intellectuals, activists in various NGOs, and the news media—are determined to implement a liberal multiculturalism based on the Western model.[67] At present, multiculturalism in Korea is still mainly at the level of discourse with little in the way of policy implementation, except for some limited policies on behalf of foreign brides. However, Korea's early efforts to achieve multiculturalism are sincere and genuine. Even if Korea is not traditionally an immigrant nation, Korea has a history of accommodating various ethnic and racial groups from the dawn of its civilization until the late nineteenth century, when ethnic nationalism came into being in response to Japanese domination. Now there is a call to return to the ethos of civil harmony among heterogeneous people.

Many Koreans are so eager, at least in rhetoric, to create a multicultural society that Korea may have a good chance of achieving a Western liberal model of multiculturalism. For a nation to realize such a model, Will Kymlicka has outlined five key foundations of the Western trends toward accommodating diversity:

> Demographics, right-consciousness, multiple access points for safe political mobilization help to explain why nondominant groups have become more assertive of multicultural claims; and the desecuritization[68] of ethnic relations and a consensus on human rights help to reduce the risk to dominant groups of accepting these claims.[69]

Kymlicka trusts that "when these five conditions are in place, the trend towards greater accommodation of ethnocultural diversity is likely to arise."[70]

Let us see whether Korea can meet such conditions as Kymlicka has outlined. First, in terms of demographics, Korea has the lowest birthrate of 193 nations, as cited earlier in this book. And, since life expectancy has extended to eighty years, a growing elderly population means that Korea needs more foreign immigrants to support its growing economy and rapid industrialization. Korean demographers estimate that by 2050, Korea may need one to three million foreign immigrants per year and hundreds of thousands of foreign women to marry Korean men living in rural areas.[71]

Koreans ranging from rural farmers to urbane intellectuals to politicians from both conservative and liberal parties are aware of multiculturalism and endorse the basic tenets of it. In fact, the Korean government, particularly local and municipal government, has played a pivotal role in promoting international marriages in cooperation with international marriage brokers. Some local and municipal governments have passed local laws that provide public funds to assist international marriages.[72] Also, various civic organizations have become strong advocates of human rights for immigrants. Most leading Korean newspapers and TV stations are actively campaigning to promote multiculturalism. Publications ranging from sensational stories to thoughtful scholarly works are showing up on newsstands and in bookstores.

Regarding democracy, since 1993, Korea has enjoyed a mature democracy, rotating its power base between the conservative and liberal parties, both of which endorse multiculturalism. Active NGO organizations in Korea are assertive in addressing human rights; they are the ones who suggested that the government adopt the term *multiculturalism* officially.

The issue on desecuritization in Korea is irrelevant, because there is no national minority in Korea[73] like the ethnic Koreans or Okinawans in Japan or the Uighurs in China. In fact, in July 2009, ethnic tensions arose between the 8.3 million ethnic Uighurs—a Turkish-speaking Central Asian people—and the Han Chinese in the Xinjiang region, which is a vast 1.6 million square kilometers. The region accounts for one-sixth of China's territory and reaches into Central Asia.[74]

Besides those factors Kymlicka has outlined for the prerequisites in implementing a liberal model of Western multiculturalism, the Korean economy is strong enough to accommodate many foreign immigrants and married immigrants. Most important, Korea's cultural legacy—a tradition of openness and tolerance toward immigrants before the late nineteenth and early twentieth centuries—may help pave the way for a multicultural society.

Also, the participation of some big business conglomerates and a big civic organization is promising for implementation of successful multiculturalism in Korea. As positive signs for those, on October 7, 2010, the Samsung group, the largest business conglomerate in Korea, announced the establishment of two companies exclusively devoted to supporting and educating multicultural families as they adjust to life in Korea. LG Electronics, another large business group, offers a family visitation program for foreign brides. Also, Hana Banking Group, one of the largest banking groups in Korea, has begun to launch a major campaign for multicultural families.

In addition, one large civic organization has played its part. On September 4, 2010, the Rotary Club, one of the most active and well-financed civic organizations in Korea, announced its plan to initiate an assistance program for multicultural families. As long as business conglomerates and civic organizations understand the genuine meaning of multiculturalism—not assimilation but accommodation—the full implementation of multiculturalism in Korea may be accomplished ahead of schedule. After all, businesses and private organizations can sometimes act more effectively and efficiently than government.

Another factor to consider is the Korean ethos that craves fast results— *ppali ppali* (hurry up)—an ethos that might hasten the process of implementation. Koreans have a well-earned international reputation for beating deadlines.[75] This was the case with Korea's industrialization. According to Richard M. Steers and his colleagues, "It took the United States 100 years to move from an agrarian state to an industrial economy, and it took Japan seventy years to make a similar adjustment, but it took Korea less than thirty years."[76] Even if it takes longer than one may estimate, Korea seems destined to move forward to become a true multicultural society with a liberal model of Western multiculturalism.

Notes

NOTES TO THE INTRODUCTION

1. Will Kymlicka, *Multicultural Citizenship* (New York: Oxford University Press, 1995), p. 1; see also Ted Gurr, *Minorities at Risk: A Global View of Ethnopolitical Conflicts* (Washington, DC: Institute of Peace Press, 1993); Leslie Laczko, "Canada's Pluralism in Comparative Perspective," *Ethnic and Racial Studies* 17 (1994): 20–41; Gunnar Nielsson, "States and 'Nation-Groups': A Global Taxonomy," in *New Nationalisms of the Developed West*, Edward Tiryakian and Ronald Rogowski, eds., pp. 27–56 (Boston: Allen & Unwin, 1985).

2. Kymlicka, *Multicultural Citizenship*, p. 196, n. 1.

3. Will Kymlicka, *Multicultural Odysseys: Navigating the New International Politics of Diversity* (New York: Oxford University Press, 2007), p. 62.

4. Hyung Il Pai, *Constructing "Korean" Origins: A Critical Review of Archaeology, Historiography, and Racial Myth in Korean State-Formation Theories* (Cambridge: Harvard University Asia Center, 2000), p. 1.

5. Ilyon [Iryŏn], *Samguk yusa: Legends and History of the Three Kingdoms of Ancient Korea*, trans. Ha Tae-hung and Grafton K. Mintz (Seoul: Yonsei University Press, 2007), pp. 158–73.

6. *Source*: Press report of the Ministry of Public Administration and Security, June 11, 2010. And see also, Yi Sŏng-mi, *Tamunhwa Code: Han'guk "Dream" haebŏp ch'atki [Multicultural Code: Seeking the Solutions for the Korean Dream]* (Seoul: Saeng'gakŭi Namu, 2010), pp. 23–35.

7. Yi, *Tamunhwa Code*, p. 25.

8. The issue is almost universal. See Will Kymlicka and Baogang He, eds., *Multiculturalism in Asia* (New York: Oxford University Press, 2005), p. 2.

9. Kim Hyun Mee, "The State and Migrant Women: Diverging Hopes in the Making of 'Multicultural Families' in Contemporary Korea," *Korea Journal* 47 (2007):

100–22, p. 103; Han Geon-Soo, "Multicultural Korea: Celebration or Challenge of Multiethnic Shift in Contemporary Korea," *Korea Journal* 47 (2007): 32–63, p. 37.

10. The emic approach is derived from the concept formulated by Kenneth Pike from the suffix of *phon-eme* to explain people's social behavior in terms of their own insider views. In contrast, *etic*, the suffix of *phon-etic*, is a label for the outsider's view of culture (Kenneth Pike, *Language in Relation to a Unified Theory of the Structure of Human Behavior*, vol. 1 [Glendale, CA: Summer Institute of Linguistics, 1954]. See also Marvin Harris, *Theories of Culture in Postmodern Times* [Walnut Creek, CA: AltaMira Press, 1999], pp. 31–33).

11. Will Kymlicka states that "the retreat from multiculturalism is far from uniform across countries; it is more pronounced in Western Europe than in North America, for example" (see Kymlicka, *Multicultural Odysseys*, p. 124).

12. Korea's birthrate has been reported slightly differently by different agencies. Some sources have indicated it as 1.24 in 2010, which would make it one of the three countries that have the lowest birthrate among 186 countries, next to Hong Kong (1.01) and Bosnia and Herzegovina (1.22). The Organisation for Economic Co-operation and Development (OECD) predicted that Korea's population is expected to shrink 0.02 percent in the cited year from a year earlier (*Korea Herald*, May 21, 2010, p. 5).

13. Life expectancy in Korea has been extended from 61.83 (58.67 male and 65.57 female) in 1970 to 79.60 (76.15 male and 82.88 female) in 2010 (*source*: The Korea National Statistical Office, ROK, November 17, 2010).

14. Chang Chae-hyŏk, the police chief on Korean Aging at the Ministry for Health and Welfare of the Korean government, has pointed out that Korea is becoming an aging society beginning in the year 2000, will become an aged society by the year 2018, and will be a superaged society by the year 2026. In this process, Korea would take only twenty-six years to become superaged, which is faster than Japan, which would take thirty-six years, the United States, which would take eighty-eight years, and France, which would take 155 years (Chang Chae-hyŏk, "Noinbogŏnbokchichŏngch'aekŭi panghyangkwa kwajae [The Directions and Tasks of the Health and Welfare Policies for the Elderly Koreans]," paper presented at the forum on the Korean Aging and Care-giving, November 17, 2010, Seoul, Korea.

15. The proportion of the Korean farming population has been reduced from 29.8 percent in the 1980s to 6.1 percent in 2010 (*source*: The Korea National Statistical Office, ROK, November 17, 2010).

16. Han Kyung-Koo, "The Archaeology of the Ethnically Homogeneous Nation-State and Multiculturalism in Korea," *Korea Journal* 47 (2007): 8–31.

17. Han, "Multicultural Korea," pp. 32–63.

18. Oh Kyŏng-sŏk et al., *Han'gukaesŏŭi tamunhwajuŭi: Hyŏnsil-gwa chaenjŏm* [*Multiculturalism in Korea: A Critical Review*] (Seoul: Han'ul Academy, 2007), pp. 37–38.

19. Kymlicka, *Multicultural Citizenship,* p. 198, n. 9.

20. Alain Finkielkraut, *La Défaite de la Pensée* [*The Undoing of Thought*], trans. Dennis O'Keeffe (London: The Claridge Press, 1988), pp. 91–92.

21. Kymlicka, *Multicultural Odysseys,* p. 7.

22. Ibid., p. 17.

23. Ibid., p. 18.

24. Charles Taylor, with commentary by K. Anthony Appiah, Jürgen Habermas, Steven C. Rockefeller, Michael Walzer, and Susan Wolf, ed. and introduced by Amy Gutmann, *Multiculturalism: Examining the Politics of Recognition* (Princeton: Princeton University Press, 1994), p. 68.

25. Finkielkraut, *La Défaite de la Pensée*, p. 64; see also Richard Caputo, "Multiculturalism and Social Justice in the United States: An Attempt to Reconcile the Irreconcilable with a Pragmatic Liberal Framework," *Race, Gender and Class* 8 (2001): 161–82, p. 164.

26. David Miller, "Multiculturalism and the Welfare State: Theoretical Reflections," in *Multiculturalism and the Welfare State: Recognition and Redistribution in Contemporary Democracies*, Keith Banting and Will Kymlicka, eds., pp. 323–38 (New York: Oxford University Press, 2006), p. 326; see also David Miller, *On Nationality* (Oxford: Oxford University Press, 1995).

27. Charles Taylor, *Multiculturalism and "The Politics of Recognition": An Essay* (Princeton: Princeton University Press, 1993).

28. Charles Taylor, "The Politics of Recognition," in *Multiculturalism: Examining the Politics of Recognition*, ed. and introduced by Amy Gutmann, pp. 25–85 (Princeton: Princeton University Press, 1994), p. 65.

29. Susan Wolf, "Comment," in *Multiculturalism: Examining the Politics of Recognition*, ed. and introduced by Amy Gutmann, pp. 75–98 (Princeton: Princeton University Press, 1994), pp. 75–98.

30. Keith Banting, Richard Johnston, Will Kymlicka, and Stuart Soroka, "Do Multiculturalism Policies Erode the Welfare State? An Empirical Analysis," in *Multiculturalism and the Welfare State: Recognition and Redistribution in Contemporary Democracies*, Keith Banting and Will Kymlicka, eds., pp. 49–91 (New York: Oxford University Press, 2006), p. 51.

31. Kymlicka, *Multicultural Citizenship*, p. 18.

32. Regarding his usage of the term *liberal*, Kymlicka states, "I do not yet know that they are 'liberal' in any meaningful sense, beyond the fact that they emerged within the framework of Western liberal democracies" (see Kymlicka, *Multicultural Odysseys*, p. 85).

33. Kymlicka, *Multicultural Odysseys*, p. 18.

34. Banting, Johnston, Kymlicka, and Soroka state that "unfortunately, there is no consensus in the literature on how to define the term 'multicultural policies.' The term has quite different connotations in different countries. Many writers employ the term without ever defining it, and those who do make an effort to define it offer very different accounts of the necessary or sufficient conditions for a policy to qualify as a 'multicultural policy'" (see Banting, Johnston, Kymlicka, and Soroka, "Do Multiculturalism Policies Erode the Welfare State?" p. 51).

35. Ibid., pp. 49–91.

36. Kim, "The State and Migrant Women," p. 103.

37. Han, "Multicultural Korea," p. 37.

38. Han, "The Archaeology of the Ethnically Homogeneous Nation-State and Multiculturalism in Korea," p. 9.

39. Kim, "The State and Migrant Women," pp. 103–4.

40. Han, "The Archaeology of the Ethnically Homogeneous Nation-State and Multiculturalism in Korea," p. 9.

41. Kim, "The State and Migrant Women," p. 109.

42. In the early 1970s, Korea launched a state-led national movement to improve the welfare of rural people, a movement that targeted thirty thousand Korean rural villages (see the details in In-Joung Whang, *Management of Rural Change in Korea: The Saemaul Undong* [Seoul: Seoul National University Press, 1981]).

43. *Source*: press release by the Bureau of Social Statistics, the Korea National Statistical Office (*T'onggyech'ŏng, Sahoet'onggye-guk*), December 13, 2010.

44. See the details in Choong Soon Kim, *Kimchi and IT: Tradition and Transformation in Korea* (Seoul: Ilchokak, 2007), pp. 167–70.

45. Kymlicka, *Multicultural Citizenship*, p. 18.

46. Wolf, "Comment," pp. 75–98.

47. The national system features an Asymmetric Digital Line (ADSL) and Wireless Broadband Internet (WiBro). Surprisingly, many Korean households, even in rural and coastal islands, have one or more PCs that are connected to the Internet. Any household that is not equipped with a PC may use one provided in the village or town halls for the public. Currently, all the components are provided in seven languages.

48. In traditional Korean society, people tended to marry at an early age. Any person beyond marriageable age was stigmatized. In 1925, for instance, most Korean women were married before the age of sixteen. The median age of marriage for women rose by about one and a half years between 1925 and 1940. In 1925, the median age at marriage for men was twenty-one; by 1940, it had risen by a little more than half a year. Ever since the Korea National Statistical Office (the census bureau) started keeping the official census in 1970, the average age of marriage among Koreans has increased steadily. In 1972, for instance, the average age of marriage for men was 26.7 and 22.6 for women. By 2004, it had increased to 30.6 for men and 27.5 for women (Kim, *Kimchi and IT*, p. 121).

49. The rate of increase has been remarkable: 1.2 percent in 1990, 3.4 percent in 2002, 8.4 percent in 2003, 11.4 percent in 2004, and 13.6 percent in 2005. In terms of number, from 1990 to 2004, over 66,000 Korean men married foreign women (*source*: the Ministry of Public Administration and Security, ROK, July 2008). In 2010, the number increased to 120,146 (see Kim Sŭng-Kwŏn et al., *2007-nyŏn chŏn'guk tamunhwakajoksilt'aechosa yŏn'gu* [*The Year 2009 Nationwide Survey on Multicultural Families*] [Seoul: The Ministry for Health, Welfare and Family Affairs, the Ministry of Justice, the Ministry of Gender Equality and Family, ROK, and the Korea Institute for Health and Social Affairs, 2010], p. 133).

50. *Source*: press report of the Ministry of Public Administration and Security, June 11, 2010.

51. When Koreans refer to overseas Koreans, those who live in Russia and Central Asian countries are called *Koryŏ-in* (people from the Koryŏ dynasty), but those who live in China, especially Manchuria, have been called *Chosŏnjok* (people from Chosŏn dynasty). Not only do Koreans in Korea address them as such but also they themselves do as well. It is just a habit without having any specific definition or

criteria. In fact, Korean migration in both Russia, especially the Maritime Province of Russia, and northern China, mostly Manchuria, had begun about the same time. In 1937, Joseph Stalin began a campaign of massive ethnic cleansing and forcibly deported everyone of Korean origin living in the coastal provinces of Far Eastern Russia to the unsettled steppe country of Central Asia 3,700 miles away. These deportees were 180,000 Korean political pawns. In this book, my designation of *Chosŏnjok* does not connote any positive or negative meaning. I simply follow a common usage.

52. Yi, *Tamunhwa Code*, p. 49.

53. A news briefing, the Ministry for Health, Welfare and Family Affairs, ROK, July 13, 2005, p. 3.

54. AP report that is quoted indirectly from the *Korea Herald,* August 12, 2008, p. 4.

55. Among the stars who have played leading roles in the *Hallyu* wave is Bae Yong-jun, for instance, who played a major role in one of the most popular Korean TV soap operas, *Kyŏul Yŏn'ga* [*Winter Sonata*], which generated four billion dollars (Internet edition of *Kyunghyang Shinmun,* November 4, 2005, n.p.). The smash-hit TV soap opera series *Taejang'gŭm* [*Jewel in the Palace*] features the actress Yi Yŏng-ae, who plays the female protagonist. The show has been so popular in China, Hong Kong, Taiwan, and other Southeast Asian counties that the networks are offering many reruns. Capitalizing on such popularity, beginning on May 10, 2006, Asiana Airlines, a Korean flagship carrier, covered its Boeing 767 jets that serve Asian countries with images from *Taejang'gŭm* and put close-up photos of Yi Yŏng-ae on the planes' tails (Kim, *Kimchi and IT,* p. 7).

56. Proportionally speaking, Korea has the largest proportion of overseas ethnic Koreans (14 percent of the total South Korean population of 49 million) as compared with China (1.8 percent out of 1.3 billion) and Japan (1.4 percent of 120 million) (Yi, *Tamunhwa Code*, p. 289).

57. Yi, *Tamunhwa Code,* pp. 42–46.

58. Francis L. K. Hsu, "Intercultural Understanding: Genuine and Spurious," *Anthropology & Education Quarterly* 8 (1977): 202–9, p. 206.

59. Indirectly quoted from Clifford Geertz, *After the Fact: Two Countries, Four Decades, One Anthropologist* (Cambridge: Harvard University Press, 1995), pp. 165–66.

60. James L. Peacock, *The Anthropological Lens: Harsh Light, Soft Focus* (New York: Cambridge University Press, 1986), p. 83.

61. James W. Fernandez, *Bwiti: An Ethnography of the Religious Imagination in Africa* (Princeton: Princeton University Press, 1982), p. xx.

62. Choong Soon Kim, *Faithful Endurance: An Ethnography of Korean Family Dispersal* (Tucson: University of Arizona Press, 1988).

63. Ch'oe Jaeseuk, *Han'guk kajokchedo yŏn'gu* [*Studies on Korean Family System*] (Seoul: Minjungsŏgwan, 1966); Kim Tu-hŏn, *Han'guk kajokchedo yŏn'gu* [*Studies on Korean Family System*] (Seoul: Seoul National University Press, 1969); Song Chun-ho, *Chosŏn sahoesa yŏn'gu* [*Social History of Chosŏn*] (Seoul: Ilchokak, 1987); Edward W. Wagner, "Two Early Genealogies and Women's Status in Early Yi

Dynasty Korea," in *Korean Women: View from the Inner Room,* Laurel Kendall and Mark Peterson, eds., pp. 23–32 (New Haven, CT: East Rock Press, 1983).

64. Kim, *Faithful Endurance*; idem, *A Korean Nationalist Entrepreneur: A Life History of Kim Sŏngsu, 1891–1955* (Albany, NY: State University of New York Press, 1998); idem, *One Anthropologist, Two Worlds: Three Decades of Reflexive Fieldwork in North America and Asia* (Knoxville: University of Tennessee Press, 2002), pp. 1–2; L. L. Langness, *The Life History in Anthropological Science* (New York: Holt, Rinehart and Winston, 1965); Pertti J. Pelto, *Anthropological Research: The Structural Inquiry* (New York: Harper & Row, 1970), pp. 98–100.

65. Pelto, *Anthropological Research,* p. 99.

66. Ibid. Also, this point is well illustrated in John Stands In Timber and Margot Liberty, *Cheyenne Memories* (New Haven: Yale University Press, 1967).

67. Oscar Lewis, *Five Families: Mexican Case Studies in the Culture of Poverty* (New York: Basic Books, 1959).

68. Kim, *Faithful Endurance.*

69. Miles Richardson, "Anthropologist—The Myth Teller," *American Ethnologist* 2 (1975): 517–33, p. 530.

NOTES TO CHAPTER 1

1. Choong Soon Kim, *Kimchi and IT: Tradition and Transformation in Korea* (Seoul: Ilchokak, 2007), p. 15.

2. Pak Ki-hyŏn, *Uri yŏksarŭl pakkun kwihwa sŏngssi: Urittang'ŭl sŏnt'aekhan kwihwainŭi paljach'wi* [*The Naturalized Surname Groups Who Changed Korean History: Track Records of Naturalized People Who Chose Korea*] (Seoul: Yŏksaŭiach'im, 2007), pp. 34–35.

3. The original report was made by Yu Yŏn-suk. Since I was unable to obtain the report, I have cited her work indirectly from Yi Sŏng-mi (see *Tamunhwa Code: Han'guk "Dream" haebŏp ch'atki* [*Multicultural Code: Seeking the Solutions for the Korean Dream*] (Seoul: Saeng'gakŭi Namu, 2010), pp. 42–46; see also *Kukmin Ilbo,* January 8, 2007, pp. 1, 5).

4. Yamagata prefecture is located in the southwest corner of Tohoku, facing Eastern Sea, and it borders Niigata and Fukushima prefectures on the south, Miyagi prefecture on the east, and Akita prefecture on the north. All of these boundaries are marked by mountains. Most of the population resides in a central plain. Yamagata has been experiencing one of the highest depopulation rates in Japan, with 5.3 percent annually. Its economy depends largely on agricultural products, especially fruits—grapes, apples, peaches, melons, persimmons, and watermelons.

5. Lam Peng-Er, "At the Margins of a Liberal-Democratic State: Ethnic Minorities in Japan," in *Multiculturalism in Asia,* Will Kymlicka and Baogang He, eds., pp. 223–43 (New York: Oxford University Press, 2005), p. 227.

6. See Choong Soon Kim, *Faithful Endurance: An Ethnography of Korean Family Dispersal* (Tucson: University of Arizona Press, 1988), pp. 23–26; Changsoo Lee and George DeVos, *Koreans in Japan: Ethnic Conflict and Accommodation*

(Berkeley: University of California Press, 1981); Peng-Er, "At the Margins of a Liberal-Democratic State," pp. 223–43.

7. Sarah M. Nelson, *The Archaeology of Korea* (New York: Cambridge University Press, 1993), p. 263; Robert Sayers and Ralph Rinzler, *The Korean Onggi Potter*, Smithsonian Folklife Studies Series, no. 5 (Washington, DC: Smithsonian Institution Press, 1987), pp. 58–63.

8. Choong Soon Kim, *One Anthropologist, Two Worlds: Three Decades of Reflexive Fieldwork in North Amereica and Asia* (Knoxvillle: University of Tennessee Press, 2002), p. xvii; idem, *Kimchi and IT*, p. 18

9. www.kakamigahara-kimuchi.com/topics.html.

10. See the idea of "pure race" in Hyung Il Pai, *Constructing "Korean" Origins: A Critical Review of Archaeology, Historiography, and Racial Myth in Korean State-Formation Theories* (Cambridge: Harvard University Asia Center, 2000), p. 465, n. 30.

11. Kim Byung-mo [Pyŏng-mo Kim], *Kim Pyŏng-mo-ŭi kokohak yŏhaeng* [*Kim Byung-mo's Archaeological Tour*], 2 vols. (Seoul: Karaesil, 2006), vol. 1, pp. 22–25.

12. A few of the works in chronological order of publication are as follows: Yi Chong-myŏng, "Koryŏ-e naet'uhan Parhaein'go [A Study on Parhae Immigrants Who Were Naturalized in Koryŏ]," *Paeksanhakpo* [*Journal of Paeksan Society*] 4 (1968): 199–225; Chŏng Pyŏng-wan, "Urinara woerae-sŏngssi-ŭi kubosŏ pigyo: Sijogo [A Comparison of Old Genealogies on Foreign Surname Groups Who Were Naturalized in Korea: On Founding Fathers]," *Pangsongt'ongsindaehak nonmunjip* [*Journal of Korea National Open University*] 13 (1991): 91–122; Hwang Un-ryong, "Kwihwasŏngssi sijo tongnaesŏl [Theories on the Naturalized Foreigners Who Came to East, Korea]," *Pusan yŏjadaehak sahak* [*History of Pusan Women's College*] 10 and 11 (1993): 297–320; Yi Chong-il, "Chung'guk-esŏ tongnaekwihwahan saram-ŭi sŏngssiwa kŭ chason-ŭi sinbunjiwi [Name of the Naturalized Surname Groups from China and the Statuses and Occupations of Their Descendants]," in *Sohŏn Nam To-yŏng paksa kohŭi kinyŏm yŏksanonch'ong* [*Commemorative Essays in Honor of Dr. Sohŏn Nam To-yŏng's 70th Birthday*], pp. 321–48 (Seoul: Minjokmunhwasa, 1993).

13. Publication of *Roots* by Alex Haley (1921–1992), winner of the Pulitzer Prize and the subsequent TV miniseries that aired on ABC in 1977, generated an enormous interest in oral history and genealogical history among the American public (see Alex Haley, *Roots: The Saga of an American Family* [New York: Doubleday, 1976]).

14. Lee Hee-Soo [Hŭi-su Yi], "Early Korea-Arabic Maritime Relations based on Muslim Sources," *Korea Journal* 31 (1991): 21–32.

15. Ch'oe Sang-su [Sang-su Ch'oe], "Relations between Korea and Arabia," *Korea Journal* 9 (1969): 14–17, 20.

16. Park Ok-kol [Pak Ok-kŏl], *Koryŏ-sidae-ŭi kwihwain yŏn'gu* [*A Study of the Naturalized People in the Koryŏ Period*] (Seoul: Kukhakcharyowŏn, 1996).

17. Some have romanized "Korea" into "Corea" or "Corée" in their early writings (see Maurice Courant, *Bibliographie Coreene* [Paris: E. Leroux, 1894–1896, Supplement, 1901; reprint, New York: B. Franklin, 1968]; Charles Dallet, *Histoire de l'Église de Corée* [Paris: V. Palme, 1874], 2 vols. [reprint, Seoul: Royal Asiatic Society, Korea Branch, 1975]; William Elliot Griffis, *Corea: The Hermit Nation* [New York: Charles Scribner's Sons, 1882]).

18. See Bruce Cumings, *Korea's Place in the Sun: A Modern History* (New York: W. W. Norton & Co., 1997), p. 89.

19. John M. Frankl, *Han'gukmunhak-e nat'anan woeguk-ŭi ŭimi* [*Images of "the Foreign" in Korean Literature and Culture*] (Seoul: Somyŏngch'ulp'an, 2008) (in Korean).

20. Andre Schmid, *Korea between Empires, 1895–1919* (New York: Columbia University Press, 2002).

21. Gi-Wook Shin, *Ethnic Nationalism in Korea: Genealogy, Politics, and Legacy* (Stanford: Stanford University Press, 2006).

22. Griffis was born in Philadelphia as the son of a sea captain and later a coal trader. Educated at Rutgers University, he fought in the American Civil War. Griffis came to Japan in 1870 to organize a school in Echizen. At the time he was writing his book on Korea, Griffis had never been in Korea. His closest experience with Korea was that he "spent a few days at Tsuruga and Mikuni, by the sea which separates Japan and Korea." His primary sources for the book were all Japanese sources, and his informants were all Japanese (see Griffis, *Corea*, p. ix).

23. Frankl, *Han'gukmunhak-e nat'anan woeguk-ŭi ŭimi*, p. 22.

24. Ibid., p. 157. Recently, Yŏn Kap-su has published a book to reevaluate the role of Hŭngsŏn Taewŏngun in the policy of isolationism (see Yŏn Kap-su, *Kojongdae chŏngch'i pyŏndong yŏn'gu* [*Studies on Political Change during the Kojong Era*] [Seoul: Ilchisa, 2008]).

25. The term *exclusionism* was introduced by Key-Hiuk Kim (see Key-Hiuk Kim, *The Last Phase of the East Asia World Order* [Berkeley: University of California Press, 1980], passim).

26. Cumings, *Korea's Place in the Sun*, p. 89.

27. Indirectly quoted from Cumings (ibid., p. 37).

28. Yi Hŭi-kun estimate its numbers would reach several tens of thousands (see Yi Hŭi-kŭn, *Urian-ŭi kŭdŭl: Sŏkkimgwa nŏmnadŭm kŭ kongjon-ŭi minjoksa* [*Those Who Live with Us: Ethnic History of Biological Mixing, Crossing Back and Forth, and Symbiosis*] [Seoul: Nŏmŏ-books, 2008], pp. 67–70).

29. Frankl, *Han'gukmunhak-e nat'anan woeguk-ŭi ŭimi*, pp. 22–59.

30. Ibid., pp. 34–35.

31. John Frankl's interview with *JoongAng Ilbo* (see *JoongAng Ilbo*, April 22, 2008, p. 29).

32. Han Kyung-Koo, "The Archaeology of the Ethnically Homogeneous Nation-State and Multiculturalism in Korea," *Korea Journal* 47 (2007): 16. According to Lhim Hag Seong, in the views of traditional Koreans, only people of Chosŏn and the Ming of China were considered to be civilized, and others were *yain,* meaning barbarians, or *orangk'ae* (Lhim Hag Seong [Yim Hak-sŏng], "Sipch'ilsegi chŏnban hojŏkcharyorŭl t'onghae pon kwihwa yain-ŭi Chosŏnesŏ-ŭi saenghwal yangsang: Ulsanhojŏk (1609) kwa Haenamhojŏk-ŭi (1639) saryaebunsŏk [The Modes of Lives of Naturalized Jurchens Appeared in the Chosŏn Census Registers in the First Half of the Seventeenth Century]," *Komunsŏ'yŏngu* [*Studies of Old Documents*] 33 [2008]: 95–128, p. 95).

33. Schmid, *Korea between Empires*, p. 173.

34. Yi, *Urian-ŭi kŭdŭl*, p. 8.

35. Ibid., passim. This book has been reviewed in several major Korean daily newspapers (see *Dong-A Ilbo,* December 5, 2008, p. A-22; *JoongAng Ilbo,* December 6, 2008, p. 16).

36. Indirectly quoted from Nelson, *The Archaeology of Korea*, p. 1.

37. Kim, *Kimchi and IT,* pp. 18–19.

38. Nelson, *The Aracheology of Korea,* passim. By and large, Kim Byung-mo concurs with Nelson's view, stating that human beings might have inhabited the peninsula around 400,000 or 500,000 years ago (Kim Byung-mo, *Han'gukin-ŭi paljach'wi* [*Footprints of Koreans*], revised ed. [Seoul: Chipmundang, 1994], p. 42). The most recent archaeological findings in Chŏn'gok-ri, Yŏnch'ŏn, of Kyŏnggi province indicate that the Korean peninsula was inhabited by Paleolithic people between 300,000 to 350,000 years ago at the earliest (Bae Kidong [Ki-dong Pae], "Chŏn'gok-ri kusŏkki yujŏk-ŭi chosagwajŏng-ŭi munjejŏm [Chŏn'gok-ri Paleolithic Site, Current Understanding]," Paper presented at the International Seminar in Memory of the Excavation of Paleolithic Site, May 3, 2002, Yŏnch'ŏn, Korea).

39. Kim, *Han'gukin-ŭi paljach'wi,* p. 91.

40. Ki-baik Lee, *A New History of Korea,* trans. Edward W. Wagner with Edward J. Schultz (Cambridge: Harvard-Yenching Institute by Harvard University Press, 1984), p. 1.

41. Ibid., p. 3. Before the Paleolithic period ended and the Neolithic period began, a relatively short Mesolithic period, beginning around 12,000 BC, was characterized less by big-game hunting and more by cultivated food sources on the Korean peninsula (Choe Chong Pil [Chŏng-p'il Ch'oe] and Martin T. Bale, "Current Perspectives on Settlement, Subsistence, and Cultivation in Prehistoric Korea," *Artic Anthropology* 39 [2002]: 95–121). Of course, the present national boundaries were then irrelevant (Nelson, *The Archaeology of Korea,* p. 109).

42. The Ainu of the northern tip of Japan, the natives of Sakhalin, and the Eskimos of the eastern coast of Siberia are all descendants of these Paleoaisan tribes (Kim, *Han'gukin-ŭi paljach'wi,* p. 92).

43. Definitive characteristics of civilization include a system of writing; cities; skilled specialists; monumental architecture; great differences in wealth and status among people; and the kind of strong, hierarchical, central political system we call the *state* (Kim, *Kimchi and IT,* p. 345, n. 10).

44. Carter J. Eckert and his associates consider that the Bronze Age in Korea lasted from about the ninth or eighth century BC until about the fourth century BC (see Carter J. Eckert et al., *Korea Old and New: A History* [Seoul: Ilchokak, 1990], p. 9). Cultural achievements of Korea in the Bronze Age were not as sophisticated as those of the Xia and Shang dynasties of China. Around 1766–1120 BC, the Shang dynasty had already invented a writing system, developed intensive agriculture, made wrought bronze tools, and established long-distance trade (Chang Kwang-chih, *The Archaeology of Ancient China,* 4th ed. [New Haven: Yale University, 1986]).

45. In older archeological accounts, rice cultivation in Korea was dated to around 1200 BC (Won-yong Kim, "Discoveries of Rice in Prehistoric Sites in Korea," *Journal of Asian Studies* 41 [1982]: 513–18), but now the dates are assumed to be earlier

than 2400 or 2100 BC (Choe Chong Pil [Chŏng-p'il Ch'oe], "Ilyuhaksangŭro pon Han'minjok kiwŏn yŏn'gu-e taehan pip'anjŏk kŏmt'o [A Critical View of Research on the Origins of Koreans and Their Culture]," *Han'guk Sang'gosa Hakpo* [*Journal of Early History of Korea*] 8 [1991]: 7–43, p. 38).

46. Nelson, *The Archaeology of Korea*, p. 116.

47. Kim Byung-mo, *Hŏ Hwang-ok route: Indo-esŏ Kaya-kkaji* [*The Route of Hŏ Hwang-ok: From India to Kaya*] (Seoul: *Yŏksa-ŭi ach'im*, 2008), p. 44. However, Sarah M. Nelson is skeptical since there is no evidence that a single ethnic group came into the Korean peninsula with rice technology (see Nelson, *The Archaeology of Korea*, p. 163).

48. Kim, *Hŏ Hwang-ok route*, p. 44; idem, *Kim Byung-mo-ŭi kokohak yŏhaeng*, pp. 50–53.

49. According to Chŏng-p'il Ch'oe, the appearance of dolmens is the most distinguished characteristic cultural trait of the Korean Bronze Age (see Kim, *Kimchi and IT*, p. 345, n. 14 [personal communication with Chŏng-p'il Ch'oe, October 1, 2005]. Dolmens can be seen in great numbers in virtually every part of Korea and appear in two basic forms of construction: table style and board style. The table style (also called the northern style) was constructed by placing several upright stones in a rough square and covering them with a flat capstone. The distribution of this kind is predominantly north of the Han River. The *paduk* (*gō* in Japanese), also known as the southern style, have a large boulder as a capstone placed atop several smaller rocks. These are found most widely in the area south of the Han River (Lee, *A New History of Korea*, p. 12).

50. Kim, *Han'gukin-ŭi paljach'wi*, p. 198.

51. Ibid., pp. 101–17.

52. Kim, *Hŏ Hwang-ok Route*, p. 45.

53. Kim Wook [Uk Kim] and Kim Chong-Youl [Chong-yŏl Kim], *Mitochondrial DNA pyŏniwa Han'gukin chiptan-ŭi kiwŏn-e kwanhan yŏn'gu* [*Modern Korean Origin and the Peopling of Korea as Revealed by mtDNA Lineages*], Seoul: Koguryŏ yŏn'gu chaedan yŏn'gu ch'ongsŏ [Koguryŏ Research Foundation], no. 13, 2005.

54. The HUGO Pan-Asian SNP Consortium, "Mapping Human Genetic Diversity in Asia," *Science* 236 (2009): 1541–45.

55. Yi-gu Kwon [Kwŏn Yi-gu], "Population of Ancient Korea in Physical Anthropological Perspective," *Korea Journal* 30 (1990): 4–12.

56. Choe, "Ilyuhaksangŭro pon Han'minjok kiwŏn," pp. 7–43; Nelson, *The Archaeology of Korea*, p. 265.

57. Se-jin Na has studied physical traits of present-day Koreans, including cranium index, the epicanthic fold, and skin color (Se-jin Na, "Physical Characteristics of Korean Nation," *Korea Journal* 3 [1963]: 9–29).

58. Chong Pil Choe (Chŏng-p'il Ch'oe) indicates that "the division of the populations of any species into biological 'race' tends to be arbitrary, but when it comes to human races, the situation is a quagmire. The population of H. [Homo] sapiens is not on its way to speciation. There are no nonadaptive physical traits. A phenotype is the result of the dynamic interaction of several genes and the environment."

59. Nelson, *The Archaeology of Korea*, p. 163.

60. To name just a few, the list of publications in chronological order includes Yi Wŏn-t'aek, "Chosŏn'jŏn'gi-ŭi kwihwa-wa kŭ sŏng'gyŏk [Naturalization and its Characteristics during the Early Chosŏn Period]," *Han'guk kukchebŏp yŏn'gu [Study of Seoul International Law]* 8 (2001): 225–46; Choi Yang-kyu [Ch'oe Yang-gyu], "Koryŏ-Chosŏn-sidae Chung'guk kwihwasŏngssi chŏngch'aek [The Settlement of the Naturalized Chinese Surname Groups during the Koryŏ and Chosŏn Periods]," unpublished MA thesis, Hongik University, Seoul, 2001; Yoon Yong-hyuk [Yun Yong-hyŏk], "Chŏng In-kyŏng-ga-ŭi Koryŏ chŏngch'ak-kwa Sŏsan [Naturalization of Chŏng In-Kyŏng during the Koryŏ Period and Sŏsan]," *The hosŏsahak [Historical Journal of hosŏ]* 48 (2007): 35–70; Lee Sŏng-mu, "Han'guk sŏngssi-wa chokpo [Korean Surname and genealogy]," Tong'asia-ŭi chokpo kukchae haksulhoeŭi [International Conference on East Asian Genealogy], Proceedings, November 21–22, 2008; Kim Pŏm-jun, "Saeroun sŏngssi chŭng'ga sokto Han'gukman mae-u nŭryŏ [Speed of Increasing Rate of New Surnames Are Very Slow in Korea]," *Kwahak'kisul [Science and Technology]* 10 (2008): 51–53; Lhim, "Sipch'ilsegi chŏnban hojŏkcharyorŭl t'onghae pon kwihwa yain-ŭi Chosŏnesŏ-ŭi saenghwal yangsang," pp. 95–128, esp. p. 103.

61. Kim Chŏng-ho, *Han'guk-ŭi kwihwa sŏngssi: Sŏngssiro pon uriminjok-ŭi kusŏng [The Naturalized Korean Surname Groups: The Composition of Ethnic Nation of Korea by Surname]* (Seoul: Chisiksanŏpsa, 2003); Lee Seo-Geon [Su-kŏn Yi], *Han'guk-ŭi sŏngssi-wa chokpo [Korean Family Names and Genealogies]* (Seoul: Seoul National University Press, 2008); Pak, *Uri yŏksarŭl pakkun kwihwa sŏngssi*; Yi, *Urian-ŭi kŭdŭl*.

62. Kim, *Han'guk-ŭi kwihwa sŏngssi*, p. 136.

63. In anthropological literature, *clan* is defined as "a set of kin whose members believe themselves to be descended from a common ancestor or ancestress but cannot specify the link back to that founder," while *lineage* can be defined as "a set of kin whose members trace descent from a common ancestor through known links" (Carol R. Ember and Melvin Ember, *Anthropology,* 9th ed. [Upper Saddle River, NJ: Prentice Hall, 1999], pp. 504, 507).

64. Lee, *Han'guk-ŭi sŏngssi-wa chokpo,* p. 80.

65. Lee, *Han'guk-ŭi sŏngssi-wa chokpo,* pp. 80–81.

66. Ibid., p. 96. On the Chinhŭng's monumental stones erected by the King Chinhŭng (540–576) in 578 during the Silla dynasty (57 BC to AD 935), for instance, no commemorated individual had a surname (ibid., pp. 72, 81–82, 96).

67. Ibid., p. 96.

68. Ibid., pp. 5, 100.

69. In principle, a person could serve the government as an official if he (always he, never she) could pass the state examination, but this opportunity was, in reality, limited to those of noble rank. Since *yangban* were exempted from the usual service obligations to the state, including corvée labor and military duty, they could devote themselves exclusively to studying for the examination.

70. Kim, *Kimchi and IT,* p. 221.

71. After the *yangban* and *chungin* (a middle class whose members were engaged in science and technology) came the *sangmin* (commoners), a class that included

people engaged in production, such as farmers and workers in manufacturing. Among them, there was also a rank order: farmers were considered the highest, followed by workers in manufacturing, then merchants at the bottom. All commoners were obliged to pay taxes, were subject to compulsory labor, and had to serve in the military (ibid., p. 222).

72. The *ch'ŏnmin* class included slaves, butchers, shamans, singing girls, and performers. Slaves who occupied the lowest layer were sold, given as gifts, and inherited. People who belonged to this class were discriminated against by the people above them (ibid.).

73. The reform of 1894, during the reign of King Kojong (1864–1907) was a sweeping one, affecting virtually every aspect of the Chosŏn administration, the economy, and sociocultural activities. One act of reform was to eliminate the hereditary class distinction between *yangban* and commoners. This reform is regarded as the starting point of Korea's modernization. After this reform, Koreans acquired surnames in growing numbers. (See Martina Deuchler, *Confucian Gentleman and Barbarian Envoys: The Opening of Korea, 1875–1885* [Seattle: University of Washington Press, 1977], p. xii; see also the details on *Kabo* reform in Young Ik Lew [Yong-ik Yu], "The *Kabo* Reform Movement: Korean and Japanese Reform Efforts in Korea," unpublished PhD dissertation, Harvard University, 1972; idem, *Kabo Kyŏngjang yŏn'gu* [*Studies on the Kabo Reform Movement*] [Seoul: Ilchokak, 1990]).

74. Lee, *Han'guk-ŭi sŏngssi-wa chokpo*, pp. 333–34.

75. Ibid., p. 334.

76. The Japanese authorities said the policy of *ch'angssi* was voluntary, but in reality it was mandatory. Often police were used to enforce the policy. Those who did not conform were thought to be anti-imperial and were discriminated against in employment and could not be enrolled in schools. Despite some vehement opposition, less than four months after the announcement of the policy over 326,105 Korean households (about 87 percent of the total) had changed their names, both surnames and personal names (Choong Soon Kim, *A Korean Nationalist Entrepreneur: A Life History of Kim Sŏngsu, 1891–1955* [Albany: State University of New York Press, 1998], p. 202, n. 27). Despite this radical change, Japanese policy could not assimilate Korean people into Japanese culture (see Mark Caprio, *Japanese Assimilation Policies in Colonial Korea, 1910–1945* [Seattle: University of Washington Press, 2009]).

77. Lee, *Han'guk-ŭi sŏngssi-wa chokpo,* pp. 194–97. I was unable to find the original names of all those who were naturalized, except some such as the Arabic name of Samga, which was dubbed Chang Sun-yong, and Tungduran from Jurchen territory, which was dubbed Yi Chi-ran, for instance.

78. The *Chosun Ilbo,* August 22, 2009, p. A-12.

79. *JoongAng Ilbo,* May 24, 2010, p. 19.

80. Genealogies recorded in the early and middle part of the Chosŏn dynasty appear to be more reliable than those published during the period of Japanese occupation (1910–1945) and Korea's subsequent liberation. At the time of Korea's liberation, there were many genealogies recorded without great concern for accuracy. Some were altered, and other genealogies falsified the ancestral past (see Lee, *Han'guk-ŭi*

sŏngssi-wa chokpo, p. 64). Some of them fabricated founding fathers from China, a result of many Koreans adoring China as an imagined place of origin (a mind-set called *mohwa sasang*). Affinity for China came from the influence of Neo-Confucianism in the seventeenth century (Choi, "Koryŏ-Chosŏn-sidae Chung'guk kwihwasŏngssi chŏngch'aek," p. 1; Park, *Koryŏ-sidae-ŭi kwihwain yŏn'gu*, pp. 37–38).

81. Chŏng, "Urinara woerae-sŏngssi-ŭi kubosŏ pigyo," pp. 91–122.

82. Hwang, "Kwihwasŏngssi sijo tongnaesŏl," pp. 297–320.

83. The Three Han, called Samhan, was a pristine state during the stage of state-building during Korea's Bronze Age period (2000 to 1000 BC). The Samhan was divided into three small states of the leagues, including Mahan, Chinhan, and Pyŏnhan, and it occupied the Han River area in the southern part of the peninsula, which was firmed during the first and third century AD (see the map of their location in Lee, *A New History of Korea*, p. 25).

84. See Arthur Cotterell, *East Asia: From Chinese Predominance to the Rise of the Pacific Rim* (New York: Oxford University Press, 1993), p. 19.

85. Kim, *Han'guk-ŭi kwihwa sŏngssi*, pp. 219–22.

86. Choi, "Koryŏ-Chosŏn sidae Chung'guk kwihassŏngssi chŏngch'ak," p. 51; Park, *Koryŏ-sidae-ŭi kwihwain yŏn'gu*, passim; Yi Wŏn-t'aek, "Chosŏn'jŏn'gi-ŭi kwihwa-wa kŭ sŏng'gyŏk [Naturalization and Its Characteristics during the Early Chosŏn Period]," *Han'guk kukchebŏp yŏn'gu* [*Study of Seoul International Law*] 8 (2001): 225–46.

87. Kim, *Han'guk-ŭi kwihwa sŏngssi*, pp. 111–12, cf. pp. 223–27.

88. Park, *Koryŏ-sidae-ŭi kwihwain yŏn'gu*, pp. 77–79.

89. Ibid.

90. Ibid., pp. 242–44.

91. Kim, *One Anthropologist, Two Worlds*, p. 35.

92. Kim, *Han'guk-ŭi kwihwa sŏngssi*, p. 225.

93. See the details in Yi Sŭng-han, *Kublai Khan-ŭi ilbonwŏnjŏng-gwa Ch'ungyŏl wang* [*Kublai Khan's Expedition of Japan and King Ch'ungyŏl*] (Seoul: P'urŭnsup, 2009), pp. 206–60, 370–72.

94. Ki-baik Lee describes that "thus Koryŏ became a 'son-in-law nation' to Yüan, in a sense an appanage under the Mongol imperial house. Subsequently it became the practice for Koryŏ crown princes to reside in Peking as hostage until called to the kingship. Even after their accession they would visit Peking frequently, leaving the throne in Kaesŏng empty. During the Mongol period the Koryŏ kings came to take Mongol names, wear their hair in Mongol style, wear Mongol dress, and use the Mongol language. The royal houses of the two nations had become a single family" (Lee, *A New History of Korea*, pp. 155–56).

95. Kim, *Han'guk-ŭi kwihwa sŏngssi*, p. 226.

96. Lee, "Chosŏn'jŏn'gi-ŭi kwihwa-wa kŭ sŏng'gyŏk," pp. 225–46.

97. Kim, *Han'guk-ŭi kwihwa sŏngssi*, pp. 227–28.

98. He came to Korea in 1963 and lectured in colleges. After the divorce, he was unable to adjust to Korean life, so he went to Japan and died July 16, 2005, at Akasaka Prince Hotel in Japan. Ironically, the hotel where he died was previously the hospital

where he had been born on December 29, 1931. The Chosŏn dynasty finally came to an end as Yi Ku died without leaving any surviving member.

99. Perhaps an exception to this will be Lhim Hag Seong's article about life patterns of ordinary Jurchens in the Chosŏn dynasty. However, descriptions are not made individually but by a summary of gregarious statistics (see Lhim, "Sipch'ilsegi chŏnban hojŏkcharyorŭl t'onghae pon kwihwa yain-ŭi Chosŏnesŏ-ŭi saenghwal yangsang," pp. 95–128).

100. Kim, *Han'guk-ŭi kwihwa sŏngssi,* pp. 267–68.

101. Iryŏn's real name before he became a monk was Kim Kyŏn-myŏng, and an exact date of publication of the memoirs is unknown, but it is assumed to be between 1281 and 1283 (see Ilyon [Iryŏn], *Samguk yusa: Legends and History of the Three Kingdoms of Ancient Korea,* trans. Ha Tae-hung and Grafton K. Mintz [Seoul: Yonsei University Press, 2007, orig. 1972], pp. 158–73).

102. Kim, *Han'guk'in-ŭi paljach'wi;* idem, *Hŏ Hwang-ok: Kim Surowangb;* idem, *Kim Suro wangbi-ŭi honin'gil* [*The Road to Marriage of Queen of King Kim Suro*] (Seoul: P'urŭnsup, 1994); idem, *Kim Byung-mo-ŭi kokohak yŏhaeng,* 2 vols.; idem, *Hŏ Hwang-ok route: Indo-esŏ Kaya-kkaji* [*The Route of Hŏ Hwang-ok: From India to Kaya*] (Seoul: Yŏksa-ŭi ach'im, 2008). See also The Association of Kimhae Kimssi An'gyŏng'gongp'a, ed*., Kimhae Kimssi an'gyŏng'gongp'a sebo* [*Genealogy of An'gyŏng Branch of Kimhae Kim Lineage*] (Seoul: The Association of Kimhae Kimssi An'gyŏng'gongp'a, 2000), esp. pp. 235–36.

103. Lee, *A New History of Korea,* p. 105.

104. Pak, *Uri yŏksarŭl pakkun kwihwa sŏngssi,* pp. 38–39.

105. Ibid., pp. 42–43.

106. Ch'oe, "Relations between Korea and Arabia," pp. 14–17, 20.

107. Pak, *Uri yŏksarŭl pakkun kwihwa sŏngssi,* p. 81.

108. See Ch'oe, "Relations between Korea and Arabia," pp. 14–17.

109. Park, *Koryŏ-sidae-ŭi kwihwain yŏn'gu,* p. 165.

110. Tŏksu Chang Chongch'inhoe, chokpop'yŏnch'an wiwŏnhoe, ed., *Tŏksu Changssi Chokpo* [*Geneaology of Tŏksu Chang Lineage*] (Seoul: Tŏksu Chang Chongch'inhoe, chokpop'yŏnch'an wiwŏnhoe [Editorial board, Association of Tŏksu Changssi], 1998), p. 191.

111. Uighur are a multiethnic and multiracial group, including Mongols, Turkish, Arabs, Iranians, and Europeans (see Pak, *Uri yŏksarŭl pakkun kwihwa sŏngssi,* p. 81).

112. See Pak, *Uri yŏksarŭl pakkun kwihwa sŏngssi,* pp. 201–03; Park, *Koryŏ-sidae-ŭi kwihwain yŏn'gu,* p. 187, 219.

113. Pak, *Uri yŏksarŭl pakkun kwihwa sŏngssi,* pp. 92–107.

114. Ibid., p. 96.

115. Ibid., p. 104.

116. Kim, *Han'gukui kwihwa sŏngssi,* p. 227.

117. Yi Kuk-chae, ed., *Ch'ŏnghaeyissi muhugongp'a sebo* [*Muhugong Branch of Ch'ŏnghaeyi Lineage*] (Seoul: Ch'ŏnghaeyissi muhugongpa'a chung'anghoe [Central Association of Muhugong Branch of Ch'ŏnghaeyi Lineage], 2006), pp. 1–89.

118. Park, *Koryŏ-sidae-ŭi kwihwain yŏn'gu,* p. 165.

119. Lee, *A New History of Korea,* p. 171.

120. According to the Association of Asan Chang lineage members, Chang Yŏng-sil's birth year was assumed to be either 1383 (tenth year of King U [1374–1388]) or 1390 (the second year of King Kongyang [1389–1392]).

121. Pak Hyŏn-mo, *Sejongch'ŏrŏm: Sot'ong'gwa hŏnsin-ŭi leadership* [*Like King Sejong: Leadership for Communication and Dedication*] (Seoul: Midasbook, 2008), pp. 380–81.

122. Lee, *A New History of Korea,* p. 196.

123. Since there was no such name in the Japanese records, there are some disputes about his identity: some believe he was Suzuki Maikotzi; others assume he may have been Harata Nobutane (see Pak, *Uri yŏksarŭl pakkun kwihwa sŏngssi,* pp. 114–16).

124. Ibid., p. 122.

125. On average, about one thousand Japanese tourists visit Urok each year (ibid., 124–25).

126. Ibid., p. 142.

127. Kang Chun-sik, *Tasi'ilnŭn Hamel-ŭi p'yoryu-gi* [*Rereading of Hamel's Ship Wreck and His Odysseys*] (Seoul: Ungjin-dot-com, 2002), passim.

128. Pak, *Uri yŏksarŭl pakkun kwihwa sŏngssi,* pp. 136–49.

129. Park, *Koryŏ-sidae-ŭi kwihwain yŏn'gu,* pp. 143–49.

130. Ibid., p. 222.

131. Lee, *A New History of Korea,* p. 72.

132. After the fall of Koguryŏ (668), Tae Cho-yŏng, a former Koguryŏ general, founded Parhae (698–926) with most of the Koguryŏ people. Its territory extended from the Sungari and Amur rivers in northern Manchuria to the northern provinces of modern Korea. Parhae gained control of most of the former Koguryŏ territory and then confronted Silla. However, later in 926 Parhae was conquered by Khitan (Kim, *Kimchi and IT,* p. 33; Park, *Koryŏ-sidae-ŭi kwihwain yŏn'gu,* p. 179).

133. Park, *Koryŏ-sidae-ŭi kwihwain yŏn'gu,* pp. 109–10, 179.

134. Ibid., pp. 183–85.

135. Lhim, "Sipch'ilsegi chŏnban hojŏkcharyorŭl t'onghae pon kwihwa yain-ŭi Chosŏnesŏ-ŭi saenghwal yangsang," pp. 95–128.

136. Ibid., p. 103.

137. Ibid., p. 121.

138. Ibid., pp. 118–19.

139. Ibid., p. 113.

140. Ibid., p. 114.

141. *Maeil Business Newspaper,* May 22, 2008, p. A-6.

142. Lhim, "Sipch'il-segi chŏnban hojŏkcharyorŭl t'onghae pon kwihwa yain-ŭi Chosŏnesŏ-ŭi saenghwal yangsang," pp. 95–128, esp. p. 122.

143. Yi, *Urian-ŭi kŭdŭl,* pp. 6–10, 111–20.

144. Kim, *Kimchi and IT,* pp. 221–22.

145. Yi Hŭi-kun estimates the number may be several tens of thousands (see Yi, *Urian-ŭi kŭdŭl,* p. 114).

146. Ibid., p. 9.

147. Ibid., p. 6.

148. Ibid., pp. 9, 120.

NOTES TO CHAPTER 2

1. The *Ŭisŏng Kim-ssi Chongbo* (the quarterly newspaper of the Ŭisŏng Kim Clan), April 1, 2009, pp. 1, 11.

2. As a nomadic tribe, the Hyungno (*Xiongnu*) occupied a vast region of northern China and Mongolia from the fifth century BC to the fifth century AD. The written documents about them are scarce.

3. Kim Chung-hwan, ed., *Ŭisŏng Kim-ssi Kaeamgong p'abo* [*Genealogy of Kaeam Branch of Ŭisŏng Kim Clan*] (Seoul: Ŭisŏng Kim-ssi Kaeamgong p'aboso, 1991), pp. 27, 67.

4. Kim Chŏng-ho, *Han'guk-ŭi kwihwa sŏngssi: Sŏngssiro pon uriminjok-ŭi kusŏng* [*The Naturalized Korean Surname Groups: The Composition of Ethnic Nation of Korea by Surname*] (Seoul: Chisiksanŏpsa, 2003), pp. 267–68.

5. See Alex Haley, *Roots: The Saga of an American Family* (New York: Doubleday, 1976).

6. Kim Byung-mo, *Hŏ Hwang-ok: Kim Suro wangbi: Ssangŏ-ŭi pimil:* [*Hŏ Hwang-ok: Queen of King Kim Suro: A Secret of "Twin-fish*] (Seoul: Chosun Ilbo, 1994); idem, *Hŏ Hwang-ok Route: Indo-esŏ Kaya-kkaji* [*The Route of Hŏ Hwang-ok: From India to Kaya*] (Seoul: Yŏksa-ŭi ach'im, 2008); idem, *Kim Suro wangbi-ŭi honin'gil* [*The Road to Marriage of Queen of King Kim Suro*] (Seoul: P'urŭnsup, 1994); idem, *Han'gukin-ŭi paljach'wi* [*Footprints of Koreans*], revised ed. (Seoul: Chipmundang, 1994); idem, *Kim Pyong-mo-ŭi kokohak yŏhaeng* [*Kim Byung-mo's Archaeological Tour*], 2 vols. (Seoul: Karaesil, 2006).

7. Assuming that her name is fictitious, I use the same name Kim Byung-mo used in his publications (see ibid.).

8. In the ancestor worship rites and rituals in Korea, women were excluded from officiating the rites (see Roger L. Janelli and Dawnhee Yim Janelli, *Ancestor Worship and Korean Society* [Stanford: Stanford University Press, 1982], pp. 13, 65–66, passim).

9. The incest taboo is almost culturally universal (see Bronislaw Malinowski, *Sex and Repression in Savage Society* [London: Kegan Paul, Trench, Trubner, 1927]; Edward Westermarck, *The History of Human Marriage* [London: Macmillan, 1894]; and Leslie A. White, *The Science of Culture: A Study of Man and Civilization* [New York: Farrar, Strauss & Cudahy, 1949]), although there have been some exceptions in the past, as in the case of Cleopatra, who was married to two of her younger brothers at different times (Russell Middleton, "Brother-Sister and Father-Daughter Marriage in Ancient Egypt," *American Sociological Review* 27 [1962]: 603–11, p. 606). In various societies, the incest taboo is extended to include a wider scope of consanguineous relatives, especially if the society is organized according to lineages and clans. The Kimhae Kim clan, Kimhae Hŏ clan, and Inch'ŏn Yi clan number 4,314,588 members (Kim, 4,124,934; Hŏ, 121,031; and Yi 68,623) in accordance with the census of the year 2000.

10. There is a mathematical formula for determining degree of relationship. The degree of relationship between husband and wife is 0 (no degree of relationship); one

generation is counted as 1 degree, and the relationship between siblings is counted as 2 degrees. On the basis of this, for instance, the distance of a cousin from Ego (focal point person) can be calculated as 1 degree (from Ego's generation to his father) + 1 degree (from Ego's cousin's generation to his father) + 2 degrees (from Ego's father to his brother) = 4 degrees (See the formula in Choong Soon Kim, *Kimchi and IT: Tradition and Transformation in Korea* [Seoul: Ilchokak, 2007], p. 358, n. 5).

11. Kwang-kyu Lee, *Han'guk kajok-ŭi sajŏk yŏn'gu* [*A Historical Study of the Korean Family*] (Seoul: Ilchisa, 1983), p. 71.

12. Ibid.

13. Kim, *Kimchi and IT*, p. 113. And rules regulating marriage customs, specifically those prohibiting marriage between close relatives, were first initiated by the tenth king of the Koryŏ dynasty (918–1392), Chŏngjong (1034–1046). During his reign, the children of close kin marriages could not be appointed to government positions. Nevertheless, such a prohibition mainly had an impact on upper-class nobility and not commoners. Some believe that such a rule reflected the influence of China, but others disagree. If Koryŏ was either forced to initiate or willingly adopted the Chinese system, the incest taboo rule might have extended to entire surname groups as in China. Instead, Koryŏ merely imposed a prohibition of marriage between close relatives (ibid.; Lee, *Han'guk kajok-ŭi sajŏk yŏn'gu*, pp. 64–65).

14. Martina Deuchler offers an explanation for the adoption of this law (Martina Deuchler, "The Tradition: Women during the Yi dynasty," in *Virtues in Conflict: Tradition and the Korean Women Today*, Sandra Mattielli, ed., pp. 1–47 [Seoul: The Royal Asiatic Society, Korea Branch, 1977], p. 4). The Chosŏn literati-official (*sadaebu*) became aware that indigenous Chosŏn customs often stood in the way of implementing reform policies, which could not be carried out successfully without legal sanctions (Kim, *Kimchi and IT*, p. 113). The adoption of the *Ta Ming Lü* was therefore an introduction of the rule of law to supplement the rule of goodness. However, Chosŏn interpreted the entire *Ta Ming Lü* so literally that lineage and clan exogamy, the rule of marriage that requires a person to marry outside his or her own group, was institutionalized in Korea.

15. Deuchler, "The Tradition," pp. 8–9.

16. In July 1977, however, the constitutional Court of Korea handed down a landmark decision ruling that prohibition of marriage between clan members beyond eight-degree relationships (third cousins) was unconstitutional. Since then, clan members whose kinship was beyond eight degrees could marry legitimately, and family registries could issue marriage licenses for such couples. Even before the court ruling, however, the incest taboo did not apply to maternal relatives who were more distantly related than third cousins. It was applied more rigidly to the patriclan (a clan tracing descent through the male line) than to a matriclan (a clan tracing descent through the female line). A court ruling handed down on February 3, 2005, followed by the passage of a new statute on March 2, 2005, changed the system of giving surnames. This in turn has altered clan exogamy.

17. Kim, *Hŏ Hwang-ok Route,* pp. 23–26.

18. Ibid., pp. 26–30.

19. Ilyon [Iryŏn], *Samguk yusa: Legends and History of the Three Kingdoms of Ancient Korea*, trans. Ha Tae-hung and Grafton K. Mintz (Seoul: Yonsei University Press, 2007, orig. 1972), pp. 58–173.

20. Sarah M. Nelson, *The Archaeology of Korea* (New York: Cambridge University Press, 1993), p. 207.

21. Before Iryŏn converted to Buddhism and became a monk, his given name was Kim Kyŏn-myŏng.

22. Nelson, *The Archaeology of Korea,* p. 207. Parenthetically, as a manifestation of such anticipation, for instance, in 2007 at tomb No. 15 of an old Kaya tomb, located in Songhyŏndong, Ch'angnyŏng county, in the south Kyŏngsang province (an old Kaya territory), a well-preserved skeleton of a Kaya woman was excavated, along with four other skulls. She was assumed to be sixteen years old, a chambermaid of a noble person, and buried when her master died. A careful reconstruction of the skeleton, mobilizing the genetic, biochemical, physical anthropological, and forensic anthropological knowledge, indicates that she died around 1,500 years ago (around 420 to 560). The reconstructed Kaya girl looks to be around 151 centimeters tall, appears slim, and resembles contemporary Korean girls of that age. The reconstructed model of her body is on display at the National Palace Museum of Korea (*Kungrip Kokung Pangmulgwan*) (see *Chosun Ilbo,* November 26, 2009, p. A-2; *JoongAng Ilbo,* November 26, 2009, p. 17; *Dong-A Ilbo,* November 26, 2009, pp. A-1, A-2).

23. Koreans commonly refer to the Three Kingdoms, but "the Three Kingdoms are thus four, Koguryo [Koguryŏ], in the far north, was the first to organize itself effectively, so we begin there, and follow with Pakche, traditionally related to Koguryo [Koguryŏ]. Kaya comes next because of its alliances with Packeche, and finally Silla" (Nelson, *The Archaeology of Korea,* p. 207).

24. Ilyon, *Samguk yusa*, p. 158.

25. *Suro* is an attempt to express in Chinese the Korean word *Soori* and *sol*, meaning "supreme" and "holy," as in Sunŭng, the posthumous title of this king (ibid., p. 172, n. 8).

26. Ibid., p. 158.

27. Ibid., p. 163.

28. Ibid., p. 161.

29. Ibid., pp. 160–61.

30. Ibid., p. 162.

31. Ibid., pp. 162–64.

32. According to *Samgu yusa*, "Kŏdŭng was crowned on 13 March 193, and reigned 39 (55) years and died on 17 September 232. His Queen was Mojŏng, daughter of Ch'ŏnpu-kyŏng Sin Po, who bore his son Map'um. The Kaihuang Calendar says, 'His family name was Kim, a corruption of Kŭm, meaning gold, because his father King Suro was born from a golden egg'" (ibid., p. 169).

33. Nelson, *The Archaeology of Korea,* p. 9.

34. Kim, *Kimchi and IT,* p. 24.

35. Nelson, *The Archaeology of Korea,* p. 9.

36. See the *sadaejuŭi* in Roy Richard Grinker, *Korea and Its Futures: Unification and the Unfinished War* (New York: St. Martin's Press, 1998), pp. 125, 142–43, 145.

37. Nelson, *The Archaeology of Korea,* p. 206.

38. John M. Frankl, *Han'gukmunhak-e nat'anan woeguk-ŭi ŭimi* [*Images of "the Foreign" in Korean Literature and Culture*] (Seoul: Somyŏngch'ulp'an, 2008) (in Korean), p. 25.

39. It is said that a map the consul showed Kim Byung-mo spelled the city as Ayodhia, but the homepage of the Uttar Paradesh spelled it as Ayodhya (Kim, *Kim Suro wangbi-ŭi honin'gil,* p. 46).

40. Rāma, the hero of the Ramayana, is a human form of the god Vishnu. In the Ramayana, he is the son and heir of an Indian king. Rāma serves as a model for Hindu men. It is said that Rāma lives in the kingdom of Ayodhya in northern India.

41. Kim, *Kim Suro wangbi-ŭi honin'gil,* pp. 51–52; idem, *Hŏ Hwang-ok route,* pp. 52–53; idem, *Hŏ Hwang-ok,* pp. 72–73.

42. Their Buddhist style of name are Kimwangbul, Kimwangdongbul, Kimwang-sangbul, Kimwanghaengbul, Kimwanghyangbul, Kimwangsŏngbul, and Kimwang-silgongbul (ibid.).

43. Ilyon, *Samguk yusa,* pp. 161–62.

44. Kim, *Kim Suro wangbi-ŭi honin'gil,* pp. 52–53.

45. Sŏkt'arhae Isagŭm (?–AD 80) was the fourth king (AD 57–80) of the Silla dynasty.

46. Kim, *Kim Suro wangbi-ŭi honin'gil,* pp. 57–58.

47. Almost every writer spells "Ayodhya" slightly differently, such as Ayuta, Ayo-dia, and Ayodhia. I adopted the official spelling of the Indian government: Ayodhya.

48. Paraphrased from Kim, *Hŏ Hwang-ok Route,* p. 58.

49. Kosala was established around the sixth century BC by Aryans, but around the first century BC Kushan was established and lasted to the middle of the fifth century AD.

50. Ibid., p. 59.

51. Ibid., pp. 59–62.

52. Ibid., p. 63.

53. Mohenjo-Daro is a well-known archeological site that revealed the remains of the Indus civilization that begun about 2500 BC.

54. Ibid., pp. 63–72.

55. Ibid., pp. 73–82.

56. The translators of *Samguk yusa,* Ha Tae-hung and Grafton K. Mintz, add an annotation: "It is interesting to note that the city of Ayuthia was at one time the capital of the kingdom of Thailand" (see Ilyon, *Samguk yusa,* p. 162; and also Arthur Cot-terell, *East Asia: From Chinese Predominance to the Rise of the Pacific Rim* [New York: Oxford University Press, 1993], pp. 151–57).

57. Kim, *Hŏ Hwang-ok Route,* pp. 64–65.

58. The conventional view on the introduction of Buddhism in Korea is that "Bud-dhism arrived on the Korean peninsula in the fourth century, during the middle of the Three Kingdoms period. The northern kingdom of Koguryŏ, which bordered on China, made the first contact with Buddhism when the Chinese monk T'udo visited the kingdom in 372, bringing with him a Buddha statue and Buddhist scripture" (Kim, *Kimchi and IT,* p. 199).

59. Indirectly quoted from Kim, *Hŏ Hwang-ok Route,* p. 104.

60. Ibid., p. 93.

61. Ibid., p. 108. "Fish Gate" in a shrine in Babylonia has a pair of engraved fish (ibid., pp. 85–89). Babylonia, an ancient empire of southwest Asia in the lower valley of the Tigris and Euphrates river, flourished in 2100–689 BC and again as "New Babylonia" in 625–538 BC.

62. Ibid., p. 140.

63. According to a linguist, Kang kil-un, by comparing the Dravidian language of India and Korean, recognized that "Karak" in Korean means "fish" in the old Dravidian, and "Kaya" in the new Dravidian language also means "fish" (indirectly quoted from ibid., p. 115).

64. Ibid., pp. 116–18.

65. Ibid., pp. 119–21.

66. According to history of the Late Han, Hŏ was not a surname, but a hereditary title of a person who teaches shamans (ibid., p. 131).

67. Ibid., pp. 121–30.

68. Even Chinese and Koreans use the same Chinese character to denote their surname, while Chinese pronounce it as Xu, Koreans pronounce it as Hŏ. So, to avoid confusion, at intervals I follow the Korean spelling with its Chinese variant inside parentheses.

69. I have found out that Luo Zhewen was in fact a native of Sichuan Sheng.

70. Ibid., pp. 143–46.

71. Ibid., pp. 151–52.

72. Ibid., pp. 173–86.

73. Ibid., pp. 191–97.

74. Ibid., pp. 200–202.

75. Ibid., p. 202.

76. Ibid., pp. 202–7.

77. Ilyon, *Samguk yusa,* p. 162.

78. Kim, *Hŏ Hwang-ok Route*, p. 208.

79. Ibid., pp. 209–10.

80. Literally, it means "a bright day." As one of the twenty-four divisions of the year, around March 15 on the lunar calendar (about April 15 on solar calendar), people celebrate the coming of spring, as signaled by blooming paulownia (empress) trees, singing skylarks instead of roaming field rats, and the occasional rainbow.

81. Most Korean names consist of three syllables, although some two-syllable names are not uncommon. The first syllable denotes the surname (*sŏng* or clan name) and either the second or third syllable indicates the name of the generation the person belongs to. Any member who belongs to the same generation from their clan progenitor shares the same generation name. One's siblings, cousins, and second or third cousins use the same generational name.

82. Ibid., pp. 210–13.

83. Kim, *Hŏ Hwang-ok.*

84. Kim, *Hŏ Hwang-ok Route,* pp. 237–38.

85. Ibid., pp. 239–41.

86. Ibid., p. 241.

87. Ibid., pp. 244–45.

88. In Hindu tradition, Manu is a title accorded to the progenitor of mankind and also the very first king to rule the earth, who saved mankind from the universal flood. Kosala was an ancient Indian kingdom that was powerful in 600 BC, and Ayodhya was once the capital of Kosala.

89. Ibid., p. 246.

90. Ibid., pp. 246–49.

91. Ibid., p. 256.

92. Ibid., pp. 258–59.

93. Ibid., pp. 256–57.

94. Recently, Kim Byung-mo has made an effort to trace the presence of twin-fish figures in Kumamoto, Japan, in order to trace a possible connection between Kaya and Japan. Interested readers can see ibid., pp. 263–86.

NOTES TO CHAPTER 3

1. Choong Soon Kim, *An Asian Anthropologist in the South: Field Experiences with Blacks, Indians, and Whites* (Knoxville: University of Tennessee Press, 1977), pp. 25–26, 75–76.

2. Korea was governed by the U.S. Army Military Government in Korea (US-AMGIC) from 1945 to 1948.

3. David E. Hunter and Phillip Whitten, eds., *Encyclopedia of Anthropology* (New York: Harper & Row, 1976), p. 140.

4. Some scholars such as Harumi Befu explain that an uneasy feeling toward foreigners might have something to do with the child-rearing process. While most American parents as a matter of course often leave their children with babysitters who are strangers to the children, Korean and Japanese children rarely have occasions to associate with nonfamily members. They receive their comfort exclusively from family members—mothers most often. Perhaps some rural American Southerners who were uneasy with me might have had experiences similar to those of most Korean and Japanese children (see Harumi Befu, *Japan: An Anthropological Introduction* [New York: Thomas Y. Crownwell, 1971], p. 155; Choong Soon Kim, *Kimchi and IT: Tradition and Transformation in Korea* [Seoul: Ilchokak, 2007], pp. 267–68).

5. See Harry H. L. Kitano and Roger Daniels, *Asian Americans: Emerging Minorities* (Englewood Cliffs, NJ: Prentice-Hall, 1995), pp. 23–24.

6. James W. Loewen, *The Mississippi Chinese: Between Black and White,* 2nd ed. (Prospect Heights, IL: Waveland Press, 1988), pp. 206–9.

7. In 1983 the Commission on Wartime Relocation and Internment of Civilians (CWRIC) created by the U.S. Congress officially recommended that the federal government formally apologize and grant each survivor a tax-free one-time payment of $20,000 (see Kitano and Daniels, *Asian Americans,* pp. 65–69).

8. Michael Breen, *The Koreans: Who They Are, What They Want, Where Their Future Lies* (New York: Thomas Dunne Books, 2004), p. 20.

9. Jürgen Habermas, "Struggles for Recognition in the Democratic Constitutional State," in *Multiculturalism: Examining the Politics of Recognition*, Amy Gutmann, ed., pp. 107–48 (Princeton: Princeton University Press, 1994), p. 136.

10. Francis L. K. Hsu, "Prejudice and Its Intellectual Effect in American Anthropology: An Ethnographic Report," *American Anthropologist* 75 (1973): 1–19, p. 5.

11. Kim, *An Asian Anthropologist in the South*, pp. 91–94.

12. Margaret Park Redfield, ed., *Human Nature and the Study of Society*, vol. 1 (Chicago: University of Chicago Press, 1962), p. 283.

13. Arthur F. Raper, *Preface to Peasantry: A Tale of Two Black Belt Counties* (Chapel Hill: University of North Carolina Press, 1936).

14. Mike Weisbart, "So Fat, So Dynamic—and So Hierachical," *Wall Street Journal*, November 8, 2010, p. R-12.

15. Kim, *An Asian Anthropologist in the South*; idem, "Can an Anthropologist Go Home Again?" *American Anthropologist* 89 (1987): 943–46; idem, *One Anthropologist, Two Worlds: Three Decades of Reflexive Fieldwork in North America and Asia* (Knoxville: University of Tennessee Press, 2002).

16. Yi Ch'am, "Essay," *Chosun Ilbo*, September 28, 2010, p. A-29.

17. Kim, *One Anthropologist, Two Worlds*, pp. 51–52.

18. Emiko Ohnuki-Tierney, "Native Anthropologist," *American Ethnologist* 11 (1984): 584–86, p. 585.

19. Wire services of the *Yŏnhap News Agency*, May 26, 2003; *Chosun Ilbo,* May 27, 2003: A-18.

20. *Korea Herald,* July 3, 2009, p. 18. Foreign wives worry about their visa status should they divorce their husbands. They think that, if divorced, they would be deported to their home country or become a denationalized citizen (*Chosun Ilbo,* January 15, 2009, p. A-12; *Hankyoreh Sinmun,* June 9, 2009, p. 11).

21. The following descriptions are from Yi Sŏng-mi, *Tamunhwa Code: Han'guk "Dream" haebŏp ch'atki* [*Multicultural Code: Seeking the Solutions for the Korean Dream*] (Seoul: Saeng'gakŭi Namu, 2010), pp. 150–57.

22. Ibid., pp. 155–57.

23. *Chosun Ilbo,* May 10, 2008, p. A-3; *Chosun Ilbo,* May 12, 2008, p. A-6.

24. *Chosun Ilbo,* May 10, 2008, p. A-13.

25. Ibid. When I inquired further into the survey results, Min Sunghye told me that she decided not to publish the results of the survey in order to protect the privacy of the children, even though their identities were not revealed. She wanted to uphold the dignity of the children and the parents who had participated in the survey (personal communication with the researcher on July 11 and 21, 2009).

26. According to Jun Hey-Jung [Hye-jŏng Chŏn] and her colleagues, immigrant women's Korean language level affects family health (see Jun Hey-Jung [Hye-jŏng Chŏn] et al., "Kyŏlhon yijuyŏsŏng kajok kŏn'gang-e yŏnghyang-ŭl mich'i-nŭn kyŏngno [Path of the Variables to Migrant Women's Families' Health]," *Han'gukkajokpokchihak* [*Korea Journal of Family Welfare*] 14 [2009]: 5–24).

27. On-line education in Korea is possible because Korea has a robust infrastructure for supporting Internet communication.

28. A press release prepared by the Ministry for Health, Welfare and Family Affairs, ROK, July 13, 2005, p. 2.

29. Ibid., p. 6.

30. Ibid.

31. *Hankyoreh Sinmun,* June 9, 2009, p. 11.

32. For instance, according to a survey made by the Ministry of Agriculture and Forestry, published on February 3, 2007, 28.1 percent (43 out of 153) suffer verbal abuse from their spouses, 9.5 percent (14 out of 147) suffer physical abuse, and 9 percent (13 out of 144) suffer sexual abuse (*Kukmin Ilbo,* February 3, 2007, p. 3). Cf. Another source indicates that three out of every ten foreign brides had experienced verbal abuse, and one out of every ten had experienced physical abuse (*Seggye Ilbo,* January 19, 2007).

33. Ibid., p. 7.

34. *Korea Herald,* April 28, 2009, p. 1.

35. Ibid.

36. *Chosun Ilbo,* April 28, 2009, p. A-10.

37. Ibid.

38. Kim Hyun Mee, "The State and Migrant Women: Diverging Hopes in the Making of 'Multicultural Families' in Contemporary Korea," *Korea Journal* 47 (2007): 100–122, p. 110. Kim's figure on the foreign currency exchange rate was based on that of 2007.

39. The survey was made by the Ministry of Gender Equality (before it was merged into the Ministry of Health, Welfare and Family Affairs in 2008) in 2006 (indirectly quoted from *Chosun Ilbo,* May 10, 2008, p. A-3).

40. *Chosun Ilbo,* May 5, 2008, p. A-3. The minimum income level is set as follows: less than 490,845 wŏn (about $409) for single person, less than 835,763 wŏn (about $696) for a two-member family, less than 1,326,609 wŏn (about $1,105) for a four-member family, etc. (the Ministry for Health, Welfare and Family Affairs, August 27, 2008).

41. Ibid.

42. While 30 percent of parents from other countries in Korea stated that their children stay home alone while they are working, 70.9 percent of working Vietnamese mothers in Korea said that their children stay home alone while they are working (*Choson Ilbo,* May 9, 2008, pp. A-1, A-3). Perhaps it has to do with cultural differences.

43. Ibid.

44. Ibid.

45. Instances of parents sending their children to live with maternal grandparents are occurring in other countries as well—for instance, in Taiwan (ibid.).

46. Indirectly quoted from *Korea Herald,* August 12, 2008, p. 4.

47. Ibid.

48. *Chosun Ilbo,* April 26, 2008, p. A-29.

49. *Joongang Ilbo,* March 14, 2008, p. 30.

50. See *Segye Ilbo,* June 26, 2006, p. 27; *Hankyoreh Sinmun,* October 30, 2008, p. 5. Taiwanese normally give about $6,000 to the international marriage brokers for the privilege of marrying Vietnamese women (*Korea Herald,* August 12, 2008, p. 4).

51. *Dong-A Ilbo,* February 17, 2009, p. A-14.

52. *Korea Times,* January 17, 2009, p. 9; *Dong-A Ilbo,* January 17, 2009, p. 1.

53. *Korea Herald,* January 17, 2009, p. 1.

54. www.donga.com, January 21, 2009, n.p.

55. It has been reported that over 44 percent of information supplied by the marriage brokers on grooms was falsified (*Kukmin Ilbo,* March 27, 2009, p. 31).

56. *Segye Ilbo,* June 23, 2009, p. 10.

57. There are numerous critical reports on ill management, deception, and false information supplied to potential overseas brides (here are just a few of those reports: *Hankyoreh Sinmun,* February 5, 2007, and November 2, 2007, p. 27; *Dong-A Ilbo,* April 30, 2008, p. 14; *Kyunghyang Sinmun*, July 8, 2008, p. 11; *Kukmin Ilbo*, March 27, 2009, p. 31; *Segye Ilbo,* June 23, 2009, p. 10, etc.).

58. Kim, "The State and Migrant Women," p. 111. Also, Kim added that "brokers invest more time and energy in providing in-warranty services in Korea than in arranging overseas weddings, as that is where they derive and maintain profits. This is why 72.9 percent of companies in the international marriage business provide in-warranty services" (ibid., p. 112).

59. Ibid., p. 112.

60. *Dong-A Ilbo*, July 10, 2010, p. A-10.

61. *Korea Herald*, July 12, 2010, p. 3.

62. *Dong-A Ilbo*, July 15, 2010, pp. 1, A-14.

63. *Korea Herald*, July 12, 2010, p. 3.

64. *Chosun Ilbo*, July 17, 2010, p. A-25.

65. *Korean Herald*, July 21, 2010, p. 1.

66. *Korea Herald*, July 20, 2010, p. 3.

67. *Korean Herald*, July 19, 2010, p. 1.

68. Ibid.

69. Laurel Kendall has given a detailed description of *massŏn* (see Laurel Kendall, *Getting Married in Korea: Of Gender, Morality, and Modernity* [Berkeley: University of California Press, 1996], pp. 103–39, esp. 109).

70. *Chosun Ilbo*, July 12, 2010, p. A-20; *JoongAng Ilbo*, July 21, 2010, p. 20.

71. *JoongAng Ilbo*, July 21, 2010, p. 20.

72. *Korea Herald,* August 12, 2008, p. 4.

73. Press report of the Ministry of Public Administration and Security, June 11, 2010.

74. Chŏn Kyŏng-su, "Sŏmun [Introduction]," in *Honhyŏl-esŏ tamunhwa [From Mixed-Blood to Multiculturalism]*, Chŏn Kyŏng-su et al., eds., pp. 12–34 (Seoul: Iljisa, 2008), pp. 17, 24.

75. *Seoul Sinmun,* March 10, 2006, p. 6.

76. *Korea Herald,* August 16, 2007, p. 4; *Maeil Business Newspaper,* November 12, 2008, p. A-30.

77. Beginning May 2009, however, under the direction of the office of the prime minister, work has begun on compiling information for a comprehensive report (*Maeil Business Newspaper,* February 23, 2009, p. 1).

78. Chŏn, "Sŏmun," p. 5.

79. *Dong-A Ilbo,* April 12, 2006, p. 3

80. See Japanese practices in Merry White, *The Japanese Overseas: Can They Go Home Again?* (Princeton: Princeton University Press, 1988), p. 66.

81. *Kyunghyang Sinmun,* November 7, 2008, p. 13.

82. *Chosun Ilbo,* May 5, 2008, p. A-1.

83. *Segye Ilbo,* October 8, 2008, p. 9.

84. *Dong-A Ilbo,* October 25, 2008, p. 26.

85. Ibid.

86. For details see Chŏn Kyŏng-su, "Ch'abyŏl-ŭi sahoewa sisŏn-ŭi chŏngch'igwajŏng-non: Tamunhwakajŏng chanyŏ-e kwanhan yebijŏk yŏn'gu [Discussions on Discriminatory Society and the Political Process]," in *Honhyŏl-esŏ tamunhwa [From Mixed-Blood to Multiculturalism]*, Chŏn Kyŏng-su et al., eds., pp. 36–85 (Seoul: Iljisa, 2008).

87. According to a press release dated February 2009, the sample size was 3,185, but a newspaper reported it as 3,175 (see *Maeil Business Newspaper,* February 19, 2009, p. A-30).

88. Ibid.

89. *Korea Herald,* June 23, 2008, p. 8.

90. *Dong-A Ilbo,* October 25, 2008, p. A-12.

91. Kim, *Kimchi and IT,* p. 233.

92. John M. Frankl, *Han'gukmunhak-e nat'anan woeguk-ŭi ŭimi [Images of "the Foreign" in Korean Literature and Culture]* (Seoul: Somyŏngch'ulp'an, 2008) (in Korean), passim.

93. Andre Schmid, *Korea between Empires, 1895–1919* (New York: Columbia University Press, 2002), passim.

94. Han Kyung-Koo, "The Archaeology of the Ethnically Homogeneous Nation-State and Multiculturalism in Korea," *Korea Journal* 47 (2007): 12.

95. Frankl, *Han'gukmunhak-e nat'anan woeguk-ŭi ŭimi,* p. 96, n. 82.

96. Han, "The Archaeology of the Ethnically Homogeneous Nation-State and Multiculturalism in Korea," p. 11.

97. Ibid., p. 13.

98. Schmid, *Korea between Empires,* p. 173.

99. Ibid., p. 174.

100. Han, "The Archaeology of the Ethnically Homogeneous Nation-State and Multiculturalism in Korea," p. 23.

101. Ibid.

102. Gi-Wook Shin, *Ethnic Nationalism in Korea: Genealogy, Politics, and Legacy* (Stanford: Stanford University Press, 2006), p. 15.

103. Ibid., pp. 15–16.

104. Pai, *Constructing "Korean" Origins,* p. 16.

105. Ibid., p. 1.

106. Han, "The Archaeology of the Ethnically Homogeneous Nation-State and Multiculturalism in Korea," p. 13.

107. Frankl, *Han'gukmunhwa-e nat'anan woeguk-ŭi ŭimi,* p. 267; James S. Gale, *Korean Sketches* (New York: Flemming H. Revell Company, 1898).

108. Hyung Il Pai, *Constructing "Korean" Origins: A Critical Review of Archaeology, Historiography, and Racial Myth in Korean State-Formation Theories* (Cambridge: Harvard University Asia Center, 2000), p. 60.

109. Ibid., p. 24; Frankl, *Han'gukmunhwa-e nat'anan woeguk-ŭi ŭimi,* p. 43, n. 79.

110. John Naisbitt, *Global Paradox* (New York: Avon Books, 1994), pp. 19–20.

111. Han, "The Archaeology of the Ethnically Homogeneous Nation-State and Multiculturalism in Korea," p. 25.

112. Shin, *Ethnic Nationalism in Korea,* p. 78; see also pp. 86–93, 103–09.

113. Ibid., p. 105.

114. The number of defectors has been on the rise annually—from 1,138 in 2002 to 16,354 in 2008 (see *Dong-A Ilbo,* July 20, 2009, p. A-10), and to 20,050 in 2010 (see *Korea Herald,* November 16, 2010, pp. 2, 4).

115. Choong Soon Kim, *Faithful Endurance: An Ethnography of Korean Family Dispersal* (Tucson: University of Arizona Press, 1988), passim.

116. Chŏng Hyŏn-sang, "Chayu-ŭi ttang-esŏ panghwanghanŭn yibangindŭl [Wandering Aliens in the Land of the Free]," *Chugan Dong-A* (*Weekly Dong-A*), 381 (April 24, 2003): 14–17, p. 17; *Chosun Ilbo,* July 8, 2009, p. A-4.

117. See *Kyunghyang Sinmun,* November 11, 2006, p. 16; *Dong-A Ilbo,* April 24, 2007, p. 30; *Hankyoreh Sinmun,* October 11, 2007, p. 30; *Chosun Ilbo,* July 8, 2009, p. A-4.

118. Cho Chŏng-a, Im Sun-hŭi, and Chŏng Chin-kyŏng, *Saet'omin-ŭi munhwagaldŭng-gwa munhwajŏk t'onghap pang'an* [*Cultural Conflict and Cultural Integration of the North Korean Escapees*] (Seoul: Korean Women's Development and Korean Institute for National Unification, 2006).

119. Ibid., pp. 94–121.

120. Ibid., pp. 58–89.

121. Ibid., pp. 47–55.

122. Ibid., 139–43.

123. *Hankyoreh Sinmun*, April 5, 2007, p. 8.

124. Ibid.

125. *Kyunghyang Sinmun,* January 1, 2007, p. 14.

126. Chŏng, "Chayu-ŭi ttang-esŏ panghwanghanŭn yibangindŭl," p. 16.

127. *Korea Herald,* July 9, 2009, p. 3.

128. Chŏng, "Chayu-ŭi ttang-esŏ panghwanghanŭn yibangindŭl," p. 17.

129. *Maeil Business Newspaper,* February 19, 2009, p. A-30.

130. Han Geon-Soo, "Multicultural Korea: Celebration or Challenge of Multiethnic Shift in Contemporray Korea," *Korea Journal* 47 (2007): 32–63, p. 49.

131. Frankl, *Han'gukmunhwa-e nat'anan woeguk-ŭi ŭimi,* p. 165; Han, "The Archaeology of the Ethnically Homogeneous Nation-State and Multiculturalism in Korea," p. 25.

132. *Korea Herald,* June 23, 2008, p. 8.

133. See Yi Kil-sang, *Segye-ŭi kyogwasŏ Han'guk-ŭl malhada* [*World School Textbooks Write about Korea*] (Seoul: P'urŭnsup, 2009); *Dong-A Ilbo,* October 8, 2008, p. A-13; *Chosun Ilbo*, October 25, 2008, p. A-12; A report prepared by the Ministry of Public Administration and Security, ROK, July 2008.

NOTES TO CHAPTER 4

1. Chosun.com, November 4, 2007, n.p.

2. Such a narrow-minded person is labeled as "redneck" in the South, referring to a rural white southerner in slang. I might be accused of being a Korean version of a redneck.

3. A major portion of this section quotes from an earlier publication of mine (see Choong Soon Kim, *Kimchi and IT: Tradition and Transformation in Korea* [Seoul: Ilchokak, 2007], pp. 109–42).

4. Choong Soon Kim, "Yŏnjul-hon or Chain String Form of Marriage Arrangement in Korea," *Journal of Marriage and the Family* 36 (1974): 575–79, p. 575.

5. Francis L. K. Hsu, *Americans & Chinese: Passage to Differences,* 3rd ed. (Honolulu: University of Hawaii Press, 1981), p. 49.

6. In the end the man was able to marry her, after overcoming many obstacles, simply because he loved her so dearly. This story has generated many movies, TV soap operas, and musicals over a long period. It is still popular among Koreans.

7. Stuart A. Queen and Robert W. Habenstein, *The Family in Various Cultures* (New York: J. B. Lippincott, 1974), p. 105.

8. Ibid., p. 336.

9. Laurel Kendall, *Getting Married in Korea: Of Gender, Morality, and Modernity* (Berkeley: University of California Press, 1996), p. 109.

10. In 1997, "only 20 percent of people in South Korea marry just for love" (Lee Kwang-kyu, *Pittsburgh Post-Gazette,* April 20, 1997, p. A-4); according to a 1999 survey conducted by a marriage consulting center named Echorus, nine out of ten respondents were in favor of free-choice marriage over arranged marriage; the respondents were six hundred adult members of the center from Seoul and its vicinities (*Kyunghyang Sinmun,* April 5, 1999, p. 18). It is unknown, however, how many of them actually married in such a way.

11. Carter J. Eckert et al., *Korea Old and New: A History* (Seoul: Ilchokak, 1990), p. 69.

12. There are reports that business conglomerate families tend to choose spouses from other conglomerate families. In a doctoral dissertation, Kong Chŏng-ja made a survey based on one hundred big business families selected randomly out of the membership firms who belong to the Federation of Korean Industries (FKI, *Chŏn'guk Kyŏngjaein Yŏnhaphoe* or *Chŏnkyŏngnyŏn*). It was found that 124 sons and 83 daughters of the 100 families married offspring of other big business families (Kong Chŏng-ja, *Han'guk taegiŏpka kajok-ŭi honmak-e kwanhan yŏn'gu* [*The Families of Korean Big Businessmen and Their Marriage Networks*], unpublished PhD dissertation, Ewha Womans University, 1989). However, according to another sociological study, of the 393 children from 52 prominent Korean businessmen's families, only 20 people (5.1 percent) married offspring of other prominent businessmen's families (Song Bok, "Han'guk sangch'ŭng-ŭi sahwoejŏk kusŏng'gwa tŭksŏng-e kwanhan yŏn'gu [A Study on the Social Structure and Characteristics of Korean Upper-Class People]," a research report, n.d.

13. Kim, "Yŏnjul-hon or Chain String Form of Marriage Arrangement in Korea," p. 577.

14. A Korean anthropologist, Cho Kang-hŭi, has documented an elaborate network of marriages among *yangban* groups in north Kyŏngsang province from the later period of the Chosŏn dynasty to the present. He claims that the boundaries of marriage were limited to some thirty clans living in geographic proximity within the province. Matches were made by the mechanism of *yŏnjulhon,* or "chain-string" forms of marriage arrangement, which operate by mobilizing networks of relatives, mainly females (see Cho Kang-hŭi, "Yŏngnam chibang-ŭi honban yŏn'gu: Chinsŏng Yissi Toegye chongson-ŭl chungsimŭro [The Marriage Network in the Kyŏngsang Region: Focusing on the Main Heir of the Chinsŏng Yi Clan]," *Minjok munhwa nonch'ong* [*The Journal of the Institute for Korean Culture*] 6 [1984]: 79–121).

15. *Seoul Economic Daily,* April 13, 2006, p. B-3.

16. Choong Soon Kim, *Faithful Endurance: An Ethnography of Korean Family Dispersal* (Tucson: University of Arizona Press, 1988), p. 38. Also, Laurel Kendall reports on Madam *Ttu* matchmakers: "In 1980, after Chun Doo-hwan's coup, the new government identified illegal matchmakers as 'elements corrupting society' and began a major crackdown. . . . Seoul gossip held that the list of marriage prospects carried by a Madam *Ttu* brought to judgment included the names of the unmarried judge who presided at her trial. The Madam *Ttu* has, by all accounts, continued to flourish" (Kendall, *Getting Married in Korea,* p. 133, n. 10). Kendall elaborates further on the Madam *Ttu* phenomenon (ibid., pp. 133–35).

17. *Seoul Economic Daily,* April 13, 2006, p. B-3.

18. Kim, *Kimchi and IT,* p. 118.

19. Investigating arranged marriage in 2005, Kim Yong-hak, a Korean sociologist, analyzed almost eight hundred megabytes of data compiled at a marriage consulting center between 2004 and 2005. He learned that men and women seeking a compatible marriage partner cared less about a person's appearance or wealth than about the person's educational background, which has become an important measure of social status. Having a degree from a reputable university was seen as highly desirable (*JoongAng Ilbo,* July 22, 2005, p. 1; *JoongAng Week,* July 22, 2005, pp. W1–W2).

20. As a new religion in Korea, Taesunjiligyo is a branch of Chŭngsangyo, headquartered in Seoul, and has grown steadily. It was established in 1969 and today has 650,000 adherents. The Chŭngsan religion was founded in 1902 by Kang Il-sun, who was once a believer in Tonghak (Eastern religion) but recognized its limitations. He proposed a new religion that preached belief in a paradise in the afterlife. It is a combination of Confucianism, Buddhism, Taoism, and the realm of diviners, geomancers, and medicine men. It teaches that the universe is a heaven that can be realized in the minds of a person through homage and prayer (see Yun Yi-hŭm et al., *Han'guk-ŭi chonggyo* [*Korean Religion*] [Seoul: Mundŏksa, 1994], pp. 217–18).

21. The amount of money the group raised and gave to Ttuet's family is disputed. Ttuet's mother told me that they received around $5,000 at one time and subsequently around $500 per year. However, the donors claim that the amount was smaller.

22. Chosun.com, May 15 and September 18, 2008.

23. When the citizenship of the shooter became known, Koreans expressed shock and a sense of public shame, while the Korean cabinet convened an emergency meeting. A candlelight vigil was held outside the embassy of the United States in Seoul.

Korean president Roh Moo-hyun expressed his deepest condolences. Korea's ambassador to the United States and several Korean American religious leaders called on Korean Americans to participate in a thirty-two-day fast, one day for each victim, for repentance.

NOTES TO CHAPTER 5

1. Choong Soon Kim, *Kimchi and IT: Tradition and Transformation in Korea* (Seoul: Ilchokak, 2007), p. 216.

2. Michael Breen, *The Koreans: Who They Are, What They Want, Where Their Future Lies* (New York: Thomas Dunne Books, 2004), p. 44.

3. Kim, *Kimchi and IT*, p. 216.

4. NYDailyNews.com, October 14, 2009; see also *The Christian Science Monitor*, October 14, 2009.

5. Yi Sŏng-mi, *Tamunhwa Code: Han'guk "Dream" haebŏp ch'atki* [*Multicultural Code: Seeking the Solutions for the Korean Dream*] (Seoul: Saeng'gakŭi Namu, 2010), pp. 53–54.

6. The Ministry of Public Administration and Security, June 11, 2010; see also Yi, *Tamunhwa Code*, p. 49, *figure*.

7. Tomoko's life story in a rural Korean town was telecast in September 2006 by a Japanese television station under the title of "A Japanese Woman Who Lives Happily in a Farming Village of Korea." Her real name was used in the film. Observing the ethical rules of anthropology, I do not identify the name of the Japanese television station in an effort to conceal her identity.

8. I used a fictitious name with Yŏngwŏl in order to protect their privacy and conceal their identities. Otherwise, it would be too easy to find out their identities.

9. Although the city was officially founded in 1889, the famous Wakayama Castle located in the center of the city was built in 1585 by order of Toyotomi Hideyoshi, who had his brother Toyotomi Hidenaga built the castle on Mt. Torafusu.

10. Thomas P. Rohlen has reported that "nine percent of the middle school students in Tokyo have private tutors. In *juku*, the focus is high school entrance or, in the case of *juku* for upper elementary school students, entrance exams to the elite private schools that admit students in seventh grade. . . . [In 1976] the poll showed that 40 percent of all fourth, fifth, and sixth graders in Tokyo were going to a *juku*. And one in ten of the country's high school students were shown to be attending *yōbiko*, the advanced analogue of *juku*." Thomas P. Rohlen, *Japan's High Schools* (Berkeley: University of California Press, 1983), p. 104. Rohlen further elaborates that "these tutoring establishments are diverse and interesting. Some belong to franchise chains, owned by large companies, that enroll thousands of students. So lucrative and flourishing was the business in the mid-1970s that a movie company, several publishing firms, and a department store all entered the market to set up their own franchise systems. Most cram schools are quite small, however, typically run at home by housewives and former teachers" (ibid.). There is a similar system in Korea as well.

11. According to Harumi Befu, "It is worth nothing that Japanese and Chinese are totally unrelated languages, genetically speaking. . . . The Chinese writing system became modified to allow the Japanese language to be recorded in the kana sylla-bary" (Harumi Befu, *Japan: An Anthropological Introduction* [New York: Thomas Y. Crownwell, 1971], pp. 17, 29).

12. Choong Soon Kim, *The Culture of Korean Industry: An Ethnography of Poongsan Corporation* (Tucson: University of Arizona Press, 1992), p. 7.

13. Even in learning or borrowing, it was amazing to know that "when opera-tions [at POSCO] commenced in 1973, local engineers reached desired normal iron production level within eight days, an unprecedented record in the history of the industry" (Lin-su Kim, "Technological Transformation of Korean Firms," in *Korean Managerial Dynamics,* Kae H. Chung and Hak Chong Lee, eds., pp. 113–29 [New York: Praeger, 1989], p. 125).

14. Francis L. K. Hsu, *Americans & Chinese: Passage to Differences,* 3rd ed. (Honolulu: University of Hawaii Press, 1981), p. 255.

15. As Hsu has said, "For the American way in religion is to be more and more exclusive, so that not only is my God the only true God while all others are false, but I cannot rest until my particular view of God has prevailed over all others. The Chinese tendency is exactly the reverse. [A] Chinese [person] may go to a Buddhist monastery to pray for a male heir, but he may proceed from there to a Taoist shrine where he beseeches a god to cure him of malaria" (ibid., pp. 255–56).

16. Befu, *Japan,* p. 96.

17. Cho Hŭng-yun and Yun Yihŭm, "Sŏmun [Introduction]," in *Han'gukin-ŭi chonggyo [Korean Religion]*, Yun Yihŭm et al., eds., pp. i–ix (Seoul: Mundŏk-sa, 1994), p. ii; see also some details in Kim, *Kimchi and IT,* pp. 180–83.

18. Kevin Sullivan and Mary Jordan, "Once-Generous Japanese become Disen-chanted with Moon's Church," *Washington Post,* August 4, 1996, p. A01.

19. Although it started out being called the Unification Theology College in 1972, it was renamed Sun Moon University in 1989 by the Unification Church, which is located in Asan City in south Ch'ungch'ŏng province. From Seoul it takes about thirty-three minutes by the Korea Train Express (KTX) to get to the city, where the main campus of the university is located. The university has 9,304 undergraduate and 694 graduate students.

20. During World War II, the Japanese authority kept Korean women at brothels for Japanese soldiers in the war zones. Thus far, the Japanese do not acknowledge their inhumane deed fully. On July 30, 2007, the U.S. House of Representatives unanimously passed a resolution calling for Japan to acknowledge its actions fully and not to distort or deny history by blaming the victims (see Kim, *Kimchi and IT,* pp. 66–67; and also see a comprehensive book by C. Sarah Soh, *The Comfort Women: Sexual Violence and Postcolonial Memory in Korea and Japan* [Chicago: University of Chicago Press, 2008]).

21. Dokdo (Tokto) is about 134.3 miles from mainland Korea and 156 miles from Japan proper. The nearest landmass is Korea's Ullŭng-do Island about 54.3 miles away, which is visible from Dokdo on fair days. The nearest Japanese territory,

known as the Oki Islands, is about 98.1 miles away. Dokdo is never visible from Japan's Oki Islands.

22. Koreans became more blusterous than ever when Japan's education ministry released its new manual on government-endorsed textbook guidelines for high-school-level geography and history. The manual claims that Japan has territorial rights to the islet of Dokdo. On March 20, 2010, Japan approved five elementary school textbooks for fifth graders that referred to Dokdo as a Japanese territory and said that Korea occupied it illegally. Koreans vehemently protested these Japanese actions (*Korea Herald,* March 31, 2010, p. 3).

23. Thomas Rohlen's ethnography on Japanese schools documents the competitiveness well (see Rohlen, *Japan's High Schools,* passim).

24. *JoongAng Ilbo,* May 5, 2010, p. 18.

25. I have intentionally not fully cited the sources in order to conceal her identity.

26. Besides the number of Koreans drafted into the Japanese military, totaling 364,186 by the end of World War II, the aggregate number of Koreans mobilized throughout the war by the Japanese government in both Korea and Japan reached almost six million (see Choong Soon Kim, *Faithful Endurance: An Ethnography of Korean Family Dispersal* [Tucson: University of Arizona Press, 1988]; idem, *A Korean Nationalist Entrepreneur: A Life History of Kim Sŏngsu, 1891–1955* [Albany: State University of New York Press, 1998], pp. 112–14).

27. Shimonoseki is a city located in Yamaguchi prefecture, Japan. It is at the southwestern tip of Honshu, facing the Tsushima Strait and also Kitakyushu across the Kanmon Straits. Since it is close to Pusan, the second largest city and the largest port city in Korea, there has been frequent and regular ferry service between Japan and Korea called the Kwanbu (Kanpu in Japanese) ferry.

28. Pertti J. Pelto, *Anthropological Research: The Structural Inquiry* (New York: Harper & Row, 1970), p. 99.

NOTES TO CHAPTER 6

1. Ch'ŏn-do was once isolated from the mainland, but in October 1984 a long bridge was constructed to connect the island to the mainland. In September 2009 the bridge was expanded due to increasing traffic.

2. In 1952, Korean immigrants constituted around 60 percent of the local population, but by 1997, their share shrank to 39.7 percent (out of a total population of 2,184,000), and by 2000 it shrank further to 32 percent.

3. In the nineteenth century, Korean immigrants migrated en masse from the Korean peninsula to China. After the foundation of the Republic of China, a second wave arrived. The immigration wave was caused by the Japanese invasion of that region of China. The Japanese were trying to use Korean immigration to diffuse the power of the Chinese in the region. After the end of World War II, many Koreans did not go back to Korea, even though their country had been liberated (as there were economic and political problems back in their country). Instead, they joined in the Chinese

civil war and were mobilized by both Chinese communists and Chinese nationalists. When the civil war was over, the new Chinese government gave Koreans their own autonomous region in 1952. Yanbian was upgraded to an ethnic autonomous prefecture in 1955.

4. The territory where modern Vladivostok is located has at different times belonged to many nations, such as Parhae (Balhae), Jurchen, the Mongol empire, and China, before Russia acquired the entire Maritime Province and the island of Sakhalin by the Treaty of Aigun (1858). China, which had just lost the Opium War with Britain, was unable to maintain its hold on the region. The Pacific coast near Vladivostok was settled mainly by Chinese, Jurchen, Manchu, and Korean peoples during the imperial Chinese Qing dynasty. The city of Vladivostok had large Korean and Chinese populations. Some Koreans who were deported from the area during Stalin's rule have since returned, particularly to Vladivostok.

5. The square was named after the Russian leader of the communist revolution of 1917, Nikolai Lenin (1870–1924).

6. According to an observation made by a local schoolteacher, the so-called miracle takes place any time there is a four-meter difference between low tide and high tide.

7. Kim Sŭng-Kwŏn et al., *2007-nyŏn chŏn'guk tamunhwakajoksilt'aechosa yŏn'gu [The Year 2009 Nationwide Survey on Multicultural Families]* (Seoul: The Ministry for Health, Welfare and Family Affairs, the Ministry of Justice, the Ministry of Gender Eqality and Family, ROK, and the Korea Institute for Health and Social Affairs, 2010), p. 164.

8. The statistics are based on the figure that was released in the year 2007 (ibid., p. 133). The 2010 figures have not yet been calculated according to all categories, including this category (The Ministry of Public Administration and Security, June 11, 2010; Yi Sŏng-mi, *Tamunhwa Code: Han'guk "Dream" haebŏp ch'atki [Multicultural Code: Seeking the Solutions for the Korean Dream]* (Seoul: Saeng'gakŭi Namu, 2010), p. 49, *figure*).

NOTES TO CHAPTER 7

1. The most recent report on November 16, 2010, puts the number of North Korean refugees living in South Korea at twenty thousand (see *Korea Herald*, November 16, 2010, p. 24). For the other categories of immigrants there are not more recent figures to report.

2. Press report of the Ministry of Public Administration and Security, June 11, 2010; Yi Sŏng-mi, *Tamunhwa Code: Han'guk "Dream" haebŏp ch'atki [Multicultural Code: Seeking the Solutions for the Korean Dream]* (Seoul: Saeng'gakŭi Namu, 2010), pp. 23–35.

3. Oh Kyŏng-sŏk, et al., Han'gukaesŏŭi tamunhwajuŭi: Hyŏnsil-gwa chaengjŏm *[Multiculturalism in Korea: A Critical Review]* (Seoul: Hasn'ul Academy, 2007), pp. 29–32.

4. Kim Hŭi-chŏng, "Han'gukŭi kwanjudohyŏng tamunhwajuŭi [The Government-led Multiculturalism in Korea]," in *Han'gukaesŏŭi tamunhwajuŭi: Hyŏnsilgwa chaengjŏm* [*Multiculturalism in Korea: A Critical Review*], Oh Kyŏng-sŏk, et al., pp. 59–79 (Seoul: Han'uk Academy, 2007), p. 58; Oh, "Han'gukaesŏŭi tamunhwajuŭi," p. 31.

5. *Chosun Ilbo*, December 17, 2010, p. A-5.

6. See Yoon In-Jin, "Han'gukchŏk tamunhwa-juŭi chŏn'agewa t'ŭksŏng: Kug'gawa siminsahoerŭl chungsimŭro [The Development and Characteristics of Multiculturalism in South Korea: With a Focus on the Relationship of the State and Civil Society]," *Han'guk sahoehak* [*Journal of Korean Sociology*] 42 (2008): 72–103, pp. 92–93.

7. Ibid., p. 99.

8. *Dong-A Ilbo,* May 14, 2010, p. B-4.

9. Vincent S. R. Brandt has stated that "contradictory forms of behaviors are found in all cultures, but they seem to have been more drastically expressed in Korea than in some other parts of the world" (Vincent S. R. Brandt, *A Korean Village: Between Farm and Sea* [Cambridge: Harvard University Press, 1971], p. 28).

10. According to a recent report by the Organization for Economic Cooperation and Development (OECD), Korea's population is expected to shrink by 0.02 percent in a year's time. In 2030, it is estimated that the population will fall by 0.25 percent over the course of year. The organization is fearful that such population decline may threaten the nation's competitiveness. A decline could reduce the number of people working and cause welfare costs to rise in response to an aging citizenry (*Korea Herald*, May 21, 2010, p. 5).

11. Will Kymlicka, *Multicultural Odysseys*: *Navigating the New International Politics of Diversity* (New York: Oxford University Press, 2007), pp. 73, 75.

12. The 1999 act reflected a bias in favor of the United States and Western Europe. In response, ethnic Koreans in China, Russia, and Central Asian countries filed complaints against it, claiming it was discriminatory. As a result of their complaints, the Constitutional Court ruled the law unconstitutional on December 31, 2003. After nine amendments were made to the law from 1999 to 2010, the law finally applied to those who emigrated from Korea before 1948. The legislated bias was thus finally eliminated.

13. Yi, *Tamunhwa Code*, p. 32.

14. Koreans think that since the term *dual or double citizenship* (*yijung-kukchŏk*) may carry a negative connotation, they prefer to use the term *plural nationality* (*poksu-kukchŏk*).

15. The only condition is that, as long as the foreign nationals live in Korea with Korean citizenship, they cannot have the privilege of being foreigners, even though they can retain citizenship in their country of origin.

16. Yi, *Tamunhwa Code*, pp. 31–32; *Chosun Ilbo*, December 17, 2010, p. A-5.

17. The term *utilitarian* as it is used here is based on common sense or the dictionary definition, meaning that the worth or value of anything is determined solely by its utility. I do not use the term in the philosophical sense associated with Jeremy Bentham and John Stuart Mill.

18. Peter A. Kraus and Karen Schönwälder, "Multiculturalism in Germany: Rhetoric, Scattered Experiments, and Future Chances," in *Multiculturalism and the Welfare State: Recognition and Redistribution in Contemporary Democracies*, Keith Banting and Will Kymlicka, eds., pp. 202–21 (New York: Oxford University Press, 2006), p. 207.

19. Jürgen Habermas, "Struggles for Recognition in the Democratic Constitutional State," in *Multiculturalism: Examining the Politics of Recognition*, Amy Gutmann, ed., pp. 107–48 (Princeton: Princeton University Press, 1994), p. 144.

20. Ibid.

21. Park Ok-kol [Pak Ok-kŏl], *Koryŏ-sidae-ŭi kwihwain yŏn'gu* [*A Study of the Naturalized People in the Koryŏ Period*] (Seoul: Kukhakcharyowŏn, 1996), pp. 183–85.

22. Han Geon-Soo, "Multicultural Korea: Celebration or Challenge of Multiethnic Shift in Contemporary Korea," *Korea Journal* 47 (2007): 32–63, p. 49.

23. See the figures in Yi, *Tamunhwa Code*, pp. 33–34.

24. Choong Soon Kim, *Kimchi and IT: Tradition and Transformation in Korea* (Seoul: Ilchokak, 2007), pp. 265–68.

25. However, in the United States, at lower levels of government such as states or cities, we find a broad range of multiculturalism policies (see Kymlicka, *Multicultural Odysseys*, p. 72).

26. Oh, *Han'gukaesŏŭi tamunhwajuŭi*, p. 33.

27. Yi, *Tamunhwa Code*, p. 263; Yoon, "Han'gukchŏk tamunhwa-juŭi chŏn'agewa t'ŭksŏng," p. 79.

28. While the residency requirement for naturalization is five years for other foreigners, foreign brides are required to have only two years of residency; and, while other foreigners are required to take 450 hours of lessons on the Korean language and Korean society, foreign brides are only required to take 150 hours (see Kim, "Han'gukŭi kwanjudohyŏng tamunhwajuŭi," pp. 71–75; Oh, *Han'gukaesŏŭi tamunhwajuŭi*, p. 32, n. 4; Yi, *Tamunhwa Code*, p. 176).

29. Han Kyung-Koo, "The Archaeology of the Ethnically Homogeneous Nation-State and Multiculturalism in Korea," *Korea Journal* 47 (2007): 9; Kim, "Han'gukŭi kwanjudohyŏng tamunhwajuŭi," p. 65; Kim Hyun Mee, "The State and Migrant Women: Diverging Hopes in the Making of 'Multicultural Families' in Contemporary Korea," *Korea Journal* 47 (2007): 100–22, pp. 101–02.

30. Yoon, "Han'gukchŏk tamunhwa-juŭi chŏn'agewa t'ŭksŏng," pp. 96–97.

31. Han, "Multicultural Korea," p. 36.

32. Kim, "The State and Migrant Women," pp. 105–6; Yi, *Tamunhwa Code*, pp. 163–64.

33. Personal communication with an official at POSCO and his memo to me dated July 30, 2008.

34. Oh et al., *Han'gukaesŏŭi tamunhwajuŭi*, p. 34.

35. Kim, "Han'gukŭi kwanjudohyŏng tamunhwajuŭi," p. 67.

36. Yi, *Tamunhwa Code*, p. 157; Oh et al., *Han'gukaesŏŭi tamunhwajuŭi*, p. 34.

37. Ibid.

38. Yoon, "Han'gukchŏk tamunhwa-juŭi chŏn'agewa t'ŭksŏng," p. 89.

39. *Dong-A Ilbo*, December 10, 2010, p. A-31.

40. Yoon, "Han'gukchŏk tamunhwa-juŭi chŏn'agewa t'ŭksŏng," p. 75.

41. Yi Song-mi has observed a similar characteristic (Yi, *Tamunhwa Code*, pp. 50–51).

42. Ibid., p. 164.

43. Yoon, "Han'gukchŏk tamunhwa-juŭi chŏn'agewa t'ŭksŏng," p. 89.

44. Ibid., p. 90.

45. Ibid., p. 98.

46. Ibid., p. 89.

47. Ibid., p. 89.

48. See Kenneth Pike, *Language in Relation to a Unified Theory of the Structure of Human Behavior*, vol. 1 (Glendale, CA: Summer Institute of Linguistics, 1954).

49. Although she attached her name to the essay, I do not disclose it here in order to protect her privacy.

50. Despite the fact that foreign brides do not particularly care for "adoptive mothers, sisters, or other forms of fictive kinship," the Ministry of Gender Equality and Family introduced, in June 2010, a program to establish fictive natal families for foreign brides. The expectation was that fictive families can play the roles of guardian, protector, and consultant as they do in real natal families (*Dong-A Ilbo*, June 5, 2010, p. A-24).

51. Although she is well known in the media, I have used a pseudonym to conceal her real name. Because she was not chosen as a candidate in the Seoul metropolitan council election of June 2, 2010, I do not consider her truly a public figure.

52. *Korea Herald*, May 12, 2010, p. 1.

53. *JoongAng Ilbo*, June 7, 2010, p. 18; idem, June 8, 2010, p. 20.

54. *JoongAng Ilbo*, June 8, 2010, p. 20.

55. Keith Banting, Richard Johnston, Will Kymlicka, and Stuart Soroka, "Do Multiculturalism Policies Erode the Welfare State? An Empirical Analysis," in *Multiculturalism and the Welfare State: Recognition and Redistribution in Contemporary Democracies*, Keith Banting and Will Kymlicka, eds., pp. 49–91 (New York: Oxford University Press, 2006), pp. 49–91.

56. Ibid., pp. 56–57.

57. Ibid., p. 86, appendix 2.1.

58. Han, "Multicultural Korea: Celebration or Challenge of Multiethnic Shift in Contemporary Korea," p. 51.

59. Baogang He, "Minority Rights with Chinese Characteristics," in *Multiculturalism in Asia*, Will Kymlicka and Baogang He, eds., pp. 56–79 (New York: Oxford University Press, 2005), p. 45.

60. Ibid., pp. 56–79.

61. Roger L. Janelli and Dawnhee Yim Janelli, *Ancestor Worship and Korean Society* (Stanford: Stanford University Press, 1982), p. 177; Choong Soon Kim, *The Culture of Korean Industry: An Ethnography of Poongsan Corporation* (Tucson: University of Arizona Press, 1992), p. 12; Edwin O. Reischauer and John K. Fairbank, *East Asia: The Great Tradition* (Boston: Houghton Mifflin, 1960), p. 426.

62. Wei-ming Tu, *Confucian Ethics Today: The Singapore Challenge* (Singapore: Federal Publications, 1984), p. 10.

63. Han, "Multicultural Korea," p. 45.

64. Ibid.

65. Mika Toyota, "Subjects of the Nation without Citizenship: The Case of 'Hill Tribes' on Thailand," in *Multiculturalism in Asia*, Will Kymlicka and Baogang He, eds., pp. 110–35 (New York: Oxford University Press, 2005), p. 134.

66. Kraus and Schönwälder, "Multiculturalsim in Germany," p. 202.

67. Oh Kyŏng-sŏk is critical about the role of broadcast media, as they tend to sensationalize stories of foreign brides (Oh, *Han'gukaesŏŭi tamunhwajuŭi*, p. 35).

68. Regarding the desecuritization, according to Kymlicka, "The first factor is geopolitical security. Where states feel insecure in geopolitical terms, fearful of neighboring enemies, they are unlikely to treat fairly their own minorities. More specifically, states will never voluntarily accord self-governing powers to minorities that they view as potential collaborators with, or as fifth-columns for, neighboring enemies. . . . In the past, this has sometimes been an issue in the West. . . . Today, however, this is essentially a nonissue throughout the established Western democracies with respect to national minorities and indegineous peoples" (Will Kymlicka, "Liberal Multiculturalism: Western Model, Global Trends, and Asian Debates," in *Multiculturalism in Asia*, Will Kymlicka and Baogang He, eds., pp. 2–55 [New York: Oxford University Press, 2005], p. 34).

69. Ibid., p. 36.

70. Ibid.

71. *Mail Business Newspaper*, May 22, 2009, pp. A-6, 29.

72. Kim, "The State and Migrant Women," p. 10.

73. Kim Nam-Kook, "Constitution and Citizenship in a Multicultural Korea: Limitations of a Republican Approach," *Korea Journal* 47 (2007): 196–220, p. 226.

74. Its population is twenty million, representing forty-seven ethnic groups, the largest being Uighurs. China has long ruled Xinjiang in various degrees and reestablished its control there in 1949 by crushing the short-lived state of Eastern Turkistan that had emerged during the Chinese civil war. Tensions led to open clashes that have continued since. Beginning July 7, 2009, more than 156 people have been killed and 1,100 people injured, and hundreds of vehicles have been damaged (*Korea Herald*, July 7, 2009, p. 1).

75. Michael Breen, *The Koreans: Who They Are, What They Want, Where Their Future Lies* (New York: Thomas Dunne Books, 2004), p. 176.

76. Richard M. Steers et al., *The Chaebol: Korea's New Industrial Might* (New York: Harper & Row, 1989), p. 136.

Bibliography

The Association of Kimhae Kimssi An'gyŏng'gongp'a, ed. *Kimhae Kimssi an'gyŏng'gongp'a sebo* [*Genealogy of An'gyŏng Branch of Kimhae Kim Lineage*]. Seoul: The Association of Kimhae Kimssi An'gyŏng'gongp'a, 2000.

Bae Kidong [Ki-dong Pae]. "Chŏn'gok-ri kusŏkki yujŏk-ŭi chosagwajŏng-ŭi munjejŏm [Chŏn'gok-ri Paleolithic Site, Current Understanding]." Paper presented at the International Seminar in Memory of the Excavation of Paleolithic Site, May 3, 2002. Yŏnch'ŏn, Korea.

Banting, Keith, Richard Johnston, Will Kymlicka, and Stuart Soroka. "Do Multiculturalism Policies Erode the Welfare State? An Empirical Analysis." In *Multiculturalism and the Welfare State: Recognition and Redistribution in Contemporary Democracies*, Keith Banting and Will Kymlicka, eds., pp. 49–91. New York: Oxford University Press, 2006.

Befu, Harumi. *Japan: An Anthropological Introduction*. New York: Thomas Y. Crownwell, 1971.

Brandt, Vincent S. R. *A Korean Village: Between Farm and Sea*. Cambridge: Harvard University Press, 1971.

Breen, Michael. *The Koreans: Who They Are, What They Want, Where Their Future Lies*. New York: Thomas Dunne Books, 2004.

Caprio, Mark. *Japanese Assimilation Policies in Colonial Korea, 1910–1945*. Seattle: University of Washington Press, 2009.

Caputo, Richard. "Multiculturalism and Social Justice in the United States: An Attempt to Reconcile the Irreconcilable with a Pragmatic Liberal Framework." *Race, Gender and Class* 8 (2001): 161–82.

Chang Chae-hyŏk. "Noinbogŏnbokchichŏngch'aekŭi panghyangkwa kwajae [The Directions and Tasks of the Health and Welfare Policies for the Elderly Koreans]." Paper presented at the forum on The Korean Aging and Care-giving, November 17, 2010. Seoul, Korea.

Chang, Kwang-chih. *The Archaeology of Ancient China*, 4th ed. New Haven: Yale University Press, 1986.

Cho Chŏng-a, Im Sun-hŭi, and Chŏng Chin-kyŏpng. *Saet'ŏmin-ŭi munhwagaldŭnggwa munhwajŏk t'onghap pang'an* [*Cultural Conflict and Cultural Integration of the North Korean Escapees*]. Seoul: Korean Women's Development and Korean Institute for National Unification, 2006.

Cho Hŭng-yun and Yun Yihŭm. "Sŏmun [Introduction]." In *Han'gukin-ŭi chonggyo* [*Korean Religion*], Yun Yihŭm et al., eds., pp. i–ix. Seoul: Mundŏk-sa, 1994.

Cho Kang-hŭi. "Yŏngnam chibang-ŭi honban yŏn'gu: Chinsŏng Yissi Toegye chongson-ŭl chungsimŭro [The Marriage Network in the Kyŏngsang Region: Focusing on the Main Heir of the Chinsŏng Yi Clan]." *Minjok munhwa nonch'ong* [*The Journal of the Institute for Korean Culture*] 6 (1984): 79–121.

Choe Chong Pil [Chŏng-p'il Ch'oe]. "Ilyuhaksangŭro pon Han'minjok kiwŏn yŏn'gu-e taehan pip'anjŏk kŏmt'o [A Critical View of Research on the Origins of Koreans and Their Culture]." *Han'guk Sang'gosa Hakpo* [*Journal of Early History of Korea*] 8 (1991): 7–43.

Choe Chong Pil [Chŏng-p'il Ch'oe] and Martin T. Bale. "Current Perspectives on Settlement, Subsistence, and Cultivation in Prehistoric Korea." *Artic Anthropology* 39 (2002): 95–121.

Ch'oe Jaeseuk. *Han'guk kajokchedo yŏn'gu* [*Studies on Korean Family System*]. Seoul: Minjungsŏgwan, 1966.

Ch'oe Sang-su [Sang-su Ch'oe]. "Relations between Korea and Arabia." *Korea Journal* 9 (1969): 14–17, 20.

Choi Yang-kyu [Ch'oe Yang-gyu]. "Koryŏ-Chosŏn-sidae Chung'guk kwihwasŏngssi chŏngch'aek [The Settlement of the Naturalized Chinese Surname Groups during the Koryŏ and Chosŏn Periods]." Unpublished MA thesis, Hongik University, Seoul, 2001.

Chŏn Kyŏng-su. "Ch'abyŏl-ŭi sahoewa sisŏn-ŭi chŏngch'igwajŏng-non: Tamunhwakajŏng chanyŏ-e kwanhan yebijŏk yŏn'gu [Discussions on Discriminatory Society and Political Process]." In *Honhyŏl-esŏ tamunhwa* [*From Mixed-Blood to Multiculturalism*], Chŏn Kyŏng-su et al., eds., pp. 36–85. Seoul: Iljisa, 2008.

———. "Sŏmun [Introduction]." In *Honhyŏl-esŏ tamunhwa* [*From Mixed-Blood to Multiculturalism*], Chŏn Kyŏng-su et al., eds., pp. 12–34. Seoul: Iljisa, 2008.

Chŏng Pyŏng-wan. "Urinara woerae-sŏngssi-ŭi kubosŏ pigyo: Sijogo [A Comparison of Old Genealogies on Foreign Surname Groups Who Were Naturalized in Korea: On Founding Fathers]." *Pangsongt'ongsindaehak nonmunjip* [*Journal of Korea National Open University*] 13 (1991): 91–122.

Cotterell, Arthur. *East Asia: From Chinese Predominance to the Rise of the Pacific Rim*. New York: Oxford University Press, 1993.

Courant, Maurice. *Bibliographie Coreenne*. Paris: E. Leroux, 1894–189; supplement, 1901; reprint, New York: B. Franklin, 1968.

Cumings, Bruce. *Korea's Place in the Sun: A Modern History*. New York: W. W. Norton, 1997.

Dallet, Charles. *Histoire de l'Église de Corée*. 2 vols. Paris: V. Palme, 1874; reprint, Seoul: Royal Asiatic Society, Korea Branch, 1975.

Deuchler, Martina. *Confucian Gentleman and Barbarian Envoys*: *The Opening of Korea, 1875–1885*. Seattle: University of Washington Press, 1977.

———. "The Tradition: Women during the Yi dynasty." In *Virtues in Conflict*: *Tradition and the Korean Women Today*, Sandra Mattielli, ed., pp. 1–47. Seoul: The Royal Asiatic Society, Korea Branch, 1977.

Eckert, Carter J. et al. *Korea Old and New*: *A History*. Seoul: Ilchokak, 1990.

Ember, Carol R., and Melvin Ember. *Anthropology*, 9th ed. Upper Saddle River, NJ: Prentice-Hall, 1999.

Fernandez, James W. *Bwiti*: *An Ethnography of the Religious Imagination in Africa*. Princeton: Princeton University Press, 1982.

Finkielkraut, Alain. *La Défaite de la Pensée* [*The Undoing of Thought*]. Trans. by Dennis O'Keeffe. London: The Claridge Press, 1988.

Frankl, John M. *Han'gukmunhak-e nat'anan woeguk-ŭi ŭimi* [*Images of "the Foreign" in Korean Literature and Culture*]. Seoul: Somyŏngch'ulp'an, 2008.

Gale, James S., *Korean Sketches*. New York: Flemming H. Revell Company, 1898.

Geertz, Clifford. *After the Fact*: *Two Countries, Four Decades, One Anthropologist*. Cambridge, MA: Harvard University Press, 1995.

Griffis, William Elliot. *Corea*: *The Hermit Nation*. New York: Charles Scribner's Sons, 1882.

Grinker, Roy Richard. *Korea and Its Futures*: *Unification and the Unfinished War*. New York: St. Martin's Press, 1998.

Gurr, Ted. *Minorities at Risk*: *A Global View of Ethnopolitical Conflict*. Washington, DC: Institute of Peace Press, 1993.

Habermas, Jürgen. "Struggles for Recognition in the Democratic Constitutional State." In *Multiculturalism*: *Examining the Politics of Recognition*, Amy Gutmann, ed., pp. 107–48. Princeton: Princeton University Press, 1994.

Haley, Alex. *Roots*: *Saga of an American Family*. New York: Doubleday, 1976.

Han Geon-Soo [Kŏn-su Han]. "Multicultural Korea: Celebration or Challenge of Multiethnic Shift in Contemporary Korea." *Korea Journal* 47 (2007): 32–63.

Han Kyung-Koo [Kyŏng-gu Han]. "The Archaeology of the Ethnically Homogeneous Nation-State and Multiculturalism in Korea." *Korea Journal* 47 (2007): 8–31.

Harris, Marvin. *Theories of Culture in Postmodern Times*. Walnut Creek, CA: AltaMira Press, 1999.

Harvey, Young S. Kim, and Soon-Hyung Chung. "The Koreans." In *Peoples and Cultures of Hawaii*, John McDermott Jr., Wen-Shing Tseng, and Thomas Maretzki, eds., pp. 135–54. Honolulu: University of Hawaii Press, 1980.

He, Baogang. "Minority Rights with Chinese Characteristics." In *Multiculturalism in Asia*, Will Kymlicka and Baogang He, eds., pp. 56–79. New York: Oxford University Press, 2005.

Hsu, Francis L. K. "The Effect of Dominant Kinship Relationships on Kin and Non-Kin Behavior." *American Anthropologist* 67 (1965): 638–61.

———. *American & Chinese*: *Purposes and Fulfillment in Great Civilizations*. Garden City, NY: The Natural History Press, 1970.

———. "Prejudice and Its Intellectual Effect in American Anthropology: An Ethnographic Report." *American Anthropologist* 75 (1973): 1–19.

———. "Intercultural Understanding: Genuine and Spurious." *Anthropology & Education Quarterly* 8 (1977): 202–9.

———. "The Cultural Problem of the Cultural Anthropologist." *American Anthropologist* 81 (1979): 517–32.

———. *Americans & Chinese: Passage to Differences,* 3rd ed. Honolulu: University of Hawaii Press, 1981.

The HUGO Pan-Asian SNP Consortium. "Mapping Human Genetic Diversity in Asia." *Science* 236 (2009): 1541–45.

Hunter, David E., and Phillip Whitten, eds. *Encyclopedia of Anthropology.* New York: Harper & Row, 1976.

Hwang Un-ryong. "Kwihwasŏngssi sijo tongnaesŏl [Theories on the Naturalized Foreigners Who Came to East, Korea]." *Pusan yŏjadaehak sahak* [*History of Pusan Women's College*] 10 and 11 (1993): 297–320.

Ilyon [Iryŏn]. *Samguk yusa: Legends and History of the Three Kingdoms of Ancient Korea.* Trans. by Ha Tae-hung and Grafton K. Mintz. Seoul: Yonsei University Press, 2007 (orig. 1972).

Janelli, Roger L., and Dawnhee Yim Janelli. *Ancestor Worship and Korean Society.* Stanford: Stanford University Press, 1982.

Jun Hey-Jung [Hye-jŏng Chŏn] et al. "Kyŏlhon yijuyŏsŏng kajok kŏn'gang-e yŏnghyang-ŭl mich'i-nŭn kyŏngno [Path of the Variables to Migrant Women's Families' Health]." *Han'gukkajokpokchihak* [*Korea Journal of Family Welfare*] 14 (2009): 5–24.

Kang Chun-sik. *Tasi'ilnŭn Hamel-ŭi p'yoryu-gi* [*Rereading of Hamel's Ship Wreck and His Odysseys*]. Seoul: Ungjin-dot-com, 2002.

Kendall, Laurel. *Getting Married in Korea: Of Gender, Morality, and Modernity.* Berkeley: University of California Press, 1996.

Kim Byung-mo [Kim Pyŏng-mo]. *Han'gukin-ŭi paljach'wi* [*Footprints of Koreans*], revised ed. Seoul: Chipmundang, 1994 (orig. 1985).

———. *Hŏ Hwang-ok: Kim Suro wangbi: Ssangŏ-ŭi pimil* [*Hŏ Hwang-ok: Queen of King Kim Suro: A Secret of "Twin-fish*]. Seoul: Chosun Ilbo, 1994.

———. *Kim Suro wangbi-ŭi honin'gil* [*The Road to Marriage of Queen of King Kim Suro*]. Seoul: P'urŭnsup, 1994.

———. *Kim Pyŏng-mo-ŭi kokohak yŏhaeng* [*Kim Byung-mo's Archaeological Tour*]. 2 vols. Seoul: Karaesil, 2006.

———. *Hŏ Hwang-ok Route: Indo-esŏ Kaya-kkaji* [*The Route of Hŏ Hwang-ok: From India to Kaya*]. Seoul: Yŏksa-ŭi ach'im, 2008.

Kim Chŏng-ho. *Han'guk-ŭi kwihwa sŏngssi: Sŏngssiro pon uriminjok-ŭi kusŏng* [*The Naturalized Korean Surname Groups: The Composition of Ethnic Nation of Korea by Surname*]. Seoul: Chisiksanŏpsa, 2003.

Kim, Choong Soon. "Yŏnjul-hon or Chain String Form of Marriage Arrangement in Korea." *Journal of Marriage and the Family* 36 (1974): 575–79.

———. *An Asian Anthropologist in the South: Field Experiences with Blacks, Indians, and Whites.* Knoxville: University of Tennessee Press, 1977.

———. "Can an Anthropologist Go Home Again?" *American Anthropologist* 89 (1987): 943–46.

———. *Faithful Endurance: An Ethnography of Korean Family Dispersal.* Tucson: University of Arizona Press, 1988.

———. *The Culture of Korean Industry: An Ethnography of Poongsan Corporation.* Tucson: The University of Arizona Press, 1992.

———. *Japanese Industry in the American South.* New York: Routledge, 1995.

———. *A Korean Nationalist Entrepreneur: A Life History of Kim Sŏngsu, 1891–1955.* Albany: State University of New York Press, 1998.

———. *One Anthropologist, Two Worlds: Three Decades of Reflexive Fieldwork in North America and Asia.* Knoxville: University of Tennessee Press, 2002.

———. *Kimchi and IT: Tradition and Transformation in Korea.* Seoul: Ilchokak, 2007.

Kim Chung-hwan, ed. *Ŭisŏng Kim-ssi Kaeamgong p'abo* [*Genealogy of Kaeam Branch of Ŭisŏng Kim Clan*]. Seoul: Ŭisŏng Kim-ssi Kaeamgong p'aboso, 1991.

Kim, Eun Mee, and Jean S. Kang. "Seoul as a Global City with Ethnic Villages." *Korea Journal* 47 (2007): 64–99.

Kim Hŭi-chŏng. "Han'gukŭi kwanjudohyŏng tamunhwajuŭi [The Government-led Multiculturalism in Korea]." In *Han'gukaesŏŭi tamunhwajuŭi: Hyŏnsilgwa chaengjŏm* [*Multiculturalism in Korea: A Critical Review*], Oh Kyŏng-sŏk et al., pp. 57–79. Seoul: Han'ul Academy, 2007.

Kim Hyun Mee. "The State and Migrant Women: Diverging Hopes in the Making of 'Multicultural Families' in Contemporary Korea." *Korea Journal* 47 (2007): 100–122.

Kim, Key-Hiuk. *The Last Phase of the East Asia World Order.* Berkeley: University of California Press, 1980.

Kim, Lin-su. "Technological Transformation of Korean Firms." In *Korean Managerial Dynamics,* Kae H. Chung and Hak Chong Lee, eds., pp. 113–29. New York: Praeger, 1989.

Kim Nam-Kook. "Constitution and Citizenship in a Multicultural Korea: Limitations of a Republican Approach." *Korea Journal* 47 (2007): 196–220.

Kim Pŏm-jun. "Saeroun sŏngssi chŭng'ga sokto Han'gukman mae-u nŭryŏ [Speed of Increasing Rate of New Surnames Are Very Slow in Korea]." *Kwahak'kisul* [*Science and Technology*] 10 (2008): 51–53.

Kim Sŭng-Kwŏn et al. *2007-nyŏn chŏn'guk tamunhwakajoksilt'aechosa yŏn'gu* [*The Year 2009 Nationwide Survey on Multicultural Families*]. Seoul: The Ministry for Health, Welfare and Family Affairs, the Ministry of Justice, the Ministry of Gender Equality and Family, ROK, and the Korea Institute for Health and Social Affairs, 2010.

Kim Tu-hŏn. *Han'guk kajokchedo yŏn'gu* [*Studies on Korean Family System*]. Seoul: Seoul National University Press, 1969.

Kim, Won-yong. "Discoveries of Rice in Prehistoric Sites in Korea." *Journal of Asian Studies* 41 (1982): 513–18.

Kim Wook [Uk Kim] and Kim Chong-Youl [Chong-yŏl Kim]. *Mitochondrial DNA pyŏniwa Han'gukin chiptan-ŭi kiwŏn-e kwanhan yŏn'gu* [*Modern Korean Origin and the Peopling of Korea as Revealed by mtDNA Lineages*]. Seoul: Koguryŏ yŏn'gu chaedan yŏn'gu ch'ongsŏ [Koguryŏ Research Foundation], no. 13, 2005.

Kitano, Harry H. L., and Roger Daniels. *Asian Americans: Emerging Minorities.* Englewood Cliffs, NJ: Prentice-Hall, 1995.

Kong Chŏng-ja. *Han'guk taegiŏpka kajok-ŭi honmak-e kwanhan yŏn'gu* [*The Families of Korean Big Businessmen and Their Marriage Networks*]. Unpublished PhD dissertation, Ewha Womans University, 1989.

Kraus, Peter A., and Karen Schönwälder. "Multiculturalism in Germany: Rhetoric, Scattered Experiments, and Future Chances." In *Multiculturalism and the Welfare State: Recognition and Redistribution in Contemporary Democracies*, Keith Banting and Will Kymlicka, eds., pp. 202–21. New York: Oxford University Press, 2006.

Kwon, Yi-gu [Kwŏn Yi-gu]. "Population of Ancient Korea in Physical Anthropological Perspective." *Korea Journal* 30 (1990): 4–12.

Kymlicka, Will. *Multicultural Citizenship.* New York: Oxford University Press, 1995.

———. "Liberal Multiculturalism: Western Model, Global Trends, and Asian Debates." In *Multiculturalism in Asia,* Will Kymlicka and Baogang He, eds., pp. 2–55. New York: Oxford University Press, 2005.

———. *Multicultural Odysseys: Navigating the New International Politics of Diversity.* New York: Oxford University Press, 2007.

Kymlicka, Will, and Baogang He, eds. *Multiculturalism in Asia.* New York: Oxford University Press, 2005.

Laczko, Leslie. "Canada's Pluralism in Comparative Perspective." *Ethnic and Racial Studies* 17 (1994): 20–41.

Langness, L. L. *The Life History in Anthropological Science.* New York: Holt, Rinehart and Winston, 1965.

Lee, Changsoo, and George DeVos. *Koreans in Japan: Ethnic Conflict and Accommodation.* Berkeley: University of California Press, 1981.

Lee Hee-Soo [Hŭi-su Yi]. "Early Korea-Arabic Maritime Relations based on Muslim Sources." *Korea Journal* 31 (1991): 21–32.

Lee, Ki-baik. *A New History of Korea.* Trans. Edward W. Wagner with Edward J. Schultz. Cambridge: Harvard-Yenching Institute by Harvard University Press, 1984.

Lee Kwang-kyu. *Han'guk kajok-ŭi sajŏk yŏn'gu* [*A Historical Study of the Korean Family*]. Seoul: Ilchisa, 1983.

———, ed., by Joseph P. Linskey.*Korean Traditional Culture.* Seoul: Jimundang, 2003.

Lee Seo-Geon [Yi Su-kŏn]. *Han'guk-ŭi sŏngssi-wa chokpo* [*Korean Family Names and Genealogies*]. Seoul: Seoul National University Press, 2008.

Lee Sŏng-mu. "Han'guk sŏngssi-wa chokpo [Korean Surname and Genealogy]." *Tong'asia-ŭi chokpo kukchae haksulhoeŭi* [International Conference on East Asian Genealogy], proceedings, November 21–22, 2008.

Lew, Young Ik [Yong-ik Yu]. "The *Kabo* Reform Movement: Korean and Japanese Reform Efforts in Korea." Unpublished PhD dissertation, Harvard University, 1972.

――――. *Kabo Kyŏngjang yŏn'gu* [*Studies on the* Kabo *Reform Movement*]. Seoul: Ilchokak, 1990.

Lewis, Oscar. *Five Families: Mexican Case Studies in the Culture of Poverty.* New York: Basic Books, 1959.

Lhim Hag Seong [Yim Hak-sŏng]. "Sipch'ilsegi chŏnban hojŏkcharyorŭl t'onghae pon kwihwa yain-ŭi Chosŏnesŏ-ŭi saenghwal yangsang: Ulsanhojŏk (1609) kwa Haenamhojŏk-ŭi (1639) saryaebunsŏk [The Modes of Lives of Naturalized Jurchens Appeared in the Chosŏn Census Registers in the First Half of the Seventeenth Century]." *Komunsŏ 'yŏngu* (*Studies of Old Documents*) 33 (2008): 95–128.

Loewen, James W. *The Mississippi Chinese: Between Black and White,* 2nd ed. Prospect Heights, IL: Waveland Press, 1988.

Malinowski, Bronislaw. *Sex and Repression in Savage Society.* London: Kegan Paul, Trench, Trubner, 1927.

Middleton, Russell. "Brother-Sister and Father-Daughter Marriage in Ancient Egypt." *American Sociological Review* 27 (1962): 603–11.

Miller, David. *On Nationality.* Oxford: Oxford University Press, 1995.

――――. "Multiculturalism and the Welfare State: Theoretical Reflections." In *Multiculturalism and the Welfare State: Recognition and Redistribution in Contemporary Democracies*, Keith Banting and Will Kymlicka, eds., pp. 323–38. New York: Oxford University Press, 2006.

Na, Se-jin. "Physical Characteristics of Korean Nation." *Korea Journal* 3 (1963): 9–29.

Naisbitt, John. *Global Paradox.* New York: Avon Books, 1994.

Nelson, Sarah M. *The Archaeology of Korea.* New York: Cambridge University Press, 1993.

Nielsson, Gunnar. "States and 'Nation-Groups': A Global Taxonomy." In *New Nationalisms of the Developed West*, Edward Tiryakian and Ronald Rogowski, eds., pp. 27–56. Boston: Allen & Unwin, 1985.

Oh Kyŏng-sŏk et al. *Han'gukaesŏŭi tamunhwajuŭi: Hyŏnsil-gwa chaengjŏm* [*Multiculturalism in Korea: A Critical Review*]. Seoul: Han'ul Academy, 2007.

Ohnuki-Tierney, Emiko. "Native Anthropologist." *American Ethnologist* 11 (1984): 584–86.

Pai, Hyung Il. *Constructing "Korean" Origins: A Critical Review of Archaeology, Historiography, and Racial Myth in Korean State-Formation Theories.* Cambridge: Harvard University Asia Center, 2000.

Pak Chong Sam. "Hanmi kukche kyŏlhon-esŏ munhwajŏk paekyŏng-ŭi ch'airo inhan ŭisajŏndal kaldŭng-ŭi ironjŏk koch'al [Theoretical Examination of Communication Conflict Resulting from Cultural Differences among International Marriages between Koreans and Americans]." *Sungjŏn Hakpo* [*Journal of Sungjŏn University*] 12 (1982): 99–136.

Pak Hyŏn-mo. *Sejongch'ŏrŏm: Sot'ong'gwa hŏnsin-ŭi leadership* [*Like King Sejong: Leadership for Communication and Dedication*]. Seoul: Midasbook, 2008.

Pak Ki-hyŏn. *Uri yŏksarŭl pakkun kwihwa sŏngssi: Urittang'ŭl sŏnt'aekhan kwihwainŭi paljach'wi* [*The Naturalized Surname Groups Who Changed Korean*

History: Track Records of Naturalized People Who Chose Korea]. Seoul: Yŏksaŭiach'im, 2007.

Park Ok-kol [Pak Ok-kŏl]. *Koryŏ-sidae-ŭi kwihwain yŏn'gu* [*A Study of the Naturalized People in the Koryŏ Period*]. Seoul: Kukhakcharyowŏn, 1996.

Peacock, James L. *The Anthropological Lens: Harsh Light, Soft Focus*. New York: Cambridge University Press, 1986.

Pelto, Pertti J. *Anthropological Research: The Structural Inquiry*. New York: Harper & Row, Publishers, 1970.

Peng-Er, Lam. "At the Margins of a Liberal-Democratic State: Ethnic Minority in Japan." In *Multiculturalism in Asia,* Will Kymlicka and Baogang He, eds., pp. 223–43. New York: Oxford University Press, 2005.

Pike, Kenneth. *Language in Relation to a Unified Theory of the Structure of Human Behavior*. Vol. 1. Glendale, CA: Summer Institute of Linguistics, 1954.

Queen, Stuart A., and Robert W. Habenstein. *The Family in Various Cultures*. New York: J. B. Lippincott Co., 1974.

Raper, Arthur F. *Preface to Peasantry: A Tale of Two Black Belt Counties*. Chapel Hill: University of North Carolina Press, 1936.

Redfield, Margaret Park, ed. *Human Nature and the Study of Society: The Papers of Robert Redfield*. Vol.1. Chicago: University of Chicago Press, 1962.

Reischauer, Edwin O., and John K. Fairbank. *East Asia: The Great Tradition*. Boston: Houghton Mifflin, 1960.

Richardson, Miles. "Anthropologist—The Myth Teller." *American Ethnologist* 2 (1975): 517–33.

Rohlen, Thomas P. *Japan's High Schools*. Berkeley: University of California Press, 1983.

Sayers, Robert, and Ralph Rinzler. *The Korean Onggi Potter*. Smithsonian Folklife Studies Series, no. 5. Washington, DC: Smithsonian Institution Press, 1987.

Schmid, Andre. *Korea between Empires, 1895–1919*. New York: Columbia University Press, 2002.

Shin, Gi-Wook. *Ethnic Nationalism in Korea: Genealogy, Politics, and Legacy*. Stanford: Stanford University Press, 2006.

Soh, C. Sarah. *The Comfort Women: Sexual Violence and Postcolonial Memory in Korea and Japan*. Chicago: University of Chicago Press, 2008.

Song Bok. "Han'guk sangch'ŭng-ŭi sahwoejŏk kusŏng'gwa tŭksŏng-e kwanhan yŏn'gu [A Study on the Social Structure and Characteristics of Korean Upper-Class People]." A research report, n.d.

Song Chun-ho. *Chosŏn sahoesa yŏn'gu* [*Social History of Chosŏn*]. Seoul: Ilchokak, 1987.

Stands In Timber, John and Margot Liberty. *Cheyenne Memories*. New Haven: Yale University Press, 1967.

Steers, Richard M. et al. *The Chaebol: Korea's New Industrial Might*. New York: Harper & Row, 1989.

Taylor, Charles. *Multiculturalism and "The Politics of Recognition": An Essay*. Princeton: Princeton University Press, 1993.

———. "The Politics of Recognition." In *Multiculturalism: Examining the Politics of Recognition*, edited and introduced by Amy Gutmann, pp. 25–85. Princeton: Princeton University Press, 1994.

Taylor, Charles with commentary by K. Anthony Appiah, Jürgen Habermas, Steven C. Rockefeller, Michael Walzer, and Susan Wolf, edited and introduced by Amy Gutmann. *Multiculturalism: Examining the Politics of Recognition*. Princeton: Princeton University Press, 1994.

Tŏksu Chang Chongch'inhoe, chokpop'yŏnch'an wiwŏnhoe, ed. *Tŏksu Changssi Chokpo* [*Geneaology of Tŏksu Chang Lineage*]. Seoul: Tŏksu Chang Chongch'inhoe, chokpop'yŏnch'an wiwŏnhoe (Editorial Board, Association of Tŏksu Changssi), 1998.

Toyota, Mika. "Subjects of the Nation without Citizenship: The Case of 'Hill Tribes' in Thailand." In *Multiculturalism in Asia*, Will Kymlicka and Baogang He, eds., pp. 110–35. New York: Oxford University Press, 2005.

Tu, Wei-ming. *Confucian Ethics Today: The Singapore Challenge*. Singapore: Federal Publications, 1984.

Wagner, Edward W. "Two Early Genealogies and Women's Status in Early Yi Dynasty Korea." In *Korean Women: View from the Inner Room*, Laurel Kendall and Mark Peterson, eds., pp. 23–32. New Haven, CT: East Rock Press, 1983.

Welty, Paul Thomas. *The Asians: Their Evolving Heritage*, 6th ed. New York: Harper & Row, 1984.

Westermarck, Edward. *The History of Human Marriage*. London: Macmillan, 1894.

Whang, In-Joung. *Management of Rural Change: The Saemaul Undong*. Seoul: Seoul National University Press, 1981.

White, Leslie A. *The Science of Culture: A Study of Man and Civilization*. New York: Farrar, Strauss & Cudahy, 1949.

White, Merry. *The Japanese Overseas: Can They Go Home Again?* Princeton: Princeton University Press, 1988.

Wolf, Susan. "Comment." In *Multiculturalism: Examining the Politics of Recognition*, edited and introduced by Amy Gutmann, pp. 75–98. Princeton: Princeton University Press, 1994.

Wong, Eugene Franklin. *On Visual Media Racism: Asians in the American Motion Pictures*. New York: Arno Press, 1978.

Yi Chong-il. "Chung'guk-esŏ tongnaekwihwahan saram-ŭi sŏngssiwa kŭ chason-ŭi sinbunjiwi [Name of the Naturalized Surname Groups from China and the Statuses and Occupations of Their Descendants]." In *Sohŏn Nam To-yŏng paksa kohŭi kinyŏm yŏksanonch'ong* [*Commemorative Essays in Honor of Dr. Sohŏn Nam To-yŏng's 70th Birthday*], pp. 321–48. Seoul: Minjokmunhwasa, 1993.

Yi Chong-myŏng. "Koryŏ-e naet'uhan Parhaein'go [A Study on Parhae Immigrants Who Were Naturalized in Koryŏ]." *Paeksanhakpo* [*Journal of Paeksan Society*] 4 (1968): 199–225.

Yi Hŭi-kŭn. *Urian-ŭi kŭdŭl: Sŏkkimgwa nŏmnadŭm kŭ kongjon-ŭi minjoksa* [*Those Who Live with Us: Ethnic History of Biological Mixing, Crossing Back and Forth, and Symbiosis*]. Seoul: Nŏmŏ-books, 2008.

Yi Kil-sang. *Segye-ŭi kyogwasŏ Han'guk-ŭl malhada* [*World School Textbooks Write about Korea*]. Seoul: P'urŭnsup, 2009.

Yi Kuk-chae, ed. *Ch'ŏnghaeyissi muhugongp'a sebo* [*Muhugong Branch of Ch'ŏnghaeyi Lineage*]. Seoul: Ch'ŏnghaeyissi muhugongpa'a chung'anghoe (Central Association of Muhugong Branch of Ch'ŏnghaeyi Lineage), 2006.

Yi Sŏng-mi. *Tamunhwa Code: Han'guk "Dream" haebŏp ch'atki* [*Multicultural Code: Seeking the Solutions for the Korean Dream*]. Seoul: Saeng'gakŭi Namu, 2010.

Yi Sŭng-han. *Kublai Khan-ŭi ilbonwŏnjŏng-gwa Ch'ungyŏl wang* [*Kublai Khan's Expedition of Japan and King Ch'ungyŏl*]. Seoul: P'urŭnsup, 2009.

Yi Wŏn-t'aek. "Chosŏn'jŏn'gi-ŭi kwihwa-wa kŭ sŏng'gyŏk [Naturalization and Its Characteristics during the Early Chosŏn Period]." *Han'guk kukchebŏp yŏn'gu* [*Study of Seoul International Law*] 8 (2001): 225–46.

Yŏn Kap-su. *Kojongdae chŏngch'i pyŏndong yŏn'gu* [*Studies on Political Change during the Kojong Era*]. Seoul: Ilchisa, 2008.

Yoon In-Jin. "Han'gukchŏk tamunhwa-juŭi chŏn'agewa t'ŭksŏng: Kug'gawa siminsahoerŭl chungsimuro [The Development and Characteristics of Multiculturalism in South Korea: With a Focus on the Relationship of the State and Civil Society]." *Han'guk sahoehak* [*Journal of Korean Sociology*] 42 (2008): 72–103.

Yoon Yong-hyuk [Yun Yong-hyŏk]. "Chŏng In-kyŏng-ga-ŭi Koryŏ chŏngch'ak-kwa Sŏsan [Naturalization of Chŏng In-Kyŏng during the Koryŏ Period and Sŏsan]." *The hosŏsahak* [*Historical Journal of Hosŏ*] 48 (2007): 35–70.

Yun Yi-hŭm et al. *Han'guk-ŭi chonggyo* [*Korean Religion*]. Seoul: Mundŏksa, 1994.

Index

About the Author

Choong Soon Kim, formerly a university faculty scholar and professor of anthropology at the University of Tennessee at Martin, is president of the Cyber University of Korea in Seoul, Korea. His articles have been published in various scholarly journals, and he is the author of numerous books written in English, including: *An Asian Anthropologist in the South: Field Experiences with Blacks, Indians, and Whites* (1977); *Faithful Endurance: An Ethnography of Korean Family Dispersal* (1988); *The Culture of Korean Industry: An Ethnography of Poongsan Corporation* (1992); *Japanese Industry in the American South* (1995); *Anthropological Studies of Korea by Westerners* (2000); *A Korean Nationalist Entrepreneur: A Life History of Kim Sŏngsu, 1891–1955* (1998); *One Anthropologist, Two Worlds: Three Decades of Reflexive Fieldwork in North America and Asia* (2002); and *Kimchi and IT: Tradition and Transformation in Korea* (2007).